grzimek's
Student Animal Life Resource

• • • •

grzimek's
Student Animal Life Resource

• • • •

Insects and Spiders
volume 1

Sea spiders to Stick leaf insects

Arthur V. Evans, D.Sc., author

Madeline S. Harris, project editor
Neil Schlager and Jayne Weisblatt, editors

THOMSON
™
GALE

Detroit • New York • San Francisco • San Diego • New Haven, Conn. • Waterville, Maine • London • Munich

THOMSON

★ ™

GALE

Grzimek's Student Animal Life Resource: Insects

Arthur V. Evans, D.Sc

Project Editor
Madeline S. Harris

Editorial
Kathleen J. Edgar, Melissa Hill,
Heather Price

Indexing Services
Synapse, the Knowledge Link
Corporation

Rights and Acquisitions
Sheila Spencer, Mari Masalin-Cooper

Imaging and Multimedia
Randy Bassett, Michael Logusz, Dan
Newell, Chris O'Bryan, Robyn Young

Product Design
Tracey Rowens, Jennifer Wahi

Composition
Evi Seoud, Mary Beth Trimper

Manufacturing
Wendy Blurton, Dorothy Maki

LIBRARY OF CONGRESS CATALOGING-IN-PUBLICATION DATA

Evans, Arthur V.
Grzimek's student animal life resource. Insects and spiders / Arthur V. Evans ;
Neil Schlager and Jayne Weisblatt, editors.
  p. cm.
  Includes bibliographical references and index.
  ISBN 0-7876-9243-3 (hardcover 2 vol. set : alk. paper) — ISBN 0-7876-9244-1
(vol. 1) — ISBN 0-7876-9245-X (vol. 2)
  1. Insects—Juvenile literature. 2. Spiders—Juvenile literature. I. Schlager, Neil,
1966- II. Weisblatt, Jayne. III. Title.
  QL467.2.E36 2005
  595.7—dc22   2005000144

ISBN 0-7876-9402-9 (21-vol set), ISBN 0-7876-9243-3 (2-vol set), ISBN 0-7876-9244-1 (vol 1), ISBN 0-7876-9245-X (vol 2)

This title is also available as an e-book
Contact your Thomson Gale sales representative for ordering information.

Printed in Canada
10 9 8 7 6 5 4 3 2 1

Contents

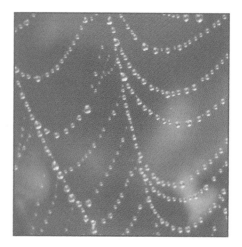

INSECTS AND SPIDERS: VOLUME 2

Reader's Guide

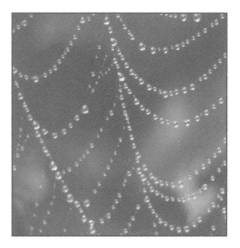

Grzimek's Student Animal Life Resource: Insects and Spiders offers readers comprehensive and easy-to-use information on Earth's insects and spiders. Entries are arranged by taxonomy, the science through which living things are classified into related groups. Each entry includes sections on physical characteristics; geographic range; habitat; diet; behavior and reproduction; animals and people; and conservation status. All entries are followed by one or more species accounts with the same information as well as a range map and photo or illustration for each species. Entries conclude with a list of books, periodicals, and Web sites that may be used for further research.

ADDITIONAL FEATURES

Each volume of *Grzimek's Student Animal Life Resource: Insects and Spiders* includes a pronunciation guide for scientific names, a glossary, an overview of Insects and Spiders, a list of species in the set by biome, a list of species by geographic range, and an index. The set has 236 full-color maps, photos, and illustrations to enliven the text, and sidebars provide additional facts and related information.

NOTE

Grzimek's Student Animal Life Resource: Insects and Spiders has standardized information in the Conservation Status section. The IUCN Red List provides the world's most comprehensive inventory of the global conservation status of plants and animals. Using a set of criteria to evaluate extinction risk, the IUCN recognizes the following categories: Extinct, Extinct in the Wild, Critically Endangered, Endangered, Vulnerable, Conservation Dependent, Near Threatened, Least Concern, and Data Deficient. These terms are defined where they are used in the text, but for a complete explanation of each category, visit the IUCN web page at http://www.iucn.org/themes/ssc/redlists/RLcats2001booklet.html.

ACKNOWLEDGEMENTS

Gale would like to thank several individuals for their assistance with this set. Dr. Arthur V. Evans wrote the entire text. At Schlager Group Inc., Neil Schlager and Jayne Weisblatt coordinated the writing and editing of the set, while Marcia Merryman Means and Leah Tieger also provided valuable assistance.

Special thanks are also due for the invaluable comments and suggestions provided by the *Grzimek's Student Animal Life Resource: Insects and Spiders* advisors:

- Mary Alice Anderson, Media Specialist, Winona Middle School, Winona, Minnesota
- Thane Johnson, Librarian, Oklahoma City Zoo, Oklahoma City, Oklahoma
- Debra Kachel, Media Specialist, Ephrata Senior High School, Ephrata, Pennsylvania
- Nina Levine, Media Specialist, Blue Mountain Middle School, Courtlandt Manor, New York
- Ruth Mormon, Media Specialist, The Meadows School, Las Vegas, Nevada

COMMENTS AND SUGGESTIONS

We welcome your comments on *Grzimek's Student Animal Life Resource: Insects and Spiders* and suggestions for future editions of this work. Please write: Editors, *Grzimek's Student Animal Life Resource: Insects and Spiders*, U•X•L, 27500 Drake Rd., Farmington Hills, Michigan 48331-3535; call toll free: 1-800-877-4253; fax: 248-699-8097; or send e-mail via www.gale.com.

Pronunciation Guide for Scientific Names

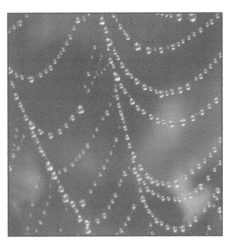

Acherontia atropos ah-KER-on-tee-uh at-TRUH-pohs

Acyrthosiphon pisum as-er-THOS-ih-fon PY-sum

Aedes aegypti ay-EE-deez ee-JIP-ty

Allopauropus carolinensis al-oh-puh-ROP-uhs kar-uh-LINE-en-sis

Anthophiloptera dryas an-thoh-FILL-op-tuh-ruh DRY-uhs

Apis mellifera AY-puhs muh-LIF-uh-ruh

Arachnida uh-RAK-nuh-duh

Atta sexdens ATE-tuh SEKS-dunz

Attacus atlas AT-uh-kuhs AT-luhs

Basilia falcozi buh-SIL-ee-ay FAL-koh-zy

Blatta orientalis BLAY-tuh or-ee-EN-tuh-lis

Blattella germanica BLAY-tell-uh jer-MAN-ih-kuh

Blattodea BLAD-uh-dee

Bombyx mori BOM-biks MOR-ee

Carausius morosos kuh-RAW-see-uhs muh-ROH-suhs

Ceratitis capitata sair-uh-TID-is kap-ih-TOT-ah

Chelifer cancroides KEL-uh-fer kan-KROY-deez

Chilopoda ky-LOP-uh-duh

Chiloporter eatoni ky-LOP-uh-der ee-uh-TOH-ny

Cimex lectularius SY-meks lek-choo-LAR-ee-uhs

Coleoptera KOH-lee-OP-tuh-ruh

Collembola kuh-LEM-buh-luh

Colossendeis megalonyx KALL-uh-SEN-days MEG-uh-LON-iks

Columbicola columbae kuh-lim-BIH-koh-luh kuh-LUM-bay

Conocephalus discolor KON-oh-SEF-uh-luhs dis-KUH-ler

Corydalus cornutus kuh-RID-uh-luhs KOR-nuh-tuhs

Cubacubana spelaea KYOO-buh-kyoo-BAH-nuh spuh-LAY-ee-uh

Cyrtodiopsis dalmanni ser-toh-DY-op-sis DALL-muh-nee

Demodex folliculorum DEM-uh-deks fuh-LIK-yuh-LOR-um

Dermacentor andersoni DER-muh-SEN-ter an-der-SOH-ny

Dermaptera der-MOP-tuh-ruh

Deroplatys lobata der-OP-luh-teez LOH-bah-duh

Diapheromera femorata DY-uh-FER-ah-mer-uh fem-uh-RAW-tuh

Diplopoda duh-PLAW-puh-duh

Diplura duh-PLER-uh

Diptera DIP-tuh-ruh

Dorcadia ioffi dor-KAY-dee-uh EYE-oh-fee

Dynastes hercules DY-nuh-steez her-KYOO-leez

Dytiscus marginalis dy-TIS-cuhs MAR-gih-NAL-is

Embioptera EM-bee-OP-tuh-ruh

Ephemera vulgata uh-FEM-uh-ruh vuhl-GAW-tuh

Ephemeroptera uh-FEM-uh-ROP-tuh-ruh

Euclimacia torquata YOO-kluh-MAY-see-uh tor-KWAH-tuh

Eumenes fraternus YOO-muh-neez fruh-TER-nuhs

Extatosoma tiaratum EK-stat-TOH-suh-muh TEE-ar-uh-tum

Forficula auricularia for-FIK-yoo-luh oh-RIK-yoo-LAR-ee-uh

Frankliniella occidentalis FRANK-lin-ee-EL-luh AWK-sih-DEN-tuh-lis

Galeodes arabs GAY-lee-OH-deez AIR-rubs

Glomeris marginata GLAW-mer-is mar-GIH-nah-tuh

Glossina palpalis glaw-SEE-nuh pal-PUH-lis

Gongylus gongylodes GON-jih-luhs gon-JIH-loh-DEEZ

Grylloblatta campodeiformis GRIL-oh-BLAH-duh KAM-poh-DAY-for-mis

Grylloblattodea GRILL-oh-BLAD-uh-DEE

Halictophagus naulti huh-LIK-tuh-FAY-guhs NALL-ty

Halobates micans huh-LOH-buh-teez MY-kunz

Hemiptera heh-MIP-tuh-ruh

Heteropteryx dilitata HED-er-OP-ter-iks DIL-uh-TAH-tuh

Holijapyx diversiuguis huh-LIJ-uh-piks dih-VER-see-uh-gwis

Hymenoptera HY-muh-NOP-tuh-ruh

Hymenopus coronatus HY-muh-NAW-puhs KUH-ruh-NAW-tuhs

Inocellia crassicornis IN-uh-SEE-lee-uh KRAS-sih-KOR-nis

Isoptera eye-SOP-tuh-ruh

Labidura herculeana luh-BIH-der-uh her-KYOO-lee-ah-nuh

Lepidoptera LEP-uh-DOP-tuh-ruh

Lepisma saccharina luh-PIZ-muh SAK-uh-REE-nuh

Lethocerus maximus luh-THAW-suh-ruhs mak-SIH-muhs

Limulus polyphemus lim-YUH-luhs PAW-lih-FUH-muhs

Liposcelis bostrychophila LIP-uh-SEL-is buh-STRIK-uh-FEE-lee-uh

Lucanus cervus LOO-kah-nuhs SER-vuhs

Lymantria dispar LY-mon-tree-uh DIS-per

Macrotermes carbonarius MAK-roh-TER-meez KAR-buh-NAR-ee-uhs

Maculinea arion MAK-yoo-LIN-ee-uh uh-REE-uhn

Magicicada septendecim MAJ-uh-SIK-uh-duh SEP-ten-DEE-sum

Mallada albofascialis muh-LAH-duh AL-boh-FOS-ee-uh-lis

Mantis religiosa MAN-tuhs ruh-LIH-jee-OH-suh

Mantodea man-TOH-dee-uh

Mantophasmotodea MAN-tuh-FAZ-muh-TOH-dee-uh

Mastigoproctus giganteus MAS-tuh-goh-PROK-tuhs JY-gan-TEE-uhs

Mecoptera meh-KOP-tuh-ruh

Megalithone tillyardi MEG-uh-LITH-uh-NEE til-YER-dy

Megaloprepus caerulatus MEG-uh-LAH-prih-puhs kee-ROO-lah-tuhs

Megaloptera MEG-uh-LOP-tuh-ruh

Megarhyssa nortoni MEG-uh-RY-suh NOR-tuh-ny

Merostomata MER-uh-STOH-muh-duh

Microcoryphia MY-kroh-KUH-rih-fee-uh

Mimetica mortuifolia MIH-meh-TIH-kuh mor-CHOO-ih-FOH-lee-uh

Morpho menelaus MOR-foh MEN-uh-LAY-uhs

Mutilla europaea myoo-TIL-uh yer-OH-pee-uh

Myrmeleon formicarius mer-MUH-lee-uhn for-MUH-kar-ee-uhs

Nasutitermes nigriceps nuh-SOO-duh-ter-meez NY-gruh-seps

Nemoptera sinuata nuh-MOP-tuh-ruh sin-YOO-ah-tuh

Neuroptera new-ROP-tuh-ruh

Nicrophorus americanus ny-KRAW-fuh-ruhs uh-MAIR-uh-KAN-uhs

Notonecta sellata NOD-uh-NEK-tuh SUH-lah-tuh

Ocypus olens AH-sih-puhs OH-lenz

Odonata OH-duh-NOD-uh

Oligotoma saundersii uh-LIG-uh-TOH-muh sawn-DER-see-eye

Orthoptera ar-THAP-tuh-ruh

Pandinus imperator pan-DEE-nuhs im-PAIR-uh-tor

Panorpa nuptialis puh-NOR-puh nup-CHEE-ah-lis

Pantala flavescens pan-TUH-luh fluh-VEH-sunz

Pauropoda pah-ROP-uh-duh

Pediculus humanas peh-DIK-yoo-luhs HYOO-mah-nuhs

Pepsis grossa PEP-suhs GRAH-suh

Periplaneta americana PAIR-uh-pluh-NEH-tuh uh-MAIR-ih-KAN-uh

Petrobius brevistylis PUH-troh-BEE-uhs bruh-VIS-tuh-lis

Phalangium opilio fuh-LAN-jee-um oh-PIL-ee-oh

Phasmida FAZ-mih-duh

Pholcus phalangioides FALL-kuhs fuh-LAN-jee-OY-deez

Phrynus parvulus FRY-nuhs PAR-vuh-luhs

Phthiraptera ther-OP-tuh-ruh

Phyllium bioculatum FIL-ee-um by-AWK-yoo-LAY-dum

Plecoptera pluh-COP-tuh-ruh

Plodia interpunctella PLOH-dee-uh IN-ter-PUNK-tel-luh

Polyancistrus serrulatus PAW-lee-AN-sis-truhs suh-ROO-lah-tuhs

Polydesmus angustus paw-LEE-deez-muhs an-GUS-tuhs

Praedatophasma maraisi pre-DAT-uh-FAZ-muh muh-RAY-sy

Protura PRUH-tyer-uh

Psocoptera soh-KOP-tuh-ruh

Pteronarcys californica TAIR-uh-NAR-seez KAL-ih-FOR-nih-kuh

Pycnogonida PIK-nuh-GON-uh-duh

Raphidioptera ruh-FID-ee-OP-tuh-ruh

Reticulitermes flavipes ruh-TIK-yoo-luh-TER-meez FLAV-uh-peez

Rhabdotogryllus caraboides RAB-doh-TAH-grih-luhs KAR-uh-BOY-deez

Rhyparobia maderae RY-puh-ROH-bee-uh muh-DER-ee

Salticus scenicus SALL-tih-kuhs SEN-ih-kuhs

Scarabaeus sacer SKAR-uh-BEE-uhs SAY-ser

Scolopendra morsitans SKALL-uh-PEN-druh MOR-sih-TAWNZ

Scutigera coleoptrata SKYOO-tij-er-uh KOH-lee-OP-truh-tuh

Scutigerella immaculata skyoo-TIJ-uh-REL-uh ih-MAK-yoo-LAH-duh

Sinetomon yoroi SY-nuh-TOH-mun YOR-oy

Siphonaptera SY-fuh-NOP-tuh-ruh

Sminthuris viridis smin-THOOR-uhs vuh-RID-is

Strepsiptera strep-SIP-tuh-ruh

Supella longipalpa SOO-pel-uh LAWN-gih-PALL-puh

Symphyla SIM-fuh-luh

Tabanus punctifer tuh-BAY-nus PUNK-tih-fer

Tachycines asynamorus TAK-uh-SEE-neez A-sih-NAW-muh-ris

Tenodera aridifolia sinensis tuh-NAH-duh-ruh uh-RID-uh-FOH-lee-uh sih-NEN-sis

Termes fatalis TER-meez FAY-tal-is

Thysanoptera THY-suh-NOP-tuh-ruh

Thysanura THY-suh-NER-uh

Tipula paludosa TIP-yuh-luh PAL-uh-DOH-suh

Trachelophorus giraffa TRAK-uh-luh-FOR-uhs jih-RAF-uh

Triaenodes bicolor try-ee-NUH-deez BY-kuh-ler

Trialeurodes vaporariorum TRY-uh-LER-uh-deez VAY-poh-rar-ee-OR-um

Trichoptera truh-KOP-tuh-ruh

Trissolcus basalis TRIH-sohl-KUHS BAS-uh-lis

Tunga Penetrans TUNG-uh PEN-uh-tronz

Zonocerus variegatus ZOH-nuh-SUH-ruhs VAIR-ee-uh-GAH-tuhs

Zootermopsis laticeps ZOO-der-MOP-sis LAD-ih-seps

Zoraptera zuh-ROP-tuh-ruh

Zorotypus hubbardi ZOR-uh-TIP-is huh-BAR-dy

Words to Know

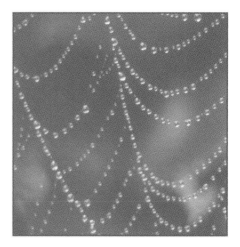

A

Adaptations: Physical features, behaviors, and other characteristics that help an organism to survive and reproduce.

Agile: Able to move quickly and with grace.

Algae: Tiny plantlike organisms that live in water and lack true roots, stems, or leaves.

Ametabolous: Lacking metamorphosis; larvae resemble small versions of wingless adults and are unable to reproduce.

Anamorphosis: A type of metamorphosis where the larva hatches with fewer abdominal segments than the adult.

Antennae: Structures that act like "feelers," or sense organs; sensitive to smell or touch.

Aposematic coloration: Bright or distinctive colors that serve as a warning.

Appendages: Mouthparts, antennae, legs, wings, and tail-like projections.

Aquatic: Living in water.

Arachnologist: A scientist who studies spiders and their relatives.

Arthropod: An animal with a hard outer skeleton and several pairs of jointed limbs.

B

Bacteria: Tiny living things that are made up of only one cell.

Bay: An inlet of the sea.

Binocular vision: The ability to use two eyes to focus on objects.

Biodiversity: The diversity of all life at all levels in a particular place.

Biological control: Using a pest's own natural enemies, such as predators, parasites, parasitoids, and diseases, to control it.

Bioluminescence: Light produced by living organisms.

Bioluminescent: Describing organisms that produce their own light.

Brackish: Salty.

Bristles: Short, stiff hairs.

C

Carapace: An upper platelike shield that covers all or part of certain arachnids; a shield-like plate covering the body of some animals.

Carnivore: An animal that eats the flesh of other animals.

Carnivorous: Meat eating.

Chimera: A single organism that has features of two or more species.

Chitin: A material similar to fingernails that is the main component of the outer skeletons of some animals.

Cholesterol: A substance in animals' cells and body fluids that "cleans" the blood; too much of it can be unhealthy.

Chrysalis: The pupa of a butterfly.

Clutch: A group of eggs.

Coevolution: Description of two or more groups of organisms that influence each other's evolution.

Colony: A grouping of animals that typically lives in a cluster, or mass; such groups of sea organisms are found together on a solid object, such as a coral reef.

Compound eyes: Eyes made up of many lenses.

Contamination: The act of making impure, or dirty, by adding a harmful substance.

Coral: A tiny sea-dwelling animal whose hard skeleton, also called coral, forms reefs in the ocean, often pinkish rose in color.

Courtship: An animal's activities that are meant to attract a mate.

Cove: A small, sheltered inlet of the sea.

Critically Endangered: Facing an extremely high risk of extinction in the wild in the near future.

Crustacean: An animal that lives in water and has a soft, segmented body covered by a hard shell, such as lobsters and shrimp.

Crypsis: A form of camouflage in which an animal imitates specific objects in the environment.

D

Decomposed: Decayed, rotted, disintegrated.

Deforestation: Clearing land of trees to use the timber or to make room for human settlement or farming.

Detritus: Tiny bits of plant and animal remains that have decomposed, or disintegrated.

Diapause: A period of rest or inactivity.

Digestive organs: The body parts that break down food and take it into the body.

Distribution: Geographic range of an animal, where it roams and feeds.

E

Ectoparasite: Parasitic organism that lives on the outside of its host organism.

Eggs: The reproductive cells that are made by female animals and that are fertilized by sperm, or reproductive cells of male animals.

Elytra: The hard, leathery forewings of beetles.

Endangered: Facing a very high risk of extinction in the wild.

Endoparasite: Parasitic organism that lives on the inside of its host organism.

Engorge: To fill up with blood.

Entomologist: A scientist who studies insects.

Estuary: The wide part at the lower end of a river, where the river meets the sea.

Evolution: Gradual process of change over time.

Exoskeleton: An animal's outer covering or supportive structure; the external skeleton or hard outer covering of some animal, especially arthropods.

Extinct: No longer alive.

F

Forage: To search for food.

Fossils: The remains, or parts, of animals that lived long ago, usually found preserved in rock or earth, amber, or other materials.

G

Galls: Abnormal plant growths caused by insects, mites, funguses, and disease.

Ganglia (sing. ganglion): Masses of nerve cells.

Geologist: A scientist who studies the history of Earth through rocks.

Gill: An organ for obtaining oxygen from water.

Gynandromorph: An individual having both male and female characteristics.

H

Hair follicle: A small cavity surrounding the root of a hair.

Harvest: To collect or gather.

Herbivore: A plant-feeding animal.

Heredity: Physical features passed from parent to offspring through genes.

Hibernation: A period of inactivity during the winter.

Hormones: Chemicals that circulate in the blood that stimulate tissues and organs.

Hydrozoans: A group of water-dwelling organisms without backbones that includes jellyfish.

Hypermetamorphosis: Development of insect larvae that have two or more distinctive body forms.

I

Instar: The stage between molts in arthropods.

Invertebrate: An animal without a backbone, such as an insect or earthworm.

Invertebrate zoologist: A scientist who studies animals without backbones.

L

Larva (plur. larvae): The early, or young, form of an animal, which must go through metamorphosis, or certain changes in form, before becoming an adult.

Lek: A group of animals gathered together to find mates.

Lichens: Plantlike growths of funguses and algae living together.

Loamy: Used in reference to soil and meaning soil that is made up of bits of plant material, clay, sand, and silt.

M

Metamorphosis: Process of change, development, and growth in animals.

Migrate: To move from one area or climate to another to breed or feed.

Migration: Movement from one area or climate to another to breed or feed.

Mimics: Organisms that imitate the appearance of another species.

Molt: To shed feathers, shell, or some other outer body part, typically at certain times of the year.

Myiasis: Disease or injury inside or outside the body caused by an infestation of fly larvae.

Myriapodologist: A scientist who studies millipedes, centipedes, and their kin.

N

Near Threatened: At risk of becoming threatened with extinction in the future.

Nymph: A young arachnid; replaced by larva in insects.

O

Omnivore: An animal that eats plants and animals.

Omnivorous: Feeding on both plant and animal materials.

Overwinter: Last through the winter weather; survive.

Ovipositor: The egg-laying tube on the abdomen of many insects and some arachnids.

Ovoviviparity: Act of retaining eggs inside the body until they hatch.

P

Paleontologist: A scientist who studies fossils of plants and animals.

Palp: Fingerlike appendages associated with mouthparts of many arthropods.

Paralyze: To make helpless or unable to move.

Parasite: An animal that lives on another organism, called a "host," from which it obtains its food; the host is seldom killed.

Parasitic: Living on another plant or animal without helping it and often harming it.

Parasitoid: A parasite that slowly kills its host.

Parthenogenesis: Development of young from unfertilized eggs.

Pedipalps: Leg-like appendages of the mouthparts of arthropods.

Pheromones: Chemicals produced by animals that affect the behavior of other individuals in the same species.

Polar: Referring to the cold regions of the world that are farthest north (the Arctic) and farthest south (the Antarctic), where temperatures never rise above 50°F (10°C).

Pollution: Poison, waste, or other material that makes the environment dirty and harmful to health.

Postures: Body positions.

Predator: An animal that hunts and kills other animals for food.

Prey: An animal hunted and caught for food.

Proboscis: A long, flexible, tubelike snout; a strawlike sucking structure of some insects.

Prolegs: Fleshy leglike structures on the abdomen of some insect larvae.

Protozoan: A single-celled, microscopic organism with a nucleus that is neither plant nor animal.

Pulsating: Beating rhythmically.

Pupa: The transition stage between larvae and adult that does not feed or walk.

R

Rainforest: A tropical woodland area of evergreen trees that has heavy rainfall all year long.

Raptorial: Grasping.

Reproductive organs: The body parts that produce young.

Resilin: A rubberlike protein found in the bodies of insects.

Resin: A sticky substance produced by plants.

Rheumatism: Any disorder that causes pain and stiffness in the joints of limbs or back.

S

Scavenger: Animal that eats decaying flesh.

Sea anemone: A small sea animal with long, thin, armlike body parts called tentacles, which looks much like a flower.

Second-growth forest: Forest that grows naturally after cutting or a fire.

Seep: A spot where water has oozed to the ground surface and formed a pool.

Setae (sing. seta): Hair-like structures on the arthropod exoskeleton.

Silt: Fine, tiny specks of earth that settle out of water or fall to the bottom; also, soil material containing very fine particles of rock.

Span: The spread, or distance between two limits, such as the ends of an insect's unfolded wings.

Species: A group of animals that share many traits and can mate and produce young with one another.

Spawn: To produce or release eggs.

Sperm: The reproductive cells that are made by male animals and that fertilize the eggs of female animals.

Spiracles: Breathing holes on the bodies of many arthropods.

Stationary: Unmoving, fixed in position.

Subphyla (sing. subphylum): The major subdivisions of a phylum.

Subtropics: Regions that border on the tropics.

Suture: A thread, wire, or something similar used to close a wound.

T

Telson: The end segment of the body of an arthropod.

Temperate: Mild; used in reference to climate.

Tentacles: Long, thin, armlike body parts used for touching and grasping.

Territorial: Protective of a living or breeding area.

Thigmotactic: Describing animals that must maintain contact with a solid surface, usually by hiding in cracks and crevices.

Thorax: Midsection of an arthropod's body.

Tidal pool: A pool of water that remains after an ocean tide has risen and fallen.

Toxin: A poison produced by a plant or animal.

Trachea: Tubes that transport air throughout the body of most arthropods.

Transparent: See-through, clear.

Tropical: Referring to a climate with an average annual temperature more than 68°F (20°C).

V

Vaccine: Inactive, or dead, germs of a disease that are administered to human beings to help protect against the disease.

Venom: Poison.

Viviparity: Act of producing live offspring inside the body.

Vulnerable: Facing a high risk of extinction in the wild.

W

Wetland: Land that is covered with shallow water or that has very wet soil.

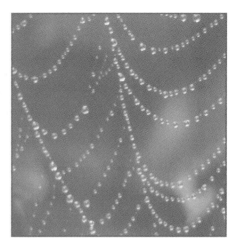

Getting to Know Insects and Spiders

WHAT ARE INSECTS AND SPIDERS?

Insects, spiders, and their relatives are all arthropods (ar-thro-pawds), or animals with a hard outer skeleton and several pairs of jointed limbs. Arthropods form the largest group of animals on Earth. They are found almost everywhere, from the deepest ocean trenches to the tallest mountain peaks. There are nearly one million species of insects known, nearly half of all the different plants and animals combined. There may be as many as ten to thirty million insect species total. Even a "typical" backyard may be the home to several thousand species of insects and spiders. Estimates of species numbers vary because scientists still know so very little about them. Millions of new species await discovery, especially among insects and mites on land and crustaceans in the ocean.

It is estimated that for every human being alive today, there are as many as two hundred million individual insects. Just the total weight of all the ants in the world, all nine thousand different kinds, is twelve times greater than the weight of all the humans on the planet. Despite their amazing numbers and the fact that they are found virtually everywhere, insects and other arthropods are still very alien to us, as if they were beings from another planet. They move on six or more legs, stare with unblinking eyes, breathe without noses, and have hard skinless bodies made up of rings and plates, yet there is something strangely familiar about them, too. Arthropods have to do all the things people do to survive, such as find food, defend themselves from their enemies, and reproduce. They also rely on their finely tuned senses to see, touch, hear, smell, and taste the world around them.

Because of their numbers and the fact that they eat almost everything that is plant, fungus, or animal, arthropods have a huge impact on all the species sharing their habitats. They pollinate flowers, disperse seeds, recycle dead organisms, and bury animal waste. Plant-feeding species provide a natural pruning service that keeps plant growth and populations in check, while flesh-eaters control the populations of other animals. They, in return, are an important food source for fishes, reptiles, amphibians, birds, mammals, and other arthropods.

Many different kinds of scientists study the lives of insects, spiders, and their relatives. Entomologists (EHN-tih-MA-luh-jists) examine the lives of insects, while arachnologists (uh-rak-NA-luh-jists) look at spiders and their relatives. Myriapodologists (mi-RI-ah-po-DAL-luh-jists) focus their attentions on millipedes, centipedes, and their kin. Invertebrate zoologists (in-VER-teh-breht zu-AH-luh-jists)and some marine biologists study marine crustaceans, sea spiders, and horseshoe crabs. It is the work of all these scientists that has provided the information found on these pages.

OLDER THAN DINOSAURS

Arthropods were swimming in lakes, crawling on land, and flying through the air long before dinosaurs. In fact, millipedes are one of the oldest land animals on Earth and have been around for about four hundred million years. Insects are more than 380 million years old. Scientists know this by studying their fossils (FAH-suhls), or remains of animals that lived long ago, usually found set into rock or earth. Scientists who study fossils are called paleontologists (PAY-li-un-TA-luh-jists). Paleontologists study fossils to understand how life has developed and changed over time. The location and chemical makeup of fossils helps paleontologists to determine their age. By studying fossils scientists know that some groups of organisms, such as horseshoe crabs, millipedes, silverfish, and cockroaches, have changed very little over millions of years. The process of organisms changing over time is called evolution (EH-vuh-LU-shun). Organisms must adapt in form and behavior to survive in an environment that is also changing. Studying fossils not only reveals clues about the evolution of these ancient animals but also gives a glimpse of the environments in which they lived.

How to become a fossil

For arthropods, the process of fossilization (FAH-suhl-ih-ZAY-shun) begins when footprints, bodies, or body parts are quickly covered in mud or sand made up of fine particles. The finer the particles, the greater the detail preserved in the fossil. Under just the right circumstances, the mud and sand will be compressed, or squeezed, as more mud and sand settle on the remains, until it becomes rock. This process takes millions of years. Fossils are only impressions of the ancient animals. Their tissues are replaced, molecule by molecule, with surrounding minerals. In time, the remains of the arthropod are transformed physically and chemically and resemble the surrounding rock.

Some of the most detailed remains of ancient arthropods are preserved in hardened tree sap called amber (AM-bur). Amber comes from the sticky sap, or resin (REH-zin), of trees. Trees produce resin to heal wounds and to defend against insect borers. Insects, spiders, and other organisms became trapped and

Some of the most detailed remains of ancient arthropods are preserved in hardened tree sap called amber. (JLM Visuals. Reproduced by permission.)

completely encased in the sticky stuff. The resin quickly hardened and eventually fell to the ground, where it was buried by decomposing plants and soil. Storms washed the hardened resin into low-lying areas that were eventually covered by the ocean. These ancient sea bottoms eventually changed into layers of limestone and sandstone that are now filled with scattered bits and chunks of fossilized resin, or amber. Over millions of years, as new mountains and islands formed, the sea bottoms were lifted above sea level, exposing pieces of amber with the ancient remains of arthropods. The oldest known insect fossils in amber are about one hundred twenty million years old.

Only a tiny fraction of all the arthropods that ever lived during ancient times were preserved as fossils. The remains of species living on land were less likely to be preserved than those living in freshwater and marine habitats. Fossilization in stone or amber depends on animals dying in the right place, at the right time, and under the right circumstances. The odds of this all happening are extremely low. Even today arthropods are quickly eaten by other animals or decompose and break up within hours or days of their deaths.

Flights of fancy

Insects are one of only four groups of animals (with pterosaurs, birds, and bats) to have achieved true flight and were the first to take to the air. The power of flight gives many insects the opportunity to find food and mates over wide areas. Flying insects also have the ability to avoid being eaten by other animals and to colonize new and suitable habitats. Birds, bats, and pterosaurs all evolved wings from their forelimbs, or front legs, but insects did not have to give up a pair of legs to fly. So where did insect wings come from?

Based on the study of fossils, the first winged insects appeared between three hundred fifty and three hundred million years ago. Their wings may have evolved from flexible structures that were first used as gills for breathing underwater. Or they may have developed from stiff projections growing out of their midsection, or thorax, and eventually evolved into more flexible, winglike structures. But why did the first insect wings evolve? Did the oldest winged insects use them for gliding through their habitat, or did they use them as solar panels to collect heat to warm their bodies? The discovery of even older fossils of winged insects may help to unravel the mystery.

DRESSED FOR SUCCESS

One way to measure the success of any group of animals is to look at biodiversity (BI-o-dih-VUHR-seh-tee), or the variety of species in a particular place. Another way is to count the numbers of individuals of a particular species. By either measure, arthropods are the most successful group of animals on Earth. The physical features that make them so successful are the size and structure of their bodies. Most arthropods range in length from 0.04 to 0.4 inches (1 to 10 millimeters). This allows them to live in numerous small habitats where larger animals cannot hope to make a living. Furthermore, their bodies are wrapped in a hard, protective, external covering called the exoskeleton (EHK-so-SKEH-leh-tin). Small and armored, arthropods are perfectly suited for living and reproducing on land or in the water.

A suit of armor

The exoskeleton works both as skin and skeleton. It protects the animal from harm as it swims, crawls, burrows, or flies through the habitat, and it provides a means of support for the muscles and internal organs inside. The exoskeleton is made up of several layers that are composed mostly of chitin (KYE-tehn), a complex material that is made of fibers and combines with a protein to make the exoskeleton light, tough, and flexible, just like fiberglass. The surface of the exoskeleton is covered with small pits, spines, and hairlike structures called setae (SIH-tee). Some setae are sensitive to touch and sometimes help to protect the body from injury. In most insects and spiders, a waxy layer covering the exoskeleton helps to maintain the moisture levels inside the body. Millipedes, centipedes, and crustaceans do not have this protection.

The exoskeleton is divided into two or three body regions. Each region is made up of a series of armored plates that are sometimes closely joined together to increase strength or distinctly segmented to maintain flexibility. The appendages (mouthparts, antennae, legs) are jointed, or divided into segments to increase their flexibility. In fact, the name arthropod means "jointed foot." All plates and segments are joined together by a thin, flexible membrane of pure chitin.

The mouthparts of arthropods are made up of two to four pairs of appendages. These appendages come in a variety of forms and are used as lips, jaws, and fangs. Insect jaws may

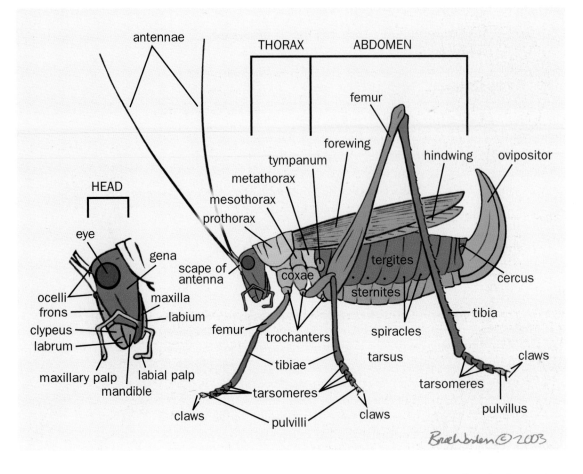

antennae

THORAX   ABDOMEN

femur

forewing

tympanum   hindwing   ovipositor

metathorax

mesothorax

prothorax

HEAD

eye

gena

scape of
antenna

tergites

coxae

ocelli

frons

clypeus

labrum

maxilla

labium

femur

trochanters

sternites

cercus

spiracles

tibia

tarsus

claws

maxillary palp   labial palp

mandible

tibiae

tarsomeres

claws   pulvilli   claws

tarsomeres

pulvillus

Brachbrden © 2003

A lateral view showing the major features of an insect. (Illustration by Bruce Worden. Reproduced by permission.)

form piercing-sucking or lapping mouthparts for drinking plant or animal fluids.

The eyes, if present, are either compound or simple. Compound eyes are made up of several to tens of thousands of individual lenses and are used for seeing images. Some species, as well as all larval insects or young, have only simple eyes, which have just one lens for each eye. Simple eyes are used primarily to distinguish light and dark. One or two pairs of antennae (an-TEH-nee), or sense organs, are covered with setae that are especially sensitive to touch and often have special pits for detecting certain odors.

Adults have three or more pairs of jointed legs and, in many insects, one or two pairs of wings. The legs come in a variety of shapes and are used for running, jumping, climbing, digging, swimming, and grasping prey. The abdomen contains the in-

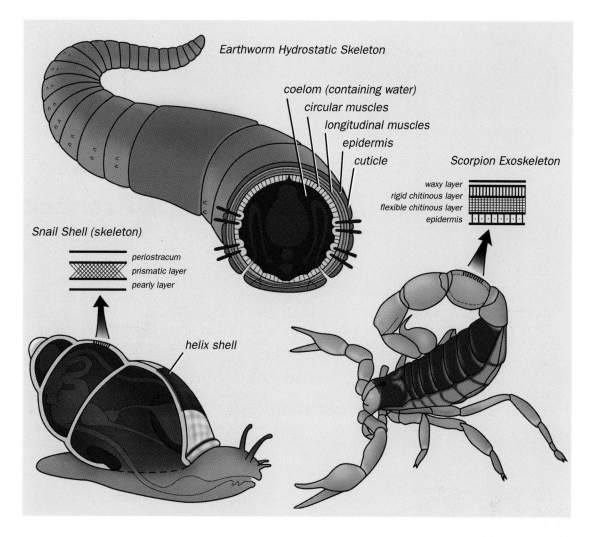

Earthworm Hydrostatic Skeleton

coelom (containing water)
circular muscles
longitudinal muscles
epidermis
cuticle

Scorpion Exoskeleton

waxy layer
rigid chitinous layer
flexible chitinous layer
epidermis

Snail Shell (skeleton)

periostracum
prismatic layer
pearly layer

helix shell

ternal and reproductive organs, as well as special appendages used for defense (as in scorpions), steering (in horseshoe crabs), or spinning silk (as in spiders). The abdomen is distinctly segmented in most arthropods but not in ticks, mites, and nearly all spiders.

A PEEK INSIDE

Inside arthropod bodies are incredibly powerful muscles that make mouthparts chew, antennae wiggle, legs dig, and wings fly. The nervous system helps to coordinate these and other movements. The brain is located inside the head. Trailing behind the brain is a nerve chord that runs along the entire length

Different types of skeletons: external (snail), hydrostatic (earthworm), and jointed (scorpion). (Illustration by Kristen Workman. Reproduced by permission.)

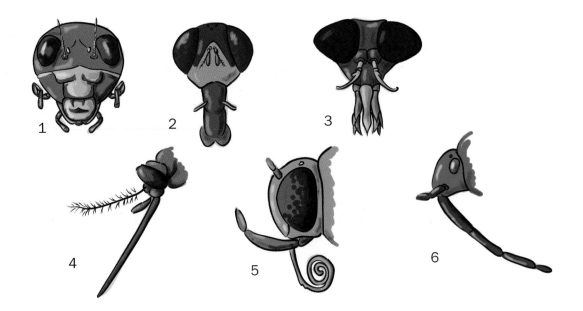

Insects have different mouth parts for feeding. 1. Cricket (chewing); 2. House fly (mopping); 3. Horse fly (piercing and sucking); 4. Mosquito (piercing and sucking); 5. Moth (sucking); 6. Froghopper (piercing and sucking). (Illustration by Ryan Burkhalter. Reproduced by permission.)

of the arthropod's underside. Along the nerve chord are bundles of nerves called ganglia (GANG-lee-uh) that help control the various parts of the body. A pair of ganglia controls each pair of appendages. All abdominal segments have a pair of ganglia except in millipedes, where each segment has two pairs. Most body segments of millipedes are actually two segments joined as one. This is also why millipedes have two pairs of legs on most of their body segments.

The blood of fishes, amphibians, reptiles, birds, and mammals circulates inside arteries and veins. This is called a closed circulatory system. But arthropods have an open circulatory system. They have a tube that runs along their backs. A series of pumps, or hearts, inside the abdomen, or body trunk, pumps the blood forward in the tube. Eventually, it spills out behind the head into various body cavities. The blood usually does not carry oxygen, but it does carry nutrients and chemicals called hormones (HOR-moans) that help the body to function. All the tissues and organs are bathed in blood. The blood eventually moves back to the abdomen where it enters the tube through tiny holes located between the hearts.

Arthropods do not have lungs. The respiratory, or breathing, system of most species living on land is made up of a series of holes and tubes. Oxygen enters the body through a series of

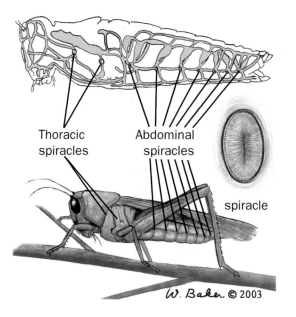

Thoracic
spiracles

Abdominal
spiracles

spiracle

W. Baker © 2003

Insect respiratory system. Oxygen and carbon dioxide move through a system of tubes (trachea) that branch to all parts of the body. Air enters via the spiracles on the insects' bodies. (Illustration by Wendy Baker. Reproduced by permission.)

holes along the sides of the body called spiracles (SPIH-reh-kuls). Each spiracle is attached to a network of tubes, or trachea (TRAY-key-uh). The trachea carry oxygen throughout the body. Carbon dioxide, a waste product of living tissues, is expelled out of the body through the same system. Some spiders have a tracheal system, but most use book lungs. Book lungs are made up of folded tissue inside the abdomen that resembles the pages of a book. Aquatic insects either trap a bubble of air over their spiracles or use gills or gill-like structures. A very thin layer of exoskeleton covers the gills, allowing dissolved oxygen in the water to pass through and enter the tracheal system. Some species have no respiratory system at all. Instead, oxygen in the water simply seeps in all over their bodies.

GETTING ORGANIZED

Animals are classified into various groups on the basis of having similar features. Sharing these similar features suggests that they share a common ancestor or history. The more features they share, the closer the relationship. Arthropods are grouped in the Phylum Arthropoda (AR-thruh-PO-duh) because they all have the following special features: exoskeletons, segmented bodies, pairs of jointed appendages, open circulatory systems, and a ventral nerve cord that runs down the underside of the animal. Arthropods are further divided into three smaller groups, or subphyla (sub-FAI-leh).

The subphylum Cheliceriformes includes sea spiders, horseshoe crabs, scorpions, spiders, ticks, mites, and their relatives. Their bodies are divided into two major regions, the forebody, sometimes called the cephalothorax (SEH-fe-lo-THO-raeks), and abdomen. The forebody has six pairs of appendages, including the pinchers or grasping arms, claw-like pedipalps (PEH-dih-paelps), and eight walking legs. They never have antennae. The reproductive organs are located at the front or rear of the abdomen. The abdomen sometimes has a tail-like structure that is used as a rudder (horseshoe crabs), a defensive weapon (scorpions), as a sensory organ (whip scorpions), or a silk-producing organ (spiders and mites). There are about sixty-one thousand species, most of which live on land.

The Uniramia includes arthropods with only one pair of antennae and legs that are not branched at their bases. Insects and their relatives have bodies that are divided into three major regions: the head, thorax, and abdomen. The head has five pairs of appendages, including the mouthparts and one pair of antennae. Adults have three pairs of legs and sometimes one or two pairs of wings. Their reproductive organs are located toward the rear of the abdomen.

Centipedes, millipedes, and their relatives have bodies that are divided into two major regions. The head is followed by a long trunk-like body. The head has four pairs of appendages, including the mouthparts and one pair of antennae. Adults have one or two pairs of legs on most body segments. Depending on the species the adults have eleven to 382 pairs of legs. Their reproductive organs are located at the end of the body or just behind the head. There are about 818,000 species of insects, millipedes, centipedes, and their relatives that live on land or in freshwater habitats.

The Crustacea include crabs, lobsters, crayfish, shrimp, barnacles, beach hoppers, pillbugs, and their relatives. Their bodies are divided into two major regions: the head, which is usually covered by a broad shield, or carapace (KARE-a-pays), and the body trunk. The head has five pairs of appendages, including the mouthparts and two pairs of antennae. The appendages of crustaceans are usually branched at their bases. The abdomen may also have paired appendages underneath. The reproductive organs are usually found on the midsection or near the front of the abdomen. There are about sixty-seven thousand species, most of which live in the ocean.

Classifications help scientists sort and identify species, as well as organize and locate information about them. But the system of classification is not carved in stone. As understanding of these animals continues to improve, classifications will also change. Groups will be combined, divided, added, or discarded. This constant state of change is sometimes frustrating, but the goal is to have a classification that reflects the true relationships of all organisms based on their evolutionary history.

TRANSFORMATIONS

Arthropods grow by breaking out of their rigid exoskeletons. Most species molt, or shed their exoskeletons, only as larvae (LAR-vee). Larvae are immature animals that are not able to reproduce. However, crustaceans, arachnids, some insects, and other arthropods will continue to grow and molt throughout their adult lives. Each stage between molts is called an instar (IHN-star). The number of instars varies among species, ranging from three to more than twenty times in insects. The number of larval molts remains the same for each species. With each molt a soft pale body escapes from its old exoskeleton through a special escape hatch. After a few hours, days, or weeks the new exoskeleton darkens and hardens. This process of change and growth is called metamorphosis (MEH-teh-MORE-feh-sihs).

There are four basic types of metamorphosis. Some millipedes and centipedes, as well relatives of insects known as proturans, develop by anamorphosis (ANN-eh-MORE-feh-sihs). Their larvae hatch from eggs with fewer body segments than they will have as adults. Additional segments and legs are added as they molt. When wingless diplurans, springtails, silverfish, and bristletails molt, the only noticeable change is that they are larger. They molt many times as larvae and will continue to molt after they reach adulthood. Grasshoppers, true bugs, dragonflies, and some other winged insects develop by gradual metamorphosis. The larvae strongly resemble the adults when they hatch, but they lack developed wings and reproductive organs. These insects stop molting once they reach the adult stage. Beetles, butterflies, moths, flies, fleas, ants, bees, wasps, and others develop by complete metamorphosis. They have four very distinct stages: egg, larva, pupa, and adult. They do not continue to grow or molt once they reach adulthood.

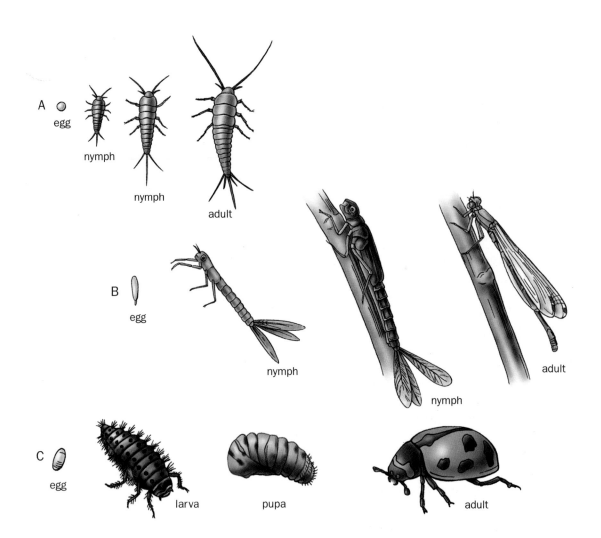

Insect metamorphosis:
A. Ametabolous development;
B. Incomplete metamorphosis;
C. Complete metamorphosis.
(Illustration by Patricia Ferrer.
Reproduced by permission.)

Spiders and other arachnids lay their eggs in a protective sac. The eggs hatch into helpless prelarvae that are unable to move. Their legs are not fully developed, and their bodies show traces of segmentation not visible in the adults. The prelarvae molt into larvae, which still show traces of segmentation on the abdomen but have legs that are more fully developed. The larvae molt into nymphs (nihmfs), or spiderlings. The very active spiderlings leave the egg sac and resemble small versions of the adults. Many arachnids continue to molt after they reach adulthood.

BEHAVIOR

Arthropods engage in all kinds of behaviors that help them to survive and reproduce. They not only have to find food, but they also need to avoid their enemies, find and select mates, and secure a future for their young.

Feeding behavior

Ecologists (ih-KA-luh-jists), scientists who study where and how organisms live, sometimes divide arthropods into different groups based on what they eat. Herbivores (URH-bih-vorz) eat plants, and carnivores (KAR-nih-vorz) eat animal flesh, while omnivores (AM-nih-vorz) eat both plants and animals. Another way to look at the feeding ecology of arthropods is by viewing them as generalists or specialists. For example, generalist herbivores eat all kinds of plants, but specialists feed on only one kind of plant or a small group of closely related species. Parasitoids (PAE-re-SIH-toyds) live and feed inside the bodies of certain kinds of animals (hosts) and eventually kill them. Parasites are also specialists, attacking only certain animal hosts but seldom killing them.

Suitable foods are found by sight, smell, touch, and taste. Herbivores chew or suck fluids from all parts of plants, including roots, trunks, stems, buds, leaves, flowers, fruits, and seeds. Some species even bleed leaves of their sticky or toxic resins before eating them. Many collect a variety of plant materials and store them as food, while others simply use them as mulch for growing their own food. Some predators (PREH-duh-ters) actively hunt their prey, while others sit and wait to ambush them. Spiders build webs that are specifically designed to trap insects and other arthropods. Omnivores are opportunists and eat any-

Centipedes are strictly carnivores and actively hunt for small animals, usually insects. Occasionally larger centipedes will catch and kill a small mammal, such as a young mouse. (Arthur V. Evans. Reproduced by permission.)

thing they find, even scavenging dead plants and animals. Some even feed on the waste products of other animals.

Defense

Insects, spiders, and other arthropods rely on many different strategies to defend themselves against predators. For example, large horned beetles avoid being eaten simply by being large and horned. Some orb-weaving spiders have hard spiny bodies that would make them an unwelcome mouthful even to the hungriest of predators. Millipedes coil up their bodies to protect their delicate heads, legs, and undersides, exposing only a series of hard plates along their backs. Others whip or kick spiny antennae and legs at their attackers. Tarantulas and other spiders rear up, flash their fangs, and adopt threatening poses. If this fails to work, many tarantulas will brush a cloud of painfully itchy hairs off their bodies into the faces of predators. While many arthropods bite, run, jump, burrow, swim, or fly to escape, others simply remain still or fall to the ground to get out of sight. Some rely on the protection of other well-defended species, such as ants.

Many insects and arachnids scavenge dead animals. This female scorpionfly and a mite are picking over the remains of a cricket. (Arthur V. Evans. Reproduced by permission.

Others startle would-be predators by suddenly flashing bright colors or eye spots. Mantids strike out with their spiny front legs to display their bright colors. The hind wings of some grasshoppers and stick insects are also brightly patterned, but they usually remain hidden under the forewings. Moths suddenly spread their plainly patterned forewings to reveal hind wings marked with large "eyes" or bright contrasting bands of color. Centipedes and caterpillars have "false heads" that either direct attacks away from sensitive parts of their bodies or simply confuse predators hoping to make a sneak attack.

Many insects and spiders use camouflage to stay out of sight, blending in with backgrounds of living or dead leaves. (Arthur V. Evans. Reproduced by permission.)

Many insects and spiders use camouflage to stay out of sight, blending in with backgrounds of living or dead leaves. Stick insects, grasshoppers, katydids, and mantids may go a step further by actually having bodies shaped like sticks, stones, leaves, or flowers. Arthropods that conceal themselves by looking like another object, living or dead, are called cryptic (KRIP-tik). They even act like the objects they mimic by remaining very still, although stick and leaf mimics sometimes gently sway back and forth, as if they were in a gentle breeze. Some spiders and caterpillars avoid detection by looking like something unappetizing, such as bird droppings.

Biting, stinging, bad tasting, and foul smelling arthropods are often brightly marked or distinctively colored as a warning to potential predators. The colors, patterns, and body shapes of harmful species, especially ants, bees, and wasps, frequently serve as models for other species that do not bite or sting. Species that resemble each other in color or behavior are called mimics.

The mating game

In some species, males are rare or unknown. The females lay unfertilized eggs that usually develop into more females. This process is called parthenogenesis (PAR-thuh-no-JEH-nuh-sihs). But most arthropods reproduce by mating. Males usually mate as many times as possible, but females mate only once, just a few times, or many times, depending on the species. In some species males and females gather at a food resource, such as a patch of flowers, sapping limbs, decomposing bodies, or piles of dung.

Some males claim these resources as territories and engage in battles with other males to win the favor of a nearby female.

Many males and females find one another by releasing pheromones (FEH-re-moans), chemicals that are especially attractive to members of the opposite sex of the same species. Others use flashing lights or sounds to attract one another. Once they get together, many species engage in courtship behaviors that help them to establish each other's suitability for mating. Courtship may involve biting, grappling, touching, leg waving, wing flapping, flashing mouthparts, and vibrating bodies.

In species that live on land, the male usually grasps the female with his legs or jaws and deposits sperm or a sperm packet directly into her body. These packets not only contain sperm but also provide nutrition for the female so she can produce bigger and better eggs. The act of mating may be brief or last several hours. To prevent the female from mating with other males, some males will remain with their mate until she lays her eggs. In some species, such as honeybees and many spiders, males leave part or all of their reproductive organs in the female's body to block mating attempts by other males.

Other groups of arthropods do not mate directly. For example, male spiders must first transfer their sperm to special containers on their pedipalps before they are ready to mate. They use the pedipalps to put the sperm directly into the female's reproductive organs. Male horseshoe crabs climb on the back of the females and release their sperm onto her eggs as she lays them in the sand. Silverfish males deposit a drop of sperm on the ground and then guide the female over it so she can pick it up with her reproductive organs. Male millipedes, centipedes, scorpions, and other arachnids put their sperm packets on the ground. Then they engage in a variety of courtship behaviors to guide the females over the packets. In some arthropods the females must find these packets without the help of males.

Parental care

Parental care is rare among arthropods. In most species it consists only of a female laying her eggs in places where they will not be eaten or destroyed, preferably near food that is suitable for the young. However, in a few species, the female keeps

the eggs inside her body until they hatch or are "born." The eggs are nourished by their own yolks. This type of development is called ovovivipary (O-vo-vai-VIH-pe-ree). Vivipary (vai-VIH-pe-ree) occurs in some flies and parasitic true bugs. The females produce only one or a few eggs at a time and keep them inside their bodies. The eggs are nourished by the mother's body, and the larvae are born alive.

Most species lay their eggs somewhere in their habitat, either singly or in batches. Some species have special egg-laying tubes called ovipositors (O-vih-PA-zih-terz) that place their eggs out of harm's way deep in the soil or wood or inside plant or animal tissues. Others have special glands that allow them to glue their eggs to surfaces or surround them in protective cases. Some species prepare special chambers for their eggs, provide them with all the food the larvae will need to develop, and then leave. Females of a few species guard the eggs until they hatch. Some will even remain with the young for a short period, but the greatest level of parental care is seen in the social insects.

Social behavior

True social behavior is defined by overlapping generations of the same species living and working together to raise their young. They also cooperate in gathering food and defending,

repairing, and expanding the nest. Insects are the only truly social arthropods. Social insects include all termites and ants but only some bees and wasps. They live in colonies with up to one million individuals. The tasks within each colony are divided among distinctly different forms or castes. The castes include workers, soldiers, and reproductives (queens and males).

Workers form the majority of the colony. They care for the young and the queen and perform all other tasks in the nest. They divide the labor among themselves on the basis of age or size. Some ants and termites also have a soldier caste. Soldiers are usually larger than the workers and sometimes equipped with powerful jaws to drive away intruders. Both workers and soldiers are sterile and cannot reproduce. The workers and soldiers of ants, bees, and wasps are always sterile females, but in termites they are male or female.

The reproductive caste consists of queens and males. Each colony has at least one queen, and she is usually the mother of the entire colony. She may live many years, laying millions of eggs in her lifetime. Males are short-lived and usually die after mating with the queen. However, termite kings usually stay with the queen long after they mate.

Social insects include all termites and ants but only some bees and wasps. (Arthur V. Evans. Reproduced by permission.)

Colony members communicate with pheromones to identify nest mates, recruit other members of the colony to find food or defend the nest, and to coordinate other activities. For example, honeybee queens use a pheromone called queen substance to hold the colony together. Workers pick up the pheromone as they lick and groom the queen. As they feed one another, they pass it along to other workers in the colony. The queen substance "tells" the workers to feed and care for the queen and her eggs and lets all the members of the colony know that she is alive and well. Every worker in the colony will know if their queen has died within a day, even though only a few workers will have actually had contact with the body.

Other arthropods occasionally gather in groups to feed, mate, or temporarily guard their young, but they are not truly social. There are about 40 species of spiders that live in groups in large webs and feed together. A huntsman spider, *Delena cancerides*, lives under bark in groups of up to three hundred individuals. These groups consist mainly of young spiders with just a few adults. They work together to attack and kill insect prey, as well as defend their shelter against spiders from other colonies.

DANCES WITH PLANTS

Arthropods, especially insects, have had a long and close relationship with flowering plants that dates back between 135 and sixty-five million years ago. From the plant's point of view this relationship is both negative and positive. A negative example is their relationship with herbivorous insects. As herbivores, insects have strongly influenced the evolution of flowering plants. Over millions of years, plants have evolved several ways of defending themselves against insects. Many have developed bad-tasting chemicals, or toxins (TAK-sihns), that discourage herbivorous insects from eating their stems and leaves. Those plants that survived insect attacks were able to pass along their characteristics to the next generation through their seeds. At the same time, the defensive strategies of plants have influenced the evolution of insects. They have evolved systems within their bodies that breakdown these toxins into harmless chemicals so they can continue to eat the plant. Those insects that were able to get enough food were able to pass their characteristics on to the next generation through their eggs. Over time, plants and insects continued to change, or evolve, into new species as they attempt to overcome the attacks and defenses of the other. The mutual influence that plants and insects have over each other's evolution continues today and is called coevolution (ko-EH-vuh-LU-shun).

From a plant's point of view, pollination is an example of a positive interaction with insects. Plants produce flowers with nectar and more pollen than they need to reproduce to attract insects. Flowers are like brightly colored, sweet-smelling road signs that encourage insect pollinators to stop and visit. These pollinators either accidentally or purposefully collect pollen from the flower. Many flowers depend on bees, flies, beetles, and thrips to carry their pollen from one flower to another so their seeds will develop. Some species of orchids rely on specific insects to pollinate them. In fact, the flowers of some species mimic female wasps. Male wasps pollinate the flowers as they attempt to "mate" with the flower. This very special type of interaction between a plant and an insect is another example of coevolution.

BENEFICIAL INSECTS AND SPIDERS

People depend on insects to pollinate their crops, ensuring that they have plenty of food, fiber, and other useful products. Honeybees are not only valued for their pollination services but also for their honey and wax. Silk from the cocoons of the silk moth, *Bombyx mori*, has been harvested for centuries. Each caterpillar must eat 125 pounds (56.7 kilograms) of mulberry leaves before it can spin a cocoon. About seventeen hundred cocoons are required to make one dress. China and Japan are the world's largest producers of silk.

Beekeeping and silkworm culture were the first forms of insect farming, but today many other insects are raised and sold for use as research animals, fish bait, and pet food. Others are used to combat weeds and insect pests. Butterflies and other tropical insects are raised and shipped alive to insect zoos and butterfly houses around the world. Money earned by butterfly farmers in Central and South America, Malaysia, and Papua New Guinea is used to support families, to maintain the farm, and to preserve or improve butterfly habitats.

Grasshoppers, termites, beetles, caterpillars, and crustaceans are important sources of food for humans and are even considered delicacies in many parts of the world. They are an excellent source of fat and protein. Western European culture has largely ignored insects as food but considers lobster, crab, and shrimp as delicacies.

Every species of arthropod is a flying, walking, or swimming pharmacy filled with potentially useful medicines and other chemical compounds. For example, venoms from insect stings are used to treat patients with rheumatism (RU-me-TIH-zem), a disease that affects the joints. The venom helps to increase blood flow to the diseased joints and stops the pain.

Arthropods also provide an early warning system for detecting changes in the environment caused by habitat destruction, pollution, and other environmental disturbances. Aquatic insects and arthropods living in the ocean are especially sensitive to even the smallest changes in water temperature and chemistry. The presence or absence of a particular species may demonstrate that a particular habitat is polluted as a result of illegal dumping, pesticides from nearby agricultural fields, or chemical waste from mining operations.

INSECTS AND SPIDERS AS SYMBOLS

People around the world have used insects as symbols to explain how the world began. There is a tribe in South America that believes a beetle created the world and, from the grains of sand left over, made men and women. In the American Southwest the Hopis believed that the world began through the activities of Spider Woman, the Earth Goddess. The sacred scarab beetle appeared in wall paintings and carvings and played an important role in the religious lives of the early Egyptians. Early Christians used insects as symbols of evil and wickedness, but eastern cultures, especially in China and Japan, often used them to signify good luck. The ancient Greeks used insects and spiders in their plays and fables about good and evil.

INSECTS AND SPIDERS IN ARTS AND CRAFTS AND IN LITERATURE

Images of insects have appeared on 6,000-year-old cave paintings, as well as on the walls of ancient Egyptian tombs. The Egyptians wore sacred scarab carvings and other insect ornaments. The ancient Greeks used insect images on jewelry and coins. Insects were also used to adorn decorative boxes, bowls, and writing sets in the Middle Ages. The hard and tough bodies of beetles have long been used to make pendants and earrings. Today, boxed collections of large tropical species are sold to tourists as decorative pieces.

Ants, bees, fleas, flies, grasshoppers, spiders, and scorpions are frequently mentioned in the Bible. Images of arthropods were once used to decorate the brightly painted borders of other important religious books and papers. They have influenced language with such words as lousy, nitpicker, grubby, and beetle-browed. Beetles have also inspired the names of a world-famous rock group and a well-known German automobile.

INSECTS AND SPIDERS AS PESTS

Insects are humanity's greatest competitors and cause huge economic losses when they feed on timber, stored foods, pastures, and crops. Termites and other insects infest and weaken wood used to build homes, businesses, floors, cabinets, and furniture. The larvae of clothes moths and carpet beetles destroy woolen clothing, rugs, and hides. Mites, moths, beetles, and other insects invade homes and infest stored foods and destroy books and other paper products. Crops lost to insect damage cause enormous economic hardship and may lead to starvation and death among hundreds or thousands of people. One-third to one-half of all food grown worldwide is lost to damage caused by insects and mites, not only by devouring the foliage but also by infecting plants with diseases.

Arthropods not only eat people's belongings, they also attack human bodies. The bites of blood-feeding mosquitoes, flies, fleas, lice, and ticks are not only irritating, they are also responsible for spreading diseases that can infect and kill people, pets, and farm animals. Over the centuries more people have died from diseases carried by arthropods than any other reason. Even today, more people die from malaria and yellow fever, diseases transmitted by mosquitoes, than from HIV/AIDS, cancer, accidents, and wars. Spiders, millipedes, centipedes, and other arthropods are not often pests but are considered nuisances when they enter homes. The venomous bites of some spiders and centipedes may be painful but are seldom life-threatening for healthy adults.

These and other pests are effectively controlled by integrated pest management, or IPM. IPM includes plowing fields to kill pests in the ground, rotating crops so that they will not have anything to eat, or planting other crops nearby that will give their enemies a place to live and prosper. Whenever possible, natural enemies are used to combat pests instead of pesticides. The use of predators, parasitoids, and diseases is called biological control. Spiders might be considered biological controls in some fields, but most species tend to eat anything they can catch, not just the pest. IPM depends on accurate identification of the pest and a thorough knowledge of its life history so that control efforts can be directed at the pest's most vulnerable life stages. However, if not used wisely, any pest control method may harm other species or their habitats.

CONSERVATION

Habitat destruction is the number one threat to all insects, spiders, and their relatives. Pollution, pesticides, land development, logging, fires, cattle grazing, and violent storms are just some of the events that damage or destroy their habitats. Introduced, or exotic, plants and animals can also have devastating effects. They compete with native arthropods for food and space. Native arthropods are usually capable of dealing with organisms that they have evolved with over millions of years, but they are often defenseless against exotic predators and diseases.

Loss of habitat and competition with exotic species affect the availability of food, mates, and egg-laying and nesting sites. The reduction or loss of any one of these resources can make a species vulnerable to extinction (ehk-STINGK-shun). Extinct species have completely died out and will never again appear on Earth. Arthropods that are widely distributed or feed on a variety of plants or animals are less likely to become extinct, but those living in small fragile habitats with specialized feeding habits are more likely to become extinct when their habitats are disturbed or destroyed. The fossil record shows that extinction is a natural process. Yet today, the loss of thousands of species of plants and animals each year, mostly arthropods, is not the result of natural events but is a direct result of human activities.

Scientists, politicians, and concerned citizens around the world have joined together to establish laws that protect arthropods and their habitats. The United States Fish and Wildlife Service helps to protect species threatened with extinction. They list seventy-seven species of arthropods as Threatened or Endangered, including forty-four insects (mostly butterflies), twelve arachnids, and twenty-one crustaceans. Some countries set aside land as preserves specifically to protect arthropods and their habitats.

The World Conservation Union (IUCN) publishes a list of species threatened by extinction. It places species in the categories Extinct, Extinct in the Wild, Critically Endangered, Endangered, Vulnerable, Near Threatened, Data Deficient, or Least Concern. In 2003 the list included 1,252 species of insects, spiders, and other arthropods. The sad fact is that scientists will probably never know just how many arthropod species are threatened with extinction and need protection. For example, tropical rainforest and coral reef habitats are disappearing so quickly that scientists have little or no time to collect and study their arthropod species before they are lost forever. Humanity's health and well-being depend on preserving all life, not just species that are big, pretty, furry, or feathered. Maybe you can be one of the scientists of the future that helps to save an insect or spider from becoming extinct.

FOR MORE INFORMATION

Books:

Brusca, R. C., and G. J. Brusca. *Invertebrates. Second edition.* Sunderland, MA: Sinauer Associates, Inc., 2003.

Craig, S. F., D. A. Thoney, and N. Schlager, editors. *Grzimek's Animal Life Encyclopedia.* Second Edition. Volume 2: *Protostomes.* Farmington, MI: Thomson Gale, 2003.

Eisner, T. *For Love of Insects.* Cambridge, MA: Harvard University Press, 2003.

Evans, A. V., R. W. Garrison, and N. Schlager, editors. *Grzimek's Animal Life Encyclopedia.* Second Edition. Volume 3: *Insects.* Farmington, MI: Thomson Gale, 2003.

Imes, R. *The Practical Entomologist.* New York: Simon & Schuster Inc., 1991.

Kritsky, G., and R. Cherry. *Insect Mythology.* San Jose, CA: Writers Club Press, 2000.

Menzel, P. *Man Eating Bugs. The Art and Science of Eating Bugs.* Berkeley, CA: Ten Speed Press, 1998.

O'Toole, C. *Alien Empire.* London: BBC Books, 1995.

Poinar, G., and R. Poinar. *The Quest for Life in Amber.* Reading, MA: Addison-Wesley Publishing Company, 1994.

Preston-Mafham, R., and K. Preston-Mafham. *The Encyclopedia of Land Invertebrate Behaviour.* Cambridge, MA: The MIT Press, 1993.

Tavoloacci, J., editor. *Insects and Spiders of the World.* New York: Marshall Cavendish, 2003.

Periodicals:

Evans, A. V. "Arthropods on Parade." *Critters USA 2000 Annual* 5 (2000): 67–75.

Hogue, C. L. "Cultural Entomology." *Annual Review of Entomology* 32 (1987): 181–199.

Web sites:

"Arthropoda." http://paleo.cortland.edu/tutorial/Arthropods/arthropods.htm (accessed on November 19, 2004).

"Directory of Entomological Societies." http://www.sciref.org/links/EntDept/index.htm (accessed on November 19, 2004).

"Directory of Entomology Departments and Institutes." http://www.sciref.org/links/EntSoc/intro.htm (accessed on November 19, 2004).

"Introduction to the Arthropods." http://www.ucmp.berkeley.edu/arthropoda/arthropoda.html (accessed on November 19, 2004).

"Information on Arachnids." The American Entomological Society. http://www.americanarachnology.org/AAS_information.html (accessed on November 19, 2004).

"Insects in Human Culture." Cultural Entomology. http://www.insects.org/ced/ (accessed on November 19, 2004).

"Insects on WWW." http://www.isis.vt.edu/~fanjun/text/Links.html (accessed on November 19, 2004).

"Phylum Arthropoda." http://animaldiversity.ummz.umich.edu/site/accounts/information/Arthropoda.html (accessed on November 19, 2004).

Videos:

Alien Empire. New York: Time Life Videos, 1995.

class
CHAPTER

PHYSICAL CHARACTERISTICS

Approximately one hundred different species, or kinds, of sea spiders live off the coasts of the United States and Canada. Most of these species are small, measuring 0.04 to 0.36 inches (1 to 9 millimeters) in length. Some deep-sea species are quite large, with legs as long as 1 foot (305 millimeters). Sea spiders are usually white or colored to blend in perfectly with their backgrounds, typically tan or brown. Sea spiders have a hard outer skeleton, called an exoskeleton. The exoskeleton is so thin that the spider can breathe through it, eliminating the need for a respiratory system, such as those found in humans and other animals. The exoskeleton is covered with tiny pits and hairlike structures. These structures require more study, but they probably help sea spiders to "taste" and "touch."

The sea spider's body is not clearly divided into distinct regions, like those of other arthropods. The first body region is the largest and contains the four small eyes and mouth. The mouth is at the end of a long, flexible tube called the proboscis (pruh-BAH-suhs). The proboscis in some sea spiders is as long as or even longer than the rest of the body. This organ is used to mix digestive chemicals into the food and suck it up into the digestive system, or those body parts that break down food for the body to absorb. The tip of the proboscis has three lips. In some species of sea spiders, the lips may have teeth, while others have spines. Leglike structures are found on either side of the proboscis and are used to handle food.

phylum
class
subclass
order
monotypic order
suborder
family

Next to the mouthparts is a pair of specialized legs used to carry eggs. In most species these egg-carrying body parts are found only in males, but some females also have them. At times of the year other than the breeding season, females use them to clean and groom themselves. During the breeding season, males use them for courting and carrying the eggs until they hatch.

The remaining body segments form the trunk of the sea spider. Attached to the trunk are four pairs of long, slender walking legs. Some sea spider species have five, or even six, pairs. Each leg has eight segments and a single claw. The trunk is very slender and contains part of the digestive system and the reproductive organs, those body parts that produce young. Both eggs, female reproductive cells, and sperm, or male reproductive cells, leave the body through openings in the legs.

GEOGRAPHIC RANGE

Sea spiders inhabit oceans worldwide, from warm tropical waters to very cold polar seas. The tropics are warm areas of the world, where the temperature is typically more than 68°F (20°C). Polar regions are the cold areas of the world near the North Pole (Arctic) and South Pole (Antarctic), where temperatures never rise above 50°F (10°C).

HABITAT

Sea spiders usually live near the shore. They are found crawling over seaweeds as well as on sea anemones (uh-NEH-muh-nees), small sea animals with long, thin, armlike body parts called tentacles (TEN-tih-kuhls); corals, the hard skeletons of certain sea creatures; and other animal colonies, or tight groupings of animals, permanently attached to the sea bottom. Some species are found at great depths, up to 23,000 feet (7,000 meters), where they live near hot water springs bubbling up from the sea floor.

DIET

Most sea spiders eat other animals and attack invertebrates (in-VER-teh-brehts), or animals without backbones, that are attached to the ocean bottom, such as corals, clams, and marine worms. A few species feed on red algae (AL-jee), a special group of plantlike ocean life that lacks true roots, stems, or leaves. Other sea spiders feed on bits of plant and animal tissues that build up under colonies of invertebrates. While some species use the teeth at the tip of the proboscis to pierce the bodies of their prey and suck out their juices, others tear their victims apart and feed on the small pieces.

BEHAVIOR AND REPRODUCTION

The habits of most sea spiders are poorly known. Some longer-legged species are good swimmers, but most sea spiders prefer to crawl about colonies of anemones, corals, and other stationary, or unmoving, prey animals, or animals that are their source of food.

Most species have both males and females, but in at least one species each spider has the reproductive organs of both sexes. In the few species of sea spider that scientists have studied, courtship, or the activity meant to attract a mate, is brief. While mating, the male and female are positioned so that they are belly to belly, head to tail.

As the female lets go of her eggs, the male releases sperm into the water over them. He then collects the fertilized eggs into a ball and attaches them to his egg-carrying structures with special "glue." Males usually mate with more than one female and are often seen carrying several batches of eggs, each batch the result of a different mating. Males typically carry the eggs until they hatch. Young seas spiders, or larvae (LAR-vee), usually swim freely in the ocean. Most species gain more pairs of legs as they grow into adulthood, although some hatch from the egg with a complete set of legs.

SEA SPIDERS AND PEOPLE

Sea spiders are rarely seen by most people. However, these penny-sized animals are sometimes easily seen in tidal pools, or pools of water that remain after an ocean tide has risen and fallen. Sea spiders are captured and stored in alcohol and other

WHAT'S IN A NAME?

The name Pycnogonida comes from the Greek words *pyknos*, meaning "thick" or "knobby," and *gony*, or "knees." These animals are called sea spiders because of their similarity to true spiders. Fossil (FAH-suhl) sea spiders, the remains of animals that lived long ago, date back almost four hundred million years. Even without fossil evidence, scientists studying living sea spiders are convinced that these animals are among the world's oldest groups of animals. There are about one thousand species of sea spiders worldwide. Although sea spiders were first discovered nearly 150 years ago, very little is known about them, especially those species living at great depths in the sea. Their unusual body form has made it difficult for scientists to figure out just how they are related to other arthropods. They are most closely related to horseshoe crabs and spiders and their relatives.

fluids to preserve them and are sold to colleges and universities as study animals.

CONSERVATION STATUS

Sea spiders are not endangered or threatened.

Colossendeis megalonyx

NO COMMON NAME
Colossendeis megalonyx

Physical characteristics: The body of this sea spider, one of the world's largest, is approximately 0.78 inches (20 millimeters) long, including the long, broadly rounded snout. The leg span is up to 27.5 inches (700 millimeters). Each leg is tipped with a long, slender claw.

Geographic range: This sea spider is found from depths of 10 to 16,400 feet (3 to 5,000 meters) around Antarctica and into the southern Atlantic Ocean, southern Indian Ocean, and southern Pacific Ocean, including the Antipodes Islands off New Zealand.

Habitat: Nothing is known about the spider's preferred living areas.

Diet: This sea spider eats soft corals and small hydrozoans attached to sponges. The hydrozoans are a group of water-dwelling organisms without backbones that includes jellyfish.

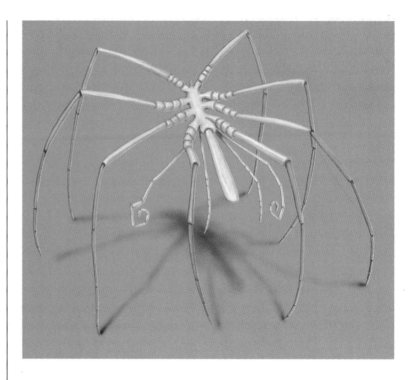

The body size of this sea spider is among the world's largest, averaging approximately 0.78 inches (20 millimeters) long. (Illustration by Joseph E. Trumpey. Reproduced by permission.)

Behavior and reproduction: Nothing is known about this sea spider's reproductive habits or other behavior.

***Colossendeis megalonyx* and people:** This species does not interact with people.

Conservation status: This species is not endangered or threatened. ∎

FOR MORE INFORMATION

Books:

Tavolacci, J., ed. *Insects and Spiders of the World*. New York: Marshall Cavendish, 2003.

Web sites:

"Arthropoda: Chelicerata Sea Spiders." *Underwater Field Guide to Ross Island and McMurdo Sound, Antarctica*. http://scilib.ucsd.edu/sio/nsf/fguide/arthropoda-2.html (accessed August 17, 2004).

"Introduction to Pycnogonida." University of California, Berkeley, Museum of Paleontology. http://www.ucmp.berkeley.edu/arthropoda/pycnogonida.html (accessed on August 17, 2004).

"Pycnogonida (Sea Spiders)." Earth-Life Web. http://www.earthlife.net/chelicerata/pycnogonida.html (accessed on August 17, 2004).

PHYSICAL CHARACTERISTICS

Adults horseshoe crabs range in length from 3.5 to 33.5 inches (89 to 850 millimeters). The females are larger than the males. Horseshoe crabs have a large, arched forebody covered by a horseshoe-shaped carapace (KARE-a-pays), or upper shell, followed by a smooth abdomen with spines on the sides, and a thin tail. There are two pairs of simple eyes, or eyes with one lens, on top of the carapace and a pair of compound eyes, or eyes with multiple lenses, on ridges toward the sides. The mouthparts are made up of a pair of pincherlike mouthparts and a pair of clawed leglike appendages. There are four pairs of clawed walking legs. The walking legs have seven segments, the last two form pinchers on the first four pairs of legs. The bases of the fourth pair of legs are fitted with special structures called flabella. The flabella are used to clean the book gills. The last pair of legs ends in four leaflike structures. These legs are used to push through, and sweep away mud, silt, and sand as the horseshoe crab burrows through the sea bottom in search of food.

The solid midsection, or abdomen, has six pairs of flaplike limbs. The first pair is joined together and protects the reproductive opening, through which the crab lays its eggs. The other five pairs form the gills, the organs through which the crab breathes underwater. They are called book gills because they resemble the pages of a book. Movable spines stick out on each side of the midsection. Different species, or types, of horseshoe crabs have different numbers of spines. A long thin tail extends from the end of the midsection and is used for steering through the water. Individual crabs that are trapped on their backs on the beach use the long tail to flip themselves over.

GEOGRAPHIC RANGE

Horseshoe crabs inhabit coastal regions of eastern North America and the Indo-Pacific. Of the four species of horseshoe crabs in the world, just one is found along the eastern and Gulf coasts of the United States.

HABITAT

Horseshoe crabs live just offshore along the coast or in salty estuaries (EHS-chew-air-eez), the wide parts at the lower ends of rivers, where the river meets the sea. They prefer coves and bays, which are small inlets of the sea, or wetland, meaning land that is covered with shallow water or that has very wet soil. The crabs like clean, sandy bottoms or muddy bottoms protected from strong wave action. Adults move onshore to mate on beaches at night.

DIET

The young, or larvae (LAR-vee), do not feed until after they molt, or shed their outer skeleton, called an exoskeleton, for the first time. Adults and older larvae both eat almost any food items they find on the bottom and also attack clams and worms, or scrape algae (AL-jee), tiny plantlike organisms, off rocks. Horseshoe crabs lack jaws and instead use their legs to grasp and crush their food. Food is ground with spines at the bases of the crab's legs. In fact, the name Merostomata comes from the Greek words *meros*, meaning leg, and *stoma*, or mouth—referring to the role the legs play in chewing food.

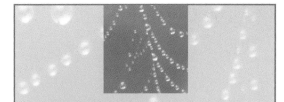

GIANT TERRORS OF ANCIENT SEAS

Despite their name, horseshoe crabs are not related to true crabs. Instead, they are related to sea spiders and true spiders and their relatives. The Merostomata are among the oldest living animals, with fossils (FAH-suhls), the remains of ancient animals, dating back 350 million years. Horseshoe crabs are the only living members of the subclass, which includes the now extinct giant water scorpions, or giant sea scorpions. They are called "living fossils" because they have changed very little over millions of years. Some 290 million years ago they were plentiful on the bottoms of ancient seas, as well as in brackish, or salty, waters and freshwaters. The sea scorpions, also called eurypterids, were similar to horseshoe crabs but thinner and longer and with a smaller shell and an abdomen divided into many segments. They were the largest arthropods ever to have roamed the earth. One species measured 9 feet (2.7 meters) in length. Giant sea scorpions probably ate fish and other giant sea scorpions.

BEHAVIOR AND REPRODUCTION

Every spring and summer adults migrate (MY-grayt), or move, from deeper waters onto nearby beaches to mate and lay eggs, or spawn. Spawning occurs at high tide on the beaches of estuaries, bays, and coves. One species swims upstream into rivers to spawn.

A male grasps the edges of the female's shell with his clawed legs, while the female digs a hollow in the sand with her legs and the front section of her body. As the female lays the eggs into this hollow, the male fertilizes (FUR-teh-lye-sez) them. The pair moves to a nearby site and begins the process all over again, using the sand dug from the new site to cover the previously laid eggs. Horseshoe crabs may spawn more than once a year, laying up to several thousand eggs after each mating.

The eggs hatch into larvae. The larvae swim constantly but soon settle to the seafloor after their first molt. They rest by burying themselves in shallow burrows in the mud and silt. Although they usually crawl on the bottom, horseshoe crabs also swim upside down using their book gills to propel themselves through the water.

Horseshoe crabs molt six times in their first year and sixteen to seventeen times during their entire lives. Males reach adulthood between nine and eleven years of age. Females become adults when they are ten to twelve years old.

HORSESHOE CRABS AND PEOPLE

Horseshoe crabs are used for food and as bait to catch various ocean-dwelling animals. Their bodies were once ground up and used as fertilizer. Certain scientific studies of their eyes have led to a better understanding of how the human eye works, resulting in improved treatments for human eye disorders. Their blood contains a substance that is used to identify bacterial contamination, or dirtying, of drugs, surgical equipment, and vaccines, or medicines that are used to protect the human body against disease. Other substances in their blood show promise in fighting viruses and cancer. Their exoskeletons are used in the manufacture of skin lotion, contact lenses, and surgical sutures, or stitches. Chitin (KYE-tehn), an important chemical component of the horseshoe crab's exoskeleton, is used to remove harmful substances from water. It also is taken as a dietary supplement.

CONSERVATION STATUS

The World Conservation Union (IUCN) lists just one species of horseshoe crab as Near Threatened, meaning that they are at risk of being threatened with extinction in the future. All horseshoe crab populations are thought to be declining world-wide owing to harvesting, or gathering by humans, and habitat destruction.

Horseshoe crab *(Limulus polyphemus)*

HORSESHOE CRAB
Limulus polyphemus

Physical characteristics: The horseshoe crab, also known as American horseshoe crab, is greenish brown to blackish brown. Males are smaller than females. The average body length of males is 14 inches (356 millimeters) and of females is 17 inches (431 millimeters).

Geographic range: The horseshoe crab inhabits the Atlantic and Gulf coasts of North America, from Long Island to the Yucatán peninsula.

Habitat: These crabs live off the coast to depths of more than 200 feet (61 meters).

Horseshoe crabs inhabit coastal regions of eastern North America and the Indo-Pacific. (© John M. Burnley/The National Audubon Society Collection/ Photo Researchers, Inc. Reproduced by permission.)

Diet: The horseshoe crab eats clams and marine worms.

Behavior and reproduction: Adults live in deeper, offshore waters during the winter, ranging as far out as 25 miles (40 kilometers). In spring they migrate into shallow waters and then onto sandy beaches to spawn. Males approach the beach as the tide rises, followed by the females. Spawning occurs mostly at night near the high-tide line.

Females bury as many as twenty thousand eggs in several clutches, or groups, which are fertilized by males. Eggs hatch after thirteen to fifteen days.

Horseshoe crabs and people: In the United States the horseshoe crab is harvested as bait for the conch and eel fisheries. From 1850 until the 1970s the horseshoe crab was processed for fertilizer. Components of its blood and exoskeleton are used for a wide variety of medical purposes.

Conservation status: This species is listed by the World Conservation Union (IUCN) as Near Threatened. It is threatened by too much harvesting and habitat destruction. ■

FOR MORE INFORMATION

Books:

Day, Nancy. *The Horseshoe Crab.* New York: Dillon Press, 1992.

Tanacredi, John T., ed. *Limulus in the Limelight: A Species 350 Million Years in the Making and in Peril?* New York: Kluwer Academic/Plenum, 2001.

Periodicals:

Rudloe, A., and J. Rudloe. "The Changeless Horseshoe Crab." *National Geographic Magazine* (April 1981) 159, no. 4: 562–572.

Web sites:

"Chitin Research." Sea Grant. http://www.ocean.udel.edu/horseshoecrab/Research/chitin.html (accessed on August 19, 2004).

"Eurypterida: All about Sea Scorpions." Palaeos: The Trace of Life on Earth. http://www.palaeos.com/Invertebrates/Arthropods/Eurypterida/ (accessed on August 19, 2004).

"Eurypterida." Eurypterids.net. http://eurypterids.net/index.html (accessed on August 19, 2004).

"The Horseshoe Crab." Ecological Research and Development Group. http://www.horseshoecrab.org/ (accessed on August 19, 2004).

"The Horseshoe Crab: Putting Science to Work to Help "Man's Best Friend." NOAA Research. http://www.oar.noaa.gov/spotlite/archive/spot_delaware.html (accessed on August 19, 2004).

SPIDERS, SCORPIONS,
MITES, AND TICKS
Arachnida

Class: Chelicerata

Subclass: Arachnida

Number of families: 570 families

subclass
CHAPTER

PHYSICAL CHARACTERISTICS

Arachnids (uh-RAK-nihds) are related to sea spiders and horseshoe crabs. Among the many members of this group are ticks and mites, scorpions, spiders, and even the common harvestman, also known as daddy longlegs—all with their own distinct appearance. Despite these differences, many adult arachnids have two distinct body regions: the front portion, a sort of head area combined with a thorax, or midsection, contains the mouthparts and six sets of paired, leglike limbs, and the second portion, the abdomen, has a stomach, reproductive opening, and lunglike structures or breathing tubes. While arachnids all have these two body parts, some have narrow waists, and others have thick waists. In some arachnids, such as mites and harvestmen, the two body parts are closely joined together to form a single region; the two parts cannot easily be seen as different from each other. The front region of arachnids is covered by a carapace (KARE-a-pays), a smooth, shield-like plate, which in some arachnids, such as harvestmen and sun spiders, is divided into three parts. In ticks, mites, and most spiders the abdomen is usually smooth, without any segments, but in all other arachnids the abdomen is plainly divided into segments.

Arachnids have mouthparts that look like small pinchers. They are used to capture and chew prey, or food animals. The mouthparts are sometimes used as fangs to inject venom, or poison, and digestive chemicals into the wounds of their prey. Arachnids also have a small set of leglike structures, called pedipalps,

phylum

class

◊ **subclass**

order

monotypic order

suborder

family

attached to either side of the mouth; in some arachnids these are used to cut and crush food, and, in others, they serve as antennae. Adult arachnids all have four pairs of legs. The legs often have bristles (brih-SUHLS), or short, stiff hairs, that can sense vibrations (vie-BRAY-shuns). The first pair is sometimes not used for walking at all and is used instead as feelers, or antennae. The other three pairs of legs are used for walking and digging, as well as for capturing prey. Some arachnids have fingerlike projections on their abdomens, used to produce silk; in spiders these structures are called spinnerets. Some arachnids have additional sensory equipment on their abdomens. Whip scorpions have a bristly and sensitive whiplike tail on the tip of the abdomen, and scorpions have comblike structures underneath the abdomen, used to detect vibrations.

GEOGRAPHIC RANGE

Arachnids are found throughout the world. About eight thousand of the ninety-seven thousand species of arachnids are found in the United States and Canada.

HABITAT

Arachnids live on land, in nearly every sort of habitat. Some live in freshwater.

DIET

Arachnids attack and kill small animals, especially insects and their relatives, and then feed on their body fluids. Many ticks and mites are parasites, meaning that they feed on the blood and tissue fluids of their victims without necessarily killing them. Some mites take the fluids and tissues of plants and funguses. Unable to chew, most arachnids must first digest their food outside their bodies. They pierce tissues with their mouthparts and inject them with digestive chemicals, turning them into fluids. The fluids are then sucked through the mouth and into the body.

BEHAVIOR AND REPRODUCTION

Most arachnids live alone, except during the mating season. They engage in an amazing variety of activity to obtain food. Some spiders trap their victims in silken webs and kill them with a poisonous bite. Others ambush their prey and overpower them with their strong legs before biting them. Scorpions use their claws to capture and kill prey, or else they kill them with a venomous sting. Pseudoscorpions (SOU-doh-skor-pee-uhns) lack a stinger, but they have claws with poison glands that drip venom into the wounds of their victims. Sun spiders use lightning speed and their massive mouthparts to outrun and tear apart prey. Ticks climb up on grass and brush along trails, spreading their legs like grappling hooks to latch on to the fur or clothing of hosts walking nearby. Mites lack the ease of movement that would allow them to travel long distances in their search for food, so some species attach themselves to larger animals not as parasites but as hitchhikers, to help them get around to find food.

When they are ready to mate, male arachnids transfer sperm, or male reproductive cells, either to special parts of the leglike organs of the mouth or onto the ground in "packets." Eventually, the sperm is moved to or picked up by the female during courtship, a set of activities meant to attract a mate. Some scorpions and other arachnids can reproduce without males. There may be one, to more than one thousand, eggs in a single brood. The eggs are laid in underground chambers, beneath stones, under tree bark, enclosed in a silken cocoon, or held in a sticky sack beneath the body of the female. Some scorpions have live young, while others keep their eggs inside the body until they hatch. Some female arachnids guard their eggs or young until their first molt, when the young shed and replace their outer covering, or exoskeleton, for the first time. Young arachnids always resemble tiny adults, although some mites hatch with only six legs and gain an additional pair as they grow into adulthood.

SMOOTH AS SILK?

Spider silk is a liquid protein played out as dry fibers through spigots mounted on six abdominal faucetlike structures called spinnerets. The spinnerets form a pump-and-valve pressure system that allows spiders to change the thickness, strength, and stretchiness of their silk. Certain kinds of spiders, called cribellate (KRIB-uh-layt) spiders, have a special plate, called the cribellum, that produces webs made up of wooly strands of silk that are sticky, like Velcro. Ecribellate (EE-krib-uh-layt) spiders lack this plate and produce webs that are tacky by virtue of glue droplets strung out like pearls along the silken strands.

ARACHNIDS AND PEOPLE

Spiders help control insect pests in gardens and parks and among field crops. Some mites eat other mites and are used to control the populations of mites that harm crops. However, many ticks and mites act as parasites on people and other animals and spread diseases. Despite their reputation, only a few spiders and scorpions have venoms strong enough to harm people. The venomous bites and stings of such spiders and scorpions are dangerous to humans, especially young children, elderly persons, or people who are already in poor health.

CONSERVATION STATUS

The World Conservation Union (IUCN) lists one arachnid species as Endangered, meaning that it faces a very high risk of extinction in the wild in the near future; nine as Vulnerable, meaning that there is a high risk of its extinction in the wild; and one as Near Threatened, meaning that it is at risk of becoming threatened with extinction in the future. These and other species of arachnids are threatened by habitat destruction.

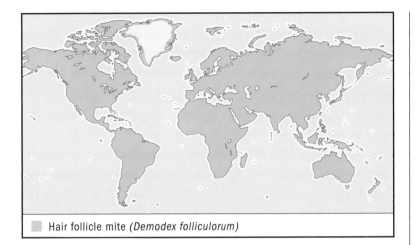

Hair follicle mite (*Demodex folliculorum*)

HAIR FOLLICLE (FAH-LIH-KUHL) MITE
Demodex folliculorum

Physical characteristics: This microscopic, wormlike, almost transparent, or see-through, parasitic mite is 0.00394 to 0.0178 inches (0.1 to 0.45 millimeters) in length. The head is distinctly separated from the body. The abdomen is finely wrinkled and tapered. Adults have eight stumplike legs, each with claws. The needlelike mouthparts are used for eating skin cells.

Geographic range: These mites live worldwide, wherever people live.

Habitat: This mite lives in human hair follicles, the small sacs that surround the root of each hair. The mite might be found anywhere on the body but prefers the follicles of the face, the roots of eyelashes, and the oil glands of the forehead, nose, and chin.

Diet: The hair follicle mite eats human skin cells.

Behavior and reproduction: Follicle mites are common parasites and spend their entire lives on their human hosts. They live in hair follicles and eyelashes, burrowing head first into the root. They move onto the skin at night at rate of 0.4 inches (1 centimeter) per hour.

Females may lay up to twenty-five oval eggs on one hair follicle. Young mites resemble adults. First-stage larvae (LAR-vee), or young

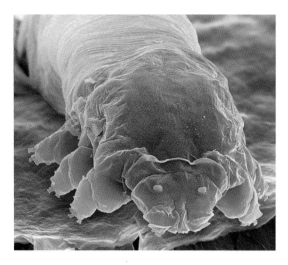

Hair follicle mites live in hair follicles and eyelashes, burrowing head first into the root. (©Andrew Syred/Photo Researchers, Inc. Reproduced by permission.)

mites, are legless, but later stages, before the mite becomes an adult, have six legs. Follicles may become tightly packed as the mite larvae grow. Adult mites leave follicles to mate and then find new follicles in which to lay eggs. The entire life cycle of the mite, from egg to adult, takes about fourteen to eighteen days.

Hair follicle mites and people: Mites are basically harmless, and humans who harbor them often show no signs of infestation. Follicle mites are not known to transmit diseases, but large numbers in a single follicle may cause itching and other skin disorders, especially in the elderly.

Conservation status: This species is not endangered or threatened. ∎

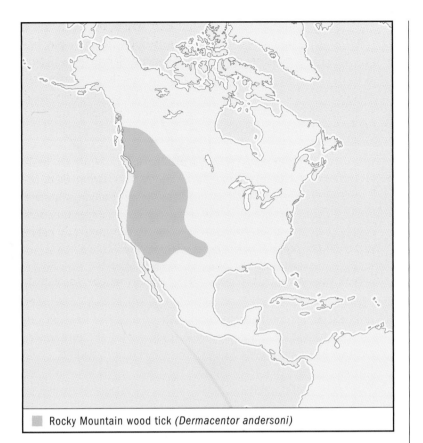

Rocky Mountain wood tick *(Dermacentor andersoni)*

ROCKY MOUNTAIN WOOD TICK
Dermacentor andersoni

Physical characteristics: Adult wood ticks typically measure 0.08 to 0.21 inches (2 to 5.3 millimeters) in length, but females filled with blood look like plump beans and may reach a length of 0.65 inches (16.5 millimeters) and a width of 0.45 inches (11.4 millimeters). Their flat, pear-shaped bodies are covered with a tough outer skeleton.

Adult females are reddish brown with a grayish white shield on the back, near the front of body; the shield turns grayish when it fills with blood. Males are spotted with brown and gray and do not have a distinctive white shield. There are eleven folds along the edge of the abdomen.

Rocky Mountain wood ticks attach themselves to their hosts by secreting a special kind of glue around their mouthparts just before inserting them into the host's flesh. (©Larry West/Photo Researchers, Inc. Reproduced by permission.)

Geographic range: The Rocky Mountain wood tick is widely distributed in North America, primarily throughout Rocky Mountain states and into southwestern Canada.

Habitat: This tick is found in spring and summer in brushy areas of foothills and mountains that are home to small mammals.

Diet: Wood ticks at the adult and larval stages feed as external parasites on the blood of reptiles, birds, and mammals and can survive for more than one year without feeding at all. When they find a host, males feed for about five days without becoming engorged, or completely filled with blood. Then they become sexually mature and ready to mate; after mating they resume feeding. Females feed for up to seven days (until they are fully engorged), during which time they mate. The body weight of a fully engorged female will increase from about 0.000176 ounces (5 milligrams) to more than 0.0247 ounces (700 milligrams).

Behavior and reproduction: Adults infest and live as parasites on large animals, such as bear, sheep, cattle, horses, dogs, and humans. Young ticks are called larvae or nymphs. Larval ticks have only six legs, while nymphs have all eight. The larvae and nymphs feed on smaller mammals, including rabbits and squirrels. Insects at all stages attack jackrabbits and porcupines. Larvae, nymphs, and adults climb grass stems and bushes while searching for a host animal. They use carbon dioxide and other chemicals associated with mammals to detect the presence of potential hosts. Ticks attach themselves to their hosts by secreting, or giving off, a special kind of glue around their mouthparts just before inserting them into the host's flesh. Only immature ticks and adult females become engorged with the host's blood. Engorged larvae, nymphs, and unfed adults normally spend the cold winter months in grasses and leaf litter.

Ticks require a blood meal before they can molt; this is also a necessity for their eggs to develop. Mating usually takes place on the host animal. After she finishes feeding, the mated female leaves the host and looks for a protected place to lay her eggs. She lays up to 7,400 eggs over a period of ten to thirty-three days and then dies. The six-legged larvae hatch and begin to search for chipmunks, mice, voles, and other small rodents. If they do not find a host within a month, they die. They feed on their first host for two to eight days before dropping to the ground and molting. At this stage they can often survive for more than year without feeding again. With their full complement of eight legs, the tick nymphs seek slightly larger hosts, such as rabbits, ground squirrels, marmots, and skunks, and feed on them until they become engorged in three to eleven days. They drop off to molt into adults in about two weeks. Adults can survive nearly two years without feeding. After finding an even larger host, partially fed adults are ready to mate.

Rocky Mountain wood ticks and people: Females may carry and transmit several diseases from small mammals to humans, including Rocky Mountain spotted fever, tularemia, and Colorado tick fever in the United States. This happens only rarely in Canada.

Conservation status: This species is not endangered or threatened.

■

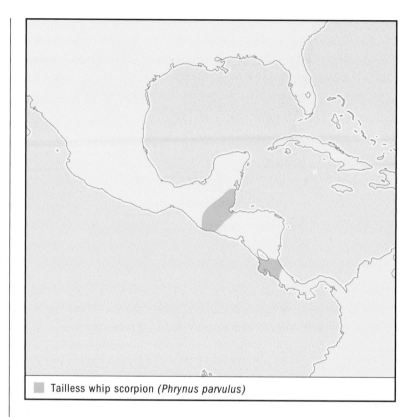

Tailless whip scorpion (*Phrynus parvulus*)

TAILLESS WHIP SCORPION
Phrynus parvulus

Physical characteristics: Whip spiders, or tailless whip scorpions, grow as long as 1.2 inches (30.4 millimeters). They lack the ability to produce silk and do not have venom glands. Their claws fold into a spiny basket, used to capture and hold prey. Young whip scorpions have reddish pedipalps and striped legs; the adults are uniformly brownish. The undivided carapace is wider than it is long. The first pair of legs is long, slender, and whiplike. Packed with special sensory structures, these legs are used not for walking but as antennae, or sense organs. The abdomen lacks a tail or defensive glands. The front of the body and abdomen are attached to each other by a narrow waist.

Geographic range: These scorpions range through Belize, Guatemala, and Costa Rica.

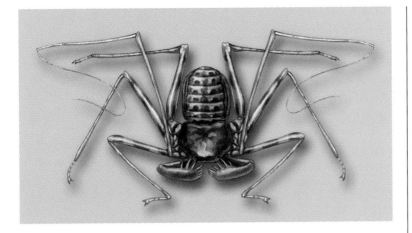

Habitat: Tailless whip scorpions live in cracks and crevices (KREH-vuh-ses) between rocks, under loose tree bark, at the base of tree trunks, or inside animal burrows, caves, and tree holes.

Diet: Tailless whip scorpions prey on small crickets, moths, and millipedes but usually avoid scorpions, centipedes, large spiders, and most ants.

Behavior and reproduction: Tailless whip scorpions are solitary animals. They are often found sitting quietly on tree trunks, waiting for insects to pass by and waving their whiplike pedipalps back and forth. Tailless whip scorpions are gentle creatures. They are very shy and run quickly when threatened. If they are attacked, they will use their spiny pedipalps as defensive weapons.

When females are nearby, males will often engage other males in combat, locking their mouthparts and claws together in battles that may last more than an hour. Males and females engage in a courtship dance that includes lots of touching and brief grabbing with the pedipalps. Once the male is accepted as a mate, he deposits a sperm packet and guides the female over it. The female lays twenty to forty eggs several months after mating. The eggs are carried underneath the body of the female until they hatch in about three or four months. After hatching, the young crawl up on the mother's back, where they remain for about a week, until they molt. They molt once or twice a year until they reach maturity. Tailless whip scorpions continue molting and growing throughout their adult lives.

Tailless whip scorpions and people: Tailless whip scorpions lack venom and are quite harmless.

Conservation status: These scorpions are not endangered or threatened. ■

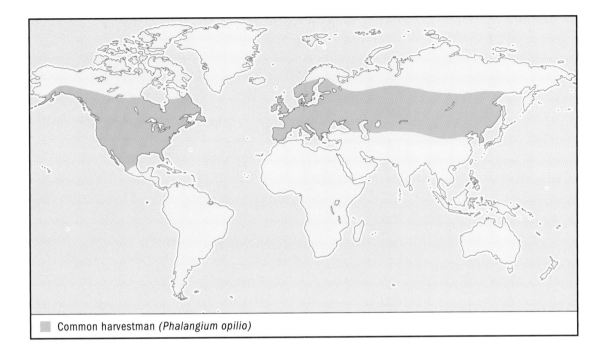

Common harvestman (Phalangium opilio)

COMMON HARVESTMAN
Phalangium opilio

Physical characteristics: The small, round bodies of common harvestmen are 0.14 to 0.35 inches (3.5 to 8.9 millimeters) in length; males typically are smaller than females. The back has various patterns and ranges in color from light gray to brown, while the underside is usually light cream colored. Both body regions are divided into segments and are joined together. Two eyes directed outward are located on top of the front body region. The common harvestman has eight very long, thin legs. These insects lack venom glands and the ability to produce silk.

Geographic range: The common harvestman lives in North America, Europe, and the temperate regions, or regions with a mild climate, of Asia.

Habitat: The common harvestman is found in gardens, parks, vacant lots, forests, woodlands, and agricultural areas.

This common harvestman is scavenging a dead honeybee. (Arthur V. Evans. Reproduced by permission.)

Diet: Harvestmen feed on small, soft-bodied invertebrates (in-VER-teh-brehts), or animals without backbones, such as aphids, caterpillars, leafhoppers, beetle larvae, mites, and slugs. They also feed on dead invertebrates and decaying plant materials, such as rotted fruit.

Behavior and reproduction: Harvestmen are active in summer and fall. At night they sometimes gather in large groups on the trunks of trees, with their legs intertwined. They fend off predators (PREH-duh-ters), or animals that hunt them for food, with a smelly, harmless fluid from scent (SENT) glands located between the first and second pairs of legs. When they are attacked, harvestmen will purposely detach a leg. The twitching limb distracts the predator until the harvestman can escape. The lost leg cannot be replaced.

Mating takes place face to face, with the male placing sperm directly into the female's body. Females lay clusters of ten to several hundred eggs in moist areas on the ground, under rocks, in cracks in soil, or in leaf litter in the autumn. One or two generations of insects are produced each year. The young hatch in spring. They look very much like the adults but have slightly shorter legs in proportion to their body size. They usually undergo seven molts, reaching maturity in two to three months.

Harvestmen and people: Harvestmen help control insect and mite pests that feed on cultivated crops. They are harmless to humans.

Conservation status: This species is not endangered or threatened.
■

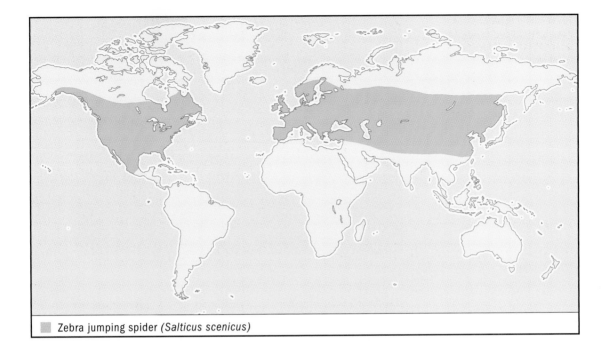

Zebra jumping spider (*Salticus scenicus*)

ZEBRA JUMPING SPIDER
Salticus scenicus

Physical characteristics: The stout-bodied adult zebra jumping spider ranges in size from 0.20 to 0.32 inches (5.1 to 8.1 millimeters). The two body regions are not segmented and are attached to each other by a narrow waist. The body is black with white hairs that form stripes on the abdomen. The eight legs are rather short and covered with sensory hairs. The fangs are large and usually hidden by the leglike mouthparts. Males are similar in appearance to females, but they have larger fangs, a darker body, and brightly colored bristly brushes on their pedipalps. Their eight eyes are arranged in three rows of four, two, and two. Jumping spiders have binocular vision: two of their eight eyes are very large and pointed directly forward, making them capable of focusing on a distant object. Binocular vision allows jumping spiders to accurately determine the distance of prey or another object. The large eyes of jumping spiders are capable of slight movement to adjust focus or to scan the scene without having to change body position. Their legs are not especially enlarged for jumping.

Geographic range: The zebra jumping spider ranges throughout the Northern Hemisphere, including most of Europe and the United States.

Habitat: This species is common in gardens, on rocks, stones, flowers, plant foliage, grass, and occasionally on trees. They are often found on vertical surfaces, such as walls, fences, decks, patios, and doorways.

Diet: They eat mostly small insects and spiders.

Behavior and reproduction: Jumping spiders jump more than they walk, and they can do so forward, sideways, and backward with equal ease and speed of movement. They do not use webs to capture their food but instead actively hunt their prey throughout the day. These spiders can catch prey up to twice their own body length, spotting them as far away as 8 feet (2.4 meters). They slowly stalk and pounce upon their prey from as far away as 6 inches (15.2 centimeters). Before jumping, the spider plays out a strand of silk and attaches it to the ground or to a branch or leaf as a safety line. Using its fangs, the spider delivers both venom and digestive chemicals. The prey is then chewed up with the spider's powerful mouthparts, and its body fluids are sucked into the spider's mouth.

Jumping spiders also build a silken cocoon or retreat into crevices, under stones and bark, or on foliage. Retreats are used as hiding places at night or shelters for molting, feeding, protecting young, and hibernation (high-bur-NAY-shun), a period of inactivity during the winter.

Before mating, males must first transfer sperm to special chambers on their leglike mouthparts. Males then court females with an elaborate and colorful display of leg waving. This dance is intended, in part, to identify the male as a potential mate for the female and not a meal. If she is willing, the male attempts to deposit the sperm into an opening underneath the female's abdomen. Females lay their eggs in silken shelters and guard them until they hatch and molt for the second time. Zebra jumping spiders mature in late spring or summer and live for about one year.

Zebra jumping spiders and people: Although the species is considered a nuisance around homes and buildings, these spiders are harmless to humans and probably eat many insects that are considered pests.

Conservation status: This species is not endangered or threatened. ■

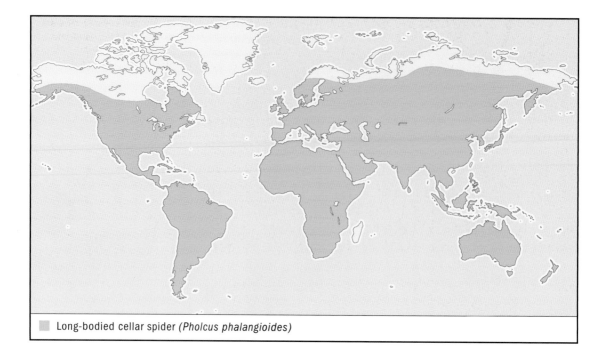

Long-bodied cellar spider (*Pholcus phalangioides*)

LONG-BODIED CELLAR SPIDER
Pholcus phalangioides

Physical characteristics: The grayish brown or tan body of the cellar spider is slender and measures 0.23 to 0.3 inches (6 to 8 millimeters) in length. These spiders have eight long, clear legs. The body regions are not divided into segments and are attached to each other by a thin waist. Males are slightly shorter than females. The abdomen is long and rectangular.

Geographic range: Long-bodied cellar spiders are found throughout world, especially in the United States and Europe.

Habitat: Long-bodied cellar spiders are usually found in homes and nearby buildings. They prefer dark, damp areas, such as crawl spaces, basements, closets, sink cabinets, ceilings, cellars, warehouses, garages, attics, and sheds. They also spin webs near open doors and windows that allow flying insects to enter. Spiders hang upside down in messy, irregular webs shaped something like umbrellas.

Long-bodied cellar spiders are usually found in homes and other buildings. (Arthur V. Evans. Reproduced by permission.)

Diet: This species eats almost any kind of insect or spider that becomes trapped in its web.

Behavior and reproduction: Prey trapped in the web either is eaten immediately or is swiftly wrapped in silk, like a mummy. The prey is bitten, injected with digestive chemicals, and then sucked dry over the next day or so. The cellar spider also invades other webs, kills the resident spider, and claims the web as its own. When these spiders are threatened, they violently shake their webs.

Courtship may take several hours, ending when the male transfers his sperm from his leglike mouth structures to the female's reproductive organs. Females produce up to three clear egg sacs, each with thirteen to sixty eggs. The sac is carried in the female's mouth. The female guards the eggs for several weeks, until they hatch. The young resemble the adults and soon strike out on their own to build their own webs nearby. They molt five times before reaching maturity and live for about two years.

Long-bodied cellar spiders and people: Urban legend has it that the venom of this spider is one of the most deadly of all, but the small and weak mouthparts prevent this spider from injecting a lethal dose to human victims. Their fangs are too small to puncture human skin, and their venom is not very strong and not dangerous to people. Cellar spiders are beneficial, in that they capture and eat household insects and other spiders.

Conservation status: This species is not endangered or threatened. ∎

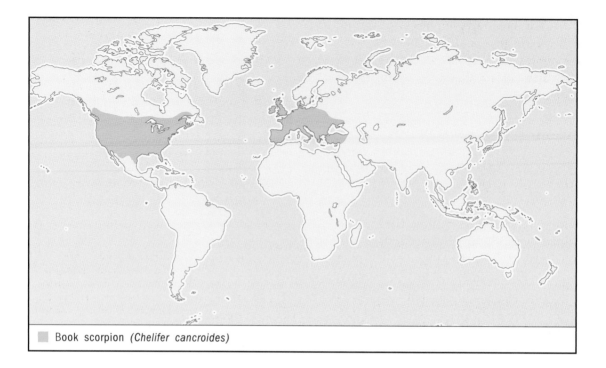

Book scorpion (*Chelifer cancroides*)

BOOK SCORPION
Chelifer cancroides

Physical characteristics: The book scorpion is very small, at 0.10 to 0.18 inches (2.6 to 4.5 millimeters), and looks somewhat like a pear-shaped scorpion without the stinging tail. The front of the body is olive brown to dark red and has no segments. The abdomen is olive green to pale brown and has distinct segments. The body regions are attached to one another. Their tiny claws contain venom glands.

Geographic range: The book scorpion is found throughout most of Europe and the United States.

Habitat: They are commonly found in homes and other buildings, including stables, barns, grain stores, and factories. They are also often found in old books in libraries.

Diet: The book scorpion eats insects, mites, and lice. Prey is grabbed, killed, and torn apart with the pedipalps, which contain venom glands. The body fluids of the prey are then sucked into the mouth.

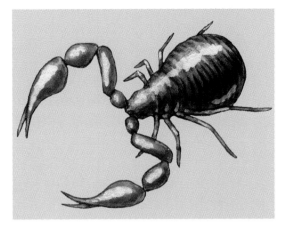

Behavior and reproduction: Books scorpions are sometimes found in large groups, with several dozen individuals. Females often use their pedipalps to grab hold of flying insects, such as house flies, to hitch a ride. Males are less likely to use this method of transportation. Their clawed pedipalps are used primarily for defense, fighting, prey capture, and building nests. Silk produced by glands in the claws is fashioned into a cocoon for molting and winter hibernation.

The book scorpion's claws contain venom glands. Prey is grabbed, killed and torn apart with the claws. (Illustration by Bruce Worden. Reproduced by permission.)

Book scorpions engage in courtship dances. The male grabs the female's claws and legs and leads her to his sperm packet. Females brood sixteen to forty eggs in a sac attached underneath their bodies. The young resemble the adults but are much paler. They molt three times and take from ten months to two years to reach maturity. They may live three to four years.

Book scorpions and people: Book scorpions eat head lice, mites, ants and other small arthropod pests living in homes and other buildings, but humans seldom notice them at all.

Conservation status: This species is not endangered or threatened. ∎

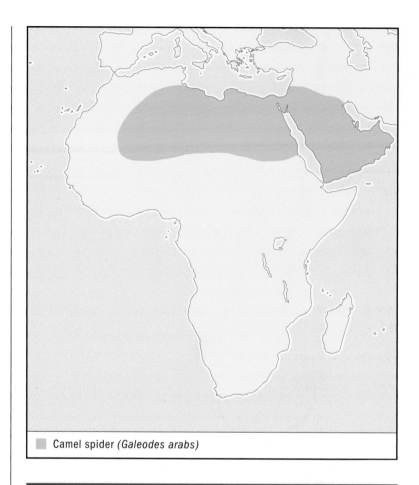

Camel spider *(Galeodes arabs)*

CAMEL SPIDER
Galeodes arabs

Physical characteristics: Camel spiders are yellowish and have a leg span up to 4.7 inches (119 millimeters), but their bodies are only 2 inches (51 millimeters) long. Males are usually smaller and more slender than females and have longer legs. Both regions of the body are divided into segments. Their entire bodies are covered with hairlike bristles. They have two small eyes set on a small bump near the front of the body. Up to one-third of the body length consists of their pincherlike mouthparts. The long and slender leglike mouthparts, as well as the first pair of legs, look and function like antennae.

In the past one hundred years soldiers stationed in North Africa and the Middle East have been fascinated by these large, fast arachnids, sometimes staging battles between captive animals. (Michael Fogden/Bruce Coleman Inc. Reproduced by permission.)

Geographic range: The camel spider lives in northern Africa and the Middle East.

Habitat: This species lives in sandy, hot, and dry habitats.

Diet: Camel spiders eat small mice, lizards, birds, amphibians, spiders, scorpions, and insects, especially termites. They use their large, powerful mouthparts to crush prey and drink water.

Behavior and reproduction: Camel spiders spend their days hiding beneath objects or in shallow burrows dug with their legs and mouthparts. They usually come out at night to hunt, locating prey with their leglike mouthparts on the ground or beneath the surface of the earth, through ground-level vibrations. Amazingly fast on their feet, camel spiders can run, in very short bursts, up to 20 inches (51 centimeters) per second, using only the back three pairs of legs.

In mating, the male roughly seizes the female with his legs and mouthparts, but he does not injure her. She becomes motionless, which prevents her from attacking the male and eating him. The male carries the female for a short distance, places her on her back, and begins stroking the underside of her abdomen. He then produces a sperm packet, picks it up in his mouth, and places it inside her body. Later, the female deposits up to 164 eggs in a deep burrow. The eggs hatch within a few days into nonmoving creatures that do not resemble the adults and do not feed. After their second molt, they begin to look more like adults, leave the burrow, and start to hunt.

Camel spiders and people: Camel spiders are not venomous and are not considered dangerous to people. In the past one hundred years soldiers stationed in North Africa and the Middle East have been fascinated by these large, fast arachnids, sometimes staging battles between captive animals.

Conservation status: This species is not endangered or threatened. ∎

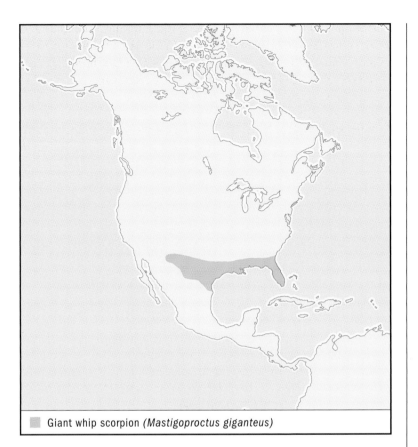

Giant whip scorpion (*Mastigoproctus giganteus*)

GIANT WHIP SCORPION
Mastigoproctus giganteus

Physical characteristics: Whip scorpions, also known as vinega-roons, mule killers, or grampas, are dark reddish brown or brownish black and measure 1 to 3.2 inches (25 to 80 millimeters) without the long, whiplike tail. The tail is usually carried straight over the back, lacks a stinger, and, at its base, has glands that release strong, defensive acids that smell like vinegar. The body is divided into two regions. The front region is undivided and covered by a carapace. It is attached to the segmented abdomen by a narrow waist. There is one pair of eyes at the front of the body, with three more pairs of eyes on the sides. The thick, spiny claws are used to grasp, tear, and place food into the mouth. There are four pairs of legs. The first pair is long and slender and used like antennae, while the remaining legs are used

for walking. Males and females are very similar in appearance, but the claws of the male are slightly longer and more slender, while they are somewhat shorter and stouter in the female.

Geographic range: The giant whip scorpion lives in the southern United States, from southeastern Arizona east to Florida and northern Mexico.

Habitat: Giant whip scorpions prefer dark, humid places and avoid bright sunlight whenever possible. They hide during the day in burrows under logs, rotting wood, rocks, and other natural debris.

Diet: Giant whip scorpions eat many different kinds of crawling invertebrates.

Behavior and reproduction: Whip scorpions hunt actively at night, using their sensitive front legs to detect ground vibrations triggered by the movements of prey. They attack and overpower prey with their mouthparts and claws. Although they are very slow, gentle animals, whip scorpions can move quickly when threatened and will squirt acid that weakens the exoskeletons of other arthropods. They will also use their claws to pinch their enemies.

Courtship involves a mating dance. The male grasps the female's antennalike front legs with his mouthparts and grabs her claws with his; then he guides her over to his sperm packet. He may assist her by placing the sperm packet directly into her reproductive opening with his claws. Afterward, the female finds a sheltered spot and produces a batch of eggs in a clear sac and carries them under her abdomen until they hatch. The pale, nearly transparent, young climb onto the mother's back and remain there until the next molt. Then they climb down to strike out on their own. They molt once a year and take three to four years to reach adulthood.

Giant whip scorpions and people: Whip scorpions are not venomous, but they are capable of spraying a mist of concentrated acetic (uh-SEE-tik) acid, the primary ingredient of vinegar. Larger individuals can inflict a painful pinch. Giant whip scorpions are sometimes kept as pets and are popular animals in insect zoos.

Conservation status: This species is not endangered or threatened. ■

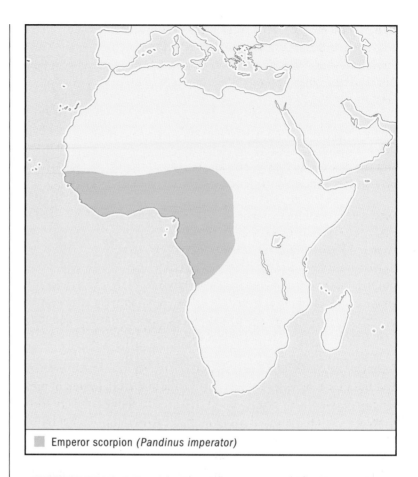

Emperor scorpion (*Pandinus imperator*)

EMPEROR SCORPION
Pandinus imperator

Physical characteristics: Emperor scorpions are shiny blue, black to greenish black, and measure 5 to 8 inches (127 to 203 millimeters) in length, including the tail. They weigh up to 1.1 ounces (35 grams), although pregnant females may weigh as much as 1.4 ounces (40 grams). The males are similar in appearance to the females, but are slightly smaller and lighter-bodied. The powerful reddish-brown claws are rough in texture. The claws, body, and tail are covered with sensory hairs. Underneath the abdomen, behind the last pair of legs, is a pair of comblike pectines. The pectines of males are longer than those of females. The six-segmented tail ends in a curved stinger.

Geographic range: This species is found in the western African countries of Senegal, Guinea-Bissau, Guinea, Ivory Coast, Sierra Leone, Ghana, Togo, Democratic Republic of Congo, Nigeria, Gabon, and Chad.

Habitat: This species prefers living in hot, humid habitats. They live in abandoned burrows of other animals or will dig their own. Individuals will also take shelter beneath rocks, logs, and tree roots.

Diet: They will hunt almost any animal smaller than themselves. Their food includes crickets, insects, other arachnids, mealworms, and millipedes. They will even catch and kill small mice and lizards. Emperor scorpions seldom run down their prey, preferring instead to ambush unsuspecting insects and other small animals that wander nearby. Digestive chemicals are used to turn their victim's tissues into liquid, which is then sucked into the mouth.

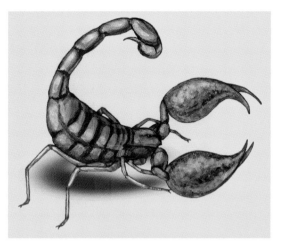

Emperor scorpions are found in the western African countries of Senegal, Guinea-Bissau, Guinea, Ivory Coast, Sierra Leone, Ghana, Togo, Democratic Republic of Congo, Nigeria, Gabon, and Chad. (Illustration by Bruce Worden. Reproduced by permission.)

Behavior and reproduction: Emperor scorpions search for mates and hunt for food at night. They detect the size and location of prey mainly through vibrations in the ground and in the air. Hungry scorpions move slowly forward, with open claws held out, and tail raised forward over the body. Young scorpions grasp their prey with their claws and quickly sting it. Larger adults crush and kill their victims with their large and powerful claws. Adults are unusually calm and very slow to sting in defense and seldom inject venom when they do.

Adult males spend most of their time looking for mates. During courtship the male uses his claws to grasp those of the female. He guides her to a hard surface where he deposits his sperm packet. He then pulls the female over the sperm packet so she can pick it up with her reproductive organs. The male leaves soon after courtship is completed to avoid being killed and eaten by a hungry female.

The female gives live birth. The young are carried inside her body from seven to nine months. Anywhere from nine to thirty-five pale white scorpions are born, one after the other. They will climb up on the mother's back and remain there until their first molt. They molt about seven times in four years before reaching adulthood. Adult females often continue to live with their young and will sometimes eat them if other kinds of food are not available. The bodies of young scorpions become darker as they grow. Their total life span is about eight years.

Emperor scorpions and people: Although large in size, emperor scorpions are not considered dangerous to healthy humans. The venom is very mild, but the sting can still be painful. Young scorpions and adult females are more likely to sting than adult males. Larger individuals can deliver a painful pinch with their claws. They are commonly sold as pets and are frequently used in films as "deadly" animals.

Conservation status: This species is not listed by the World Conservation Union (IUCN). However, because thousands of individuals are collected and sold in the pet trade every year, they have been listed as Threatened on Appendix II of the Convention on International Trade in Endangered Species of Wild Fauna and Flora (CITES). Their populations are being monitored to prevent over collecting. ■

FOR MORE INFORMATION

Books:

Edwards, G. B., and S. Marshall. *Florida's Fabulous Spiders*. Tampa, FL: World Publications, 2001.

Hurley, R. J. *A Field Guide to Spider Webs*. Westminster, MD: Pinchin Press, 1992.

Jackman, John A. *A Field Guide to Spiders and Scorpions*. Texas Monthly Field Guide Series. Houston, TX: Gulf Publishing, 2002.

Kaston, B. J. *How to Know the Spiders*. Boston, MA: WCB/McGraw-Hill, 1978.

Levi, H. W., and L. Levi. *Spiders and Their Kin*. New York: Golden Books, 1996.

McDaniel, B. *How to Know the Mites and Ticks*. Dubuque, IA: William C. Brown, 1979.

Milne, L., J. Milne, and Susan Rayfield. *National Audubon Society Field Guide to North American Insects and Spiders*. New York: Knopf, 1994.

Preston-Mafham, Rod. *The Book of Spiders*. Edison, NJ: Chartwell Books, 1998.

Preston-Mafham, Rod, and Ken Preston-Mafham. *Spiders of the World*. New York: Facts on File, 2002.

Periodicals:

Moffett, M. W. "Wind Scorpions." *National Geographic*. 206 (July 2004): 94–101.

Web sites:

"Critter Catalog: Arachnids." BioKids. http://www.biokids.umich.edu/critters/ information/Arachnida.html (accessed on September 21, 2004).

PROTURANS

Protura

Class: Entognatha
Order: Protura
Number of families: 4 families

PHYSICAL CHARACTERISTICS

Proturans have three distinct body regions (head; thorax, or midsection; and abdomen), no wings, and six legs, but they are not considered true insects. They form a group closely related to insects that includes springtails (order Collembola) and diplurans (order Diplura). All of these animals have mouthparts located inside a special pocket in their heads.

Proturans are small, pale, secretive animals ranging in size from 0.024 to 0.06 inches (0.6 to 1.5 millimeters). The head is cone-shaped and lacks eyes or antennae (an-TEH-nee). The needlelike jaws are directed straight ahead, with only their tips visible outside the head. On the top of the head is a pair of slightly raised, ringlike structures that help proturans smell their surroundings by detecting the presence of chemical compounds.

The front legs are long and bristling with sensitive, hairlike structures. These are the proturans' most important sensory structures, and they are usually curled and held high above the body like antennae. All of the legs have five segments and are tipped with a single claw. The species that live on the soil surface have longer claws than the species that burrow through the soil. Adult proturans have an eleven-segmented abdomen tipped with a distinctive taillike structure. The first three abdominal segments each have a pair of segmented appendages (uh-PEN-dih-jehz), or limblike structures, underneath. Most species breathe directly through the exoskeleton, or outer skeleton, but a few proturans have respiratory system made up of an internal network of breathing tubes.

GEOGRAPHIC RANGE

Proturans are found around the world, except in the Arctic and Antarctic.

HABITAT

Protura usually prefer to live in moist habitats with lots of rotting plant materials. They are found in meadows or in leaf litter, rotten logs, soil, and moss in wooded areas. Some species live in parks and agricultural fields. Most proturans live near the soil surface, although some are found underground as deep as 10 inches (25.4 centimeters).

DIET

Little is known of the feeding habits of proturans. Their needlelike mouthparts suggest that they feed on fluids. A few species feed on fungus, organisms related to mushrooms. They are believed to suck fluids from threadlike structures that underground funguses use to obtain nutrients from the roots of plants.

BEHAVIOR AND REPRODUCTION

Proturans move slowly through the soil with their forelegs, or front legs, held out in front of the head, while the middle and hind legs are used for walking. Some species curl the tip of the abdomen over the head to discharge a sticky fluid in the direction of their enemies. Occasionally, proturans gather together in large groups, making them easy to see.

The life cycles are known only for a few species. Among proturans, there is no courtship, or activities meant to attract a mate. Males deposit packets of sperm on the ground, which are later picked up by the females. Eggs are laid in early spring. Proturans are the only insectlike animals that add body segments and structures as they grow. Larval proturans, or young proturans, look very similar to the adults but have only eight abdominal segments. As they grow and molt, or shed and replace their skeletons, they add segments. Only after they molt for the fifth time do they reach adulthood. It is unknown whether proturans keep growing and molting after they become adults.

Species living close to the surface in cooler habitats produce one generation per year and spend the winter as adults, while species living deep in the soil may reproduce year-round. Some species spend the summer near the surface and migrate deeper into the soil with the approach of winter.

PROTURANS AND PEOPLE

Proturans are common in forest leaf litter. They help build nutrient-rich soils by breaking down dead plants. They are not considered pests.

CONSERVATION STATUS

No proturans are endangered or threatened.

Sinentomon yoroi

NO COMMON NAME
Sinentomon yoroi

Physical characteristics: The body is very spiny. The larvae (LAR-vee) have rows of small hairlike bristles on top of some of their abdominal segments.

Geographic range: This species lives in Japan.

Habitat: They live among the roots of bamboo on steep slopes with little leaf litter.

Diet: Nothing is known.

Behavior and reproduction: Nothing is known.

Sinetomon yoroi and people: The activities of this species are not known to affect people directly.

Conservation status: The species is not endangered or threatened. ■

FOR MORE INFORMATION

Books:

Tavolacci, J., ed. *Insects and Spiders of the World.* Vol. 7, *Owlet Moth–Scorpion.* New York: Marshall Cavendish, 2003.

Wooten, Anthony. *Insects of the World.* New York: Blanford Press, 1984.

Web sites:

"Insects and Their Allies: Protura." CSIRO Entomology. http://www.ento.csiro.au/education/hexapods/ protura.html (accessed on August 30, 2004).

McLaughlin, Kari. "Protura." Discover Life. http://www.discoverlife.org/ nh/tx/Insecta/Protura/ (accessed on August 30, 2004).

Sinentomon yoroi *live among the roots of bamboo on steep slopes with little leaf litter. (Illustration by John Megahan. Reproduced by permission.)*

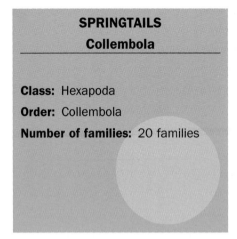

SPRINGTAILS
Collembola

Class: Hexapoda
Order: Collembola
Number of families: 20 families

order

PHYSICAL CHARACTERISTICS

Springtails have three distinct body regions (head; thorax, or midsection; and abdomen), no wings, and six legs, but they are not considered true insects. They form a group closely related to insects that includes proturans (order Protura) and diplurans (order Diplura). All of these animals have mouthparts located inside a special pocket in their head.

Springtails range in length from 0.008 to 0.4 inches (0.2 to 10 millimeters). Species living in caves, deep in leaf litter, or soil are whitish or grayish, while those living out in the open are usually darker or brighter in color. Their bodies are covered in flattened hairlike structures called scales. These insects might have no eyes at all, or they might have small groups of simple eyes, each with single lenses. The mouthparts are needle-like for sucking fluids or have grinding surfaces for chewing.

On the underside of the abdomen is a special organ that absorbs moisture from the surrounding habitat, to maintain the body's water balance. Farther back on the abdomen is a forklike structure that inspired the common name "springtail." The six-segmented abdomen does not have pinchers or a tail at the tip.

GEOGRAPHIC RANGE

Springtails are found worldwide, from the tropics to the edges of the polar ice caps.

HABITAT

Springtails live in warm, damp places. They are especially common in leaf litter and soil. Some species are found in caves, the burrows of small mammals, or the nests of ants and termites. They also live in moss, under stones, on the surfaces of ponds and lakes, and along rocky seashores. Others are found high in the trees of tropical rainforests or on the surface of snowbanks. Springtails are sometimes so common in grasslands that there are more than 596,000 individuals per square yard (500,000 per square meter).

DIET

Most springtails feed on funguses, organisms that include mushrooms, mold, and yeast. All funguses depend other plants or animals for their food. They also feed on bacteria, tiny living things that are made up of only one cell. Species living in trees or those living in the soil also eat plant material and algae (AL-jee), living things that resemble plants but do not have roots, stems, or leaves. A few species are carnivorous (KAR-nih-vuh-rus), or meat eating, feeding on tiny worms and other springtails and their eggs.

BEHAVIOR AND REPRODUCTION

Springtails "jump" not with their legs but by the springlike release of the forklike structure underneath the abdomen. When released, the "fork" snaps down against the ground and flips the springtail into the air, sometimes as high as 8 inches (20.3 centimeters). This device, present in all but a few springtails, seems to be an effective method to avoid predators, or animals that hunt the springtail for food.

Adults are capable of reproduction only every other time they molt, or shed their external skeleton. Reproduction usually requires a male and female, but some females can produce eggs without a male. Some springtails have elaborate courtship behavior, with males dancing and butting heads with females. Many males leave a sperm packet on the ground that is later picked up by the female. Others place sperm with their hind legs directly into the female's reproductive organs.

Eggs are laid singly or in large masses by several females. Some females cover their eggs with a mixture of chewed-up soil and their own waste, to protect them from mold or from becoming dried out. The eggs hatch into larvae that resemble small adults. They usually molt four or five times before reaching adulthood and continue to grow and molt for the rest of their lives. Some species, especially those living in the tropics,

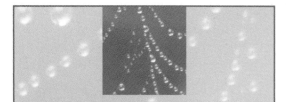

WALKING ON WATER

Some springtails live on the surfaces of still ponds, lakes, and tide pools. Their dark blue or reddish brown bodies are covered with a waxy, waterproof coating that allows them to live on the surface of the water without getting wet or sinking. Sometimes they gather by the hundreds or thousands, and, in such a group, they resemble velvety mats on the water's surface. However, they do not lay their eggs on the water and must return to land to reproduce.

produce several generations every year, and others have only one generation per year. Some Antarctic species may take as long as four years to become adults.

SPRINGTAILS AND PEOPLE

Springtails found in homes are often considered pests, but they do not cause any harm. A few plant-feeding or fungus-feeding species may become pests, damaging alfalfa crops and commercially grown mushrooms. Many springtails play an important role in the environment by breaking down and recycling dead plant materials. They are most commonly encountered in the garden under stones or in compost. Springtails swarming on snow are called "snow fleas."

CONSERVATION STATUS

No springtails are endangered or threatened.

Lucerne flea (*Sminthurus viridis*)

LUCERNE FLEA
Sminthurus viridis

Physical characteristics: Lucerne fleas, also known as varied-springtails, are round and have a distinct and well-developed "fork." They grow up to 0.1 inches (2.5 millimeters) in length. They have long, elbowed antennae (an-TEH-nee) and an irregular pattern of green, brown, and yellow coloring over the body.

Geographic range: Originally from Europe, springtails have spread worldwide.

Habitat: Lucerne fleas live in agricultural fields planted with alfalfa.

Diet: The larvae eat patches of leaves, while adults eat all of the leaf except the veins.

Behavior and reproduction: When disturbed or threatened, Lucerne fleas can jump as far as 12 inches (30.5 centimeters).

The male leaves a sperm packet on the soil or attaches it to low vegetation to be picked up later by the female. The female typically lays

Lucerne fleas, also known as varied springtails, live in agricultural fields planted with alfalfa. (Illustration by Amanda Humphrey. Reproduced by permission.)

clusters of up to forty eggs in the soil during winter. Up to three generations are produced each winter. Eggs that are laid in spring are capable of surviving hot, dry conditions. These eggs hatch the following autumn.

Lucerne fleas and people: Lucerne fleas are considered pests in fields of lupine flowers, lentils, beans, and field peas. Predatory mites are used to keep these pests under control.

Conservation status: This species is not endangered or threatened. ■

FOR MORE INFORMATION

Books:

Tavolacci, J., ed. *Insects and Spiders of the World.* Vol. 7, *Owlet Moth–Scorpion.* New York: Marshall Cavendish, 2003.

Web sites:

"Critter Catalog: Springtails." BioKids. http://www.biokids.umich.edu/critters/information/Collembola.html (accessed on September 1, 2004).

DIPLURANS
Diplura

Class: Entognatha
Order: Diplura
Number of families: 9 families

PHYSICAL CHARACTERISTICS

Diplurans have three distinct body regions (head; thorax, or midsection; and abdomen), no wings, and six legs, but they are not considered true insects. Diplurans form a group closely related to insects that includes proturans (order Protura) and springtails (order Collembola). All of these animals have chewing mouthparts inside a special pocket in their head.

Diplurans are long, slender, and cylindrical or slightly flattened animals that are 0.12 to 1.97 inches (3 to 50 millimeters) in length. They are usually white or pale yellow and are often slightly transparent, or see-through. Their bodies are covered with hairlike structures. Diplurans have no eyes, but their antennae (an-TEH-nee), or feelers, are bristling with sensory hairs. The abdomen has ten segments and is tipped with a pair of threadlike or pincherlike appendages, or limblike structures. Most of the segments have pairs of small leglike structures underneath that are used to support the long abdomen.

GEOGRAPHIC RANGE

Diplurans are widely distributed throughout the world.

HABITAT

Diplurans live in the soil and are found in moist habitats under rocks, logs, leaf litter, and tree bark. Some species live in caves.

phylum
class
subclass
● **order**
monotypic order
suborder
family

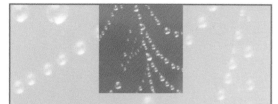

DIPLURANS ON THE EDGE?

Although no diplurans are recognized to be in danger of extinction, it is still possible that some species have had their populations reduced or eliminated altogether. Scientists know so little about these animals that the destruction of their habitats would wipe them out forever and we would never know it. However, some species appear to be able to deal with habitat destruction. For example, several species are known to live and reproduce successfully within the city limits of Vienna, Austria.

DIET

Diplurans eat both plant material and animal tissues. They feed on living and dead small, soft-bodied mites, worms, symphylans (sihm-FIE-luhns) other diplurans, and insects. They also eat funguses, living plants, and decaying vegetation.

BEHAVIOR AND REPRODUCTION

Some species burrow in loose soil, making wormlike movements with their long, slender bodies. They are also capable runners on the surface of the ground. Other species have powerful legs for pushing their way into cracks and pockets in the soil, but they are very poor runners. Many species use their mouthparts to help them dig through the soil.

Diplurans locate their food sources, or prey, with their antennae, or feelers, and stalk them until they are within striking distance. Species that have pincherlike structures at the tip of the abdomen sometimes use them to capture prey but more typically employ them for defense. Diplurans with long, flexible, taillike structures quickly lose them if they are grasped by a predator (PREH-duh-ter), hunting them for food. This allows the dipluran to escape.

Male diplurans attach sperm packets to the soil. Females search for these sperm packets and collect them to fertilize their eggs. They lay their eggs on stalks in small clutches, or groups, on leaf litter or in small cavities in the soil. In some species the female protects her eggs by wrapping her body around them. She will stay with them for a short time after they hatch.

Young diplurans, or larvae (LAR-vee), look like small versions of the adults. They are unable to feed until after they shed their external skeleton, or molt, for the first time. Diplurans reach adulthood after their second molt. Adults live as long as two years and continue to grow and molt for their entire lives. Continued molting allows them to replace broken or worn-out legs and other body parts.

DIPLURANS AND PEOPLE

A few diplurans cause minor damage to garden vegetables by eating them, but most species do not affect people in any way.

CONSERVATION STATUS

No species of diplurans is threatened or endangered.

Holjapyx diversiunguis

NO COMMON NAME
Holjapyx diversiunguis

Physical characteristics: This species measures 0.2 to 0.3 inches (6 to 8 millimeters) and can only be identified by looking at the hair-like structures on the body and the abdomen under a microscope. The body is pale yellow, while the last abdominal segment and pincher-like structures are dark brown. The antennae have twenty-six segments. Each half of the pinchers has a distinctive toothlike projection.

Geographic range: These diplurans are found in central California. They are distributed from the Pacific coast east to the crest of the Sierra Nevada mountains.

Habitat: This species lives in the soil and is often found under rocks and wet leaf litter.

Diet: Nothing is known about the food preferences of this animal.

Behavior and reproduction: This dipluran has been found down in the soil to depths of 30 inches (76 centimeters).

A female was found with eight small larvae, suggesting that she not only looks after her young, but that she probably stands guard over the eggs.

***Holijapyx diversiunguis* and people:** This species has no direct impact on people or their activities.

Conservation status: This species is not threatened or endangered. ∎

FOR MORE INFORMATION

Web sites:

"Diplura." Tree of Life Web Project. http://tolweb .org/tree?group=Diplura&contgroup=Hexapoda (accessed on September 1, 2004).

"Entognathous Hexapods: Diplura." Ecowatch. http:// www.ento.csiro.au/Ecowatch/Hexapods/diplura.htm (accessed on September 1, 2004).

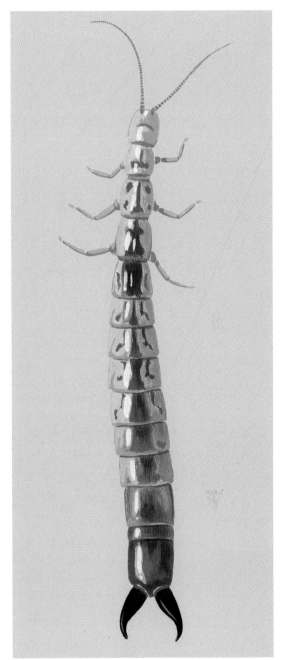

Holjapyx diversiunguis *live in the soil and are often found under rocks and wet leaf litter. (Illustration by John Megahan. Reproduced by permission.)*

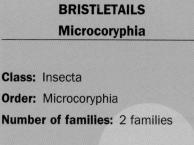

BRISTLETAILS

Microcoryphia

Class: Insecta
Order: Microcoryphia
Number of families: 2 families

order

PHYSICAL CHARACTERISTICS

Bristletails are true insects that never develop wings. They have young that look just like the adults. Their mouthparts, unlike those of diplurans, proturans, and collembolans, are not hidden inside a pocket in the head. They range in size from 0.3 to 0.8 inches (7 to 20 millimeters), not including their tails. The thorax, or midsection, is divided into three sections, each with enlarged upper and lower plates, giving the bristletail a humpback or teardrop shape. The entire body (head, thorax, and abdomen) is covered with flat scales. The head has a pair of long, threadlike antennae (an-TEH-nee), or feelers, and long, leglike mouthparts that look much like a fourth pair of legs. The large eyes consist of many lenses.

The ten-segmented abdomen is tipped with three long, bristle-like tails that are held straight out from the body. All but the first abdominal segments have paired structures underneath that help support the abdomen and keep it from dragging on the ground. Most of the abdominal segments usually have special sacs underneath that help attach the bristletail to the ground so that it can molt, or shed its external skeleton.

GEOGRAPHIC RANGE

Bristetails are found on all continents except Antarctica.

HABITAT

Bristletails are found on the soil, in leaf litter, under rocks, and on stumps and logs from sea level to 15,750 feet (4,800 meters) in the Himalayas. Species living in tropical rainforests often spend some or all of their time high up on the trunks and limbs of trees.

DIET

Bristletails eat dead leaves; algae (AL-jee); funguses; and lichens (LIE-kuhns), which are plantlike growths of funguses and algae growing together.

BEHAVIOR AND REPRODUCTION

The majority of species are active early in the evening or at night. Different species living in the same habitat sometimes group together in sheltered habitats. Bristletails seem to follow certain routes as they search for food, suggesting that they are following trails of chemicals laid down by other bristletails.

BRISTLETAILS VERSUS SILVERFISH

With their shiny, scaly bodies, bristletails closely resemble silverfish (order Thysanura). Bristletails, however, have tube-shaped bodies, while those of silverfish are flattened. The eyes of bristletails are quite large and meet over the top of the head, but those of silverfish are much smaller and are widely separated. And each jaw of a bristletail has only one point of attachment to the head, while those of silverfish and all other insects connect to the head at two points.

Bristletails jump by bending their bodies and then suddenly releasing the tip of the abdomen so that it hits the ground. They are excellent climbers, using their paired abdominal structures to grip vertical surfaces as they climb like inchworms.

Males and females engage in lots of touching with their antennae during courtship. Depending on the species, the males use a variety of methods to transfer their sperm to the female. In some species the male lays a silk thread on the ground. He deposits sperm on the web, which is later collected by the female. The males of other species attach a sperm packet to the ground and then guide a female over it. Still other species mate, with the male depositing sperm directly into the female's body.

Females lay their eggs in protected places, usually gluing them to the ground. Young bristletails molt six to eight times before reaching adulthood. Adults continue to molt and grow for the rest of their lives and are able to replace lost limbs and other structures as they molt. Bristletails may live up to three years and molt as many as sixty times.

BRISTLETAILS AND PEOPLE

Bristletails do not directly affect people or their activities.

CONSERVATION STATUS

No bristletails are threatened or endangered.

Petrobius brevistylis

NO COMMON NAME
Petrobius brevistylis

Physical characteristics: The body is as long as 0.43 inches (11 millimeters), not including the antennae and tails. Each of these structures is nearly as long as the body. They are covered with silvery gray scales, mixed with scattered patches of black scales. The antennae are completely covered with dark scales.

Geographic range: The species is originally from northern Europe and has since become established in northeastern North America.

Habitat: This bristletail is most common above the high-tide line along rocky seacoasts, living among cliffs and boulders. They prefer steep surfaces with few cracks and little loose sand. They also are found on buildings in northern Europe.

Diet: This species grazes on algae, lichens, and mosses growing on rocks.

Petrobius brevistylis *graze on algae, lichens, and mosses growing on rocks. (Illustration by Jonathan Higgins. Reproduced by permission.)*

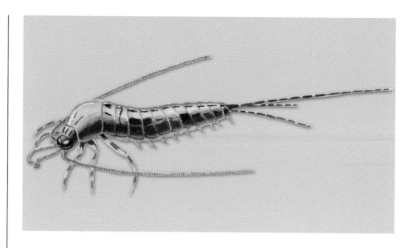

Behavior and reproduction: Individuals forage, or search, for food on the surfaces of cliffs and among boulders. They hide in cracks among the rocks or under stones.

During courtship, bristletails have very little contact. Males deposit sperm directly into the female's body. In some populations there may be very few males or no males at all, and the females can reproduce without mating. The eggs are soft and are squeezed into cracks in the rocks. After hatching, the larvae (LAR-vee), or young, take about three or four months to reach adulthood. Adults may live up to three years.

***Petrobius brevistylis* and people:** Bristletails do not directly affect people or their activities.

Conservation status: This species is not threatened or endangered. ■

FOR MORE INFORMATION

Web sites:

"Archaeognatha, Bristletails." Tree of Life Web Project. http://tolweb .org/tree?group=Archaeognatha&contgroup;=Insecta%20> (accessed on September 2, 2004).

"Insects and Their Allies: Archaeognatha: Bristletails." CSIRO Entomology. http://www.ento.csiro.au/education/insects/archaeognatha.html (accessed on September 2, 2004).

"Jumping Bristletails." http://www.ent3.orst.edu/moldenka/taxons/ Petrobius.html (accessed on September 2, 2004).

order

CHAPTER

SILVERFISH AND FIRE BRATS
Thysanura

Class: Insecta

Order: Thysanura

Number of families: 4 families

phylum

class

subclass

order

monotypic order

suborder

family

PHYSICAL CHARACTERISTICS

Thysanurans (thigh-suh-NOOR-uhns) have no wings. Their flattened bodies typically are covered with overlapping silvery gray scales. Most species are 0.4 to 0.8 inches (10.2 to 20.3 millimeters) in length, but a few species range from 0.04 to 1.9 inches (1 to 48.3 millimeters). One fossil (FAH-suhl) thysanuran, about 350 million years old and measuring 2.36 inches (60 millimeters), is the largest silverfish known. The thysanuran head may or may not have small eyes, each eye with several lenses. The antennae (an-TEH-nee), or feelers, are long and threadlike. Like those of all insects, the mouthparts of thysanurans are on the outside of the head. Each jaw is attached to the head at two points.

Silverfish and fire brats have ten-segmented abdomens. All but the first abdominal segments have paired structures underneath to help support the abdomen and keep it from dragging on the ground. The tip of the abdomen has two shorter tails and one longer, threadlike tail. Thysanuran larvae (LAR-vee), or young, look like the adults.

GEOGRAPHIC RANGE

Thysanurans are found worldwide.

HABITAT

Thysanurans are found in moist habitats, but a few are found in sandy deserts. They live under bark, rocks, rotting logs, and

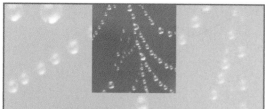

FIRE BRATS LIKE IT HOT!

Fire brats live mostly with humans and prefer homes and buildings where both the temperature and moisture levels are high. They often are found near hot-water pipes, heaters, and fireplaces as well as ovens in bakeries. Their eggs take only twelve to sixteen days to hatch at 98.6°F (37°C). At 104°F (40°C) fire brats grow quickly, shedding their external skeletons every nine to eleven days. They live for about two years and will molt forty-five to sixty times.

leaf litter. Some species prefer to live in caves, among ants or termites, or with people.

DIET

Thysanurans eat decaying or dried plants and animal remains. Species living with people feed on starchy materials, such as paper, cardboard, book bindings, wallpaper paste, and some fabrics. They also eat the starch used to make fabrics stiff. Species living with ants get food by stealing it from their hosts.

BEHAVIOR AND REPRODUCTION

The flat bodies of thysanurans allow them access to all kinds of narrow spaces as they search for food and mates at night. During the day they hide under stones or leaves. When they are alarmed, they can move with incredible speed.

Although the females of some species of silverfish can reproduce without mating, most species require males and females to produce fertilized eggs. Males deposit a sperm packet on the ground, beneath a silken thread. The packet is later picked up by the female. Females lay their eggs inside cracks and between spaces in leaf litter. The eggs are about 0.04 inches (1 millimeter) long and are longer than they are wide. At first they are soft and white, but after several hours they turn yellow and then brown. The larvae resemble small adults. Silverfish continue to molt, or shed their outer skeletons, throughout their lives and may live for up to six years.

SILVERFISH AND FIRE BRATS AND PEOPLE

Some species of silverfish are especially suited for living with people. They have been accidentally transported throughout the world. These species are considered household pests because of the damage they cause to household goods as they feed.

CONSERVATION STATUS

No species of thysanuran are threatened or endangered.

Silverfish (*Lepisma saccharina*)

SILVERFISH
Lepisma saccharina

Physical characteristics: Adult silverfish measure up to 0.4 inches (10.2 millimeters) in length. Their bodies are covered with silvery scales.

Geographic range: Silverfish probably originally came from tropical Asia; the species is now found living with people worldwide.

Habitat: This species lives in warm, damp places in the home, especially basements, closets, bookcases, shelves, and baseboards.

Diet: Immature and adult silverfish are fond of flour and starch and are sometimes found in cereal; they also feed on muslin, starched collars and cuffs, lace, carpets, fur, and leather. They are also cannibalistic, feeding on molted silverfish skins and dead and injured individuals.

Immature and adult silverfish are fond of flour and starch and are sometimes found in cereal; they also feed on muslin, starched collars and cuffs, lace, carpets, fur, and leather. (Mark Smith/Photo Researchers, Inc. Reproduced by permission.)

Behavior and reproduction: Silverfish forage, or search, for food at night. They spend their days hidden in dark, protected places.

The male spins a silk thread and deposits a packet of sperm underneath; the female picks it up and places it in her reproductive opening. Eggs are laid singly or in small batches of two to three and deposited in crevices (KREH-vuh-ses) or under objects. Under the best conditions, a female lays an average of one hundred eggs during her life span. The larvae have no scales up to the time of their third molt. After ten molts, they reach sexual maturity; the adults, with a life span of two to eight years, keep molting about four times every year.

Silverfish and people: Silverfish are considered household pests because their feeding activities damage household goods.

Conservation status: Silverfish are not threatened or endangered. ■

Cubacubana spelaea

NO COMMON NAME
Cubacubana spelaea

Physical characteristics: The long, slender body of this thysanuran grows as long as 0.47 inches (12 millimeters), without antennae or tails. The antennae are one and half times the body length, and the tails are slightly longer than the body, growing to 1.41 inches (35.8 millimeters). These thysanurans do not have eyes, and their whitish or transparent, or see-through, bodies lack scales.

Geographic range: This species is only known from the Toca da Boa Vista caves in the north of Bahia, Brazil.

Habitat: They prefer the deepest and wettest areas of the cave, near standing bodies of water.

Diet: The species feeds on dry leaves and other plant tissues carried into the cave by bats. They also probably eat the paper wrapping of markers left years ago by scientists studying the caves.

Behavior and reproduction: Very little is known about the behavior of this species. They are usually found running quickly over rock formations on the cave floor. Males are unknown, which might mean that females can reproduce without mating.

***Cubacubana spelaea* and people:** This species has no direct impact on humans or their activities.

Conservation status: This species is not threatened or endangered. ■

FOR MORE INFORMATION

Web sites:

"Critter Catalog: Silverfish." BioKids. http://www.biokids.umich.edu/critters/information/Thysanura.html (accessed on September 2, 2004).

"Thysanura: Silverfish and Firebrats." Tree of Life Web Project. http://tolweb.org/tree?group=Thysanura&contgroup=Insecta (accessed on September 2, 2004).

Class: Insecta

Order: Ephemeroptera

Number of families: 40 families

order

CHAPTER

PHYSICAL CHARACTERISTICS

Mayflies range in length from 0.04 to 3.2 inches (1 to 81.2 millimeters). They come in a variety of colors, including white, yellow, pinkish, gray, or black. The adults always have wings. In fact, this is the oldest group of winged insects alive today. One mayfly fossil (FAH-suhl), an impression of a mayfly left in mud in ancient times and hardened into stone, has a wingspan of 18 inches (45.7 centimeters). The four transparent wings of the mayfly are held together straight over the body. A network of veins supports each wing. The first pair of wings is much larger than the second; in some species the second pair of wings is very small or even missing altogether.

Males and females are usually easy to tell apart. Males have eyes that are each divided into two separate parts. The upper parts of the eyes are directed upward and mounted on short stalks. The eyes are very sensitive, so males can easily find and capture female mayflies in mating swarms or when there is little sunlight. Males have long front legs that are held out in front of the body. They also have slender bodies, and the abdomen is filled mostly with air. Females are shorter and have heavier bodies, and their abdomens are filled with eggs. The abdomens of both males and females are tipped with two or three long, threadlike structures that are used like antennae (an-TEH-nee), to help mayflies "feel" what is going on behind them. These structures are always longer in the males.

Although adult mayflies are amazingly similar to one another, their larvae (LAR-vee) come in a wide variety of shapes.

phylum

class

subclass

● **order**

monotypic order

suborder

family

They do not resemble adults. Species living in fast-moving water cling to rocks and are usually flat and shieldlike in shape. Their low, smooth bodies prevent them from being swept away by the swift current. Mayfly larvae living in the slower waters of ponds and lakes are usually free-swimming. Their bodies are slender and shaped more like a cylinder. No matter how and where they live, all mayfly larvae have chewing mouthparts.

The larvae breathe underwater with gills. The gills are attached along the sides of the abdomen. Depending on where they live and the oxygen content of the water, the gills are brushy and tuftlike or flattened into plates. Species with feathery gills often live in low-oxygen water, and the feathery gills have more surface area exposed to the water, for drawing in the oxygen. Species with flattened gills usually live in fast-moving streams. Their streamlined shape prevents them from being swept away by the current. In some species that live in fast-moving water, the gills form a sticky disk that acts like a suction cup to attach the larvae to submerged rocks. Other species use their gills as paddles for swimming.

GEOGRAPHIC RANGE

Mayflies are found on all continents except Antarctica and a few small islands in the middle of the ocean. They are most abundant in mild or tropical climates.

HABITAT

The larvae live in a wide variety of freshwater habitats, from swift mountain streams to lowland rivers, ponds, and lakes. Many live under rocks, logs, and other debris (duh-BREE). Some species burrow in living or decaying plant tissues or in the soft, muddy bottoms of rivers and lakes. Others swim freely in small ponds or in small springs and seeps, pools where water has oozed to the ground surface. Most species are sensitive to pollution, or poison, waste, or other material that makes the environment dirty and harmful to health. Some are tolerant of small levels of contamination in the form of plant debris, animal waste, and muddy water. Adults are weak fliers and usually stay very close to the body of water where they grew up.

DIET

Mayflies feed only as larvae. By the time they reach the adult stage, their mouthparts and digestive systems have mostly disappeared. Most larvae eat bits of living or dead algae (AL-jee) from the bottom of their water habitat. Burrowing species flap their abdominal gills to draw water into their burrows. They use their mouthparts and legs to strain out bits of algae from the incoming water. Other species scrape algae off rocks and logs with their mouthparts. A few species attack and eat the aquatic, or water-living, larvae of flies.

BEHAVIOR AND REPRODUCTION

Mayfly larvae are important in transferring energy in freshwater habitats. The larvae strain and eat large amounts of algae as food. They transfer the algae's energy to other animals when fishes, birds, insects, and spiders eat them.

Most larvae remain hidden during the day to avoid predators (PREH-duh-ters), or animals who hunt them for food, but others are found swimming out in the open in the daytime. Some species live in groups, especially in puddles and pools that last for only a short period of time. They usually come out of the water at dawn or just before nightfall to transform into adults, but some species leave the water at midday. Males usually surface well before the females.

Adult male mayflies sometimes take part in massive mating flights. The time, location, flight pattern, and number of participating mayflies vary with each species. Some swarms are composed of a few males, and others have hundreds or even thousands of mayflies. Females fly above the swarms and are spotted by the males swarming below. Males use their long front legs to grab the females. Sperm is transferred to the female directly. After mating, the female lays one hundred to twelve hundred eggs in the water.

Mayflies spend most of their lives in the water as eggs and larvae. The eggs take one week to one year to hatch. In most species the larvae molt, or shed their external skeletons, fifteen to twenty-five times before reaching adulthood. Depending on the species and local conditions, such as temperature and wa-

MAYFLIES ON THE COMEBACK TRAIL?

More than one hundred years ago many European rivers were the sites of spectacular swarms of mayflies numbering in the thousands every year. Since then, many populations have declined drastically or disappeared entirely. Scientists blame water pollution and larval habitat destruction caused by heavy industries located on the rivers. As factories in Communist countries started closing in the early 1990s, the water quality of many rivers in Eastern Europe began to improve, giving some mayfly populations a chance to increase their numbers.

ter quality, mayfly larvae take from three weeks to three years to reach adulthood.

Mayflies are the only order of insects that has an extra winged stage called the "subimago" (sub-ih-MAH-goh) The subimago is duller in color than the adult, or imago. It is also heavier bodied and has wings that are smoky instead of clear. The subimago is covered with water-repellent hairs that allow it to emerge from the water unharmed in preparation for adult life on land. At this stage, the mayfly has lost its larval gills and would be in danger of drowning as it makes its way to the surface, if it were not for the hairs, which keep water away from the mayfly's breathing holes. The adults live only a few days, just long enough to mate and lay eggs.

MAYFLIES AND PEOPLE

Because of their sensitivity to changes in the water, larval mayflies are often used by scientists as indicators of water quality. Their presence or absence in ponds, lakes, streams, and rivers may give evidence of changes in water temperature, oxygen levels, or chemical pollution. Mayflies are also popular with fly fishermen. They make lures called "flies" that imitate the forms of both adult and larval mayflies, using them instead of living bait to get fish to bite.

CONSERVATION STATUS

The World Conservation Union (ICUN) lists two species of mayflies as Extinct, meaning that no members of the species are still alive, and one as Vulnerable, meaning that it faces a high risk of extinction in the wild. The main reasons for declining populations of mayflies are habitat destruction by pollution; deforestation, or the clearing of land of trees, at the margins of rivers; dam construction; and introduction of foreign fish.

Chiloporter eatoni

NO COMMON NAME
Chiloporter eatoni

Physical characteristics: Adults are 0.6 to 0.9 inches (15.2 to 22.9 millimeters) in length. Their bodies and wings are yellowish. The larvae have large heads and almost circular gills covering the abdomen. The gills vary in color from pale yellow or pink to violet.

Geographic range: This species lives in southern Argentina and Chile.

Habitat: They live in cold, fast-flowing creeks and streams as well as the borders of lakes with well-oxygenated water.

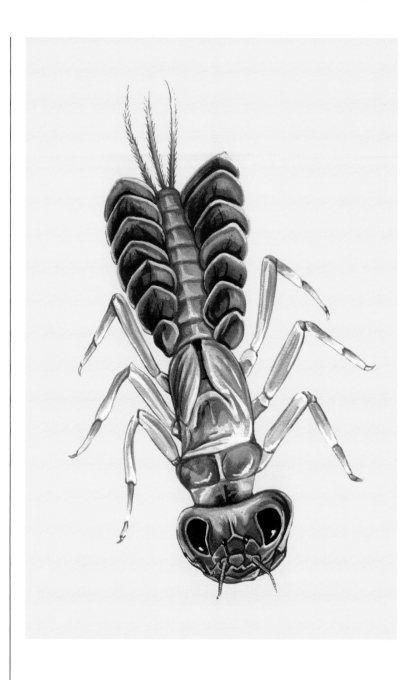

Diet: The larvae are active predators and eat the larvae of other aquatic insects.

Behavior and reproduction: The larvae crawl on the bottom and are fast swimmers. They use their gills to propel themselves through the water. When they are not feeding, they hide under rocks and other debris. The behavior of adults, including reproduction, is unknown.

***Chiloporter eatoni* and people:**   They do not affect people or their activities directly.

Conservation status: The World Conservation Union (IUCN) does not officially list this species, but their populations may be threatened by the introduction of insect-eating trout.   ■

Brown mayfly (*Ephemera vulgata*)

BROWN MAYFLY
Ephemera vulgata

Physical characteristics: Adults are 0.55 to 0.86 inches (14 to 21.8 millimeters). Their wings are spotted. The larvae have mouthparts that look like miniature elephant tusks. They use these tusklike jaws for burrowing in the mud. The large abdominal gills are fringed and used, in part, to create a water current inside the burrow, as a way to maintain a steady flow of oxygen-rich water and food particles.

Geographic range: The brown mayfly lives in western Europe, including Great Britain and Scandinavia, and areas south of the Arctic Circle, ranging east to central Siberia.

Habitat: The larvae prefer the still waters of ponds, lakes, slow-moving rivers, and the mouths of rivers that are not too cold.

Diet: The larvae strain bits of algae and plant materials from the water with their mouthparts and legs.

Behavior and reproduction: Larvae burrow in muddy and sandy bottoms or in fine gravel.

Grzimek's Student Animal Life Resource

Males fly in small to large mating swarms in the evening next to bodies of water. Females lay their eggs while they float downstream on the water surface. The life cycle is completed within two, or, rarely, three years, depending on water temperature.

Brown mayflies and people: Brown mayflies are valued by fly fishermen, who tie flies that imitate the body form of both larvae and adults.

Conservation status: This species is not threatened or endangered. ■

FOR MORE INFORMATION

Periodicals:

Szentpéteri, J. L. "Molt, Mate, Die: The Brief, Lusty Life of the Mayfly." *National Geographic* 203, no. 5 (May 2003): 72–85.

Web sites:

"Critter Case File: Mayflies." University of Kentucky Department of Entomology. http://www.uky.edu/Agriculture/CritterFiles/casefile/insects/mayflies/mayflies.htm (accessed on September 3, 2004).

"Ephemeroptera: Mayflies." Ecowatch. http://www.ento.csiro.au/Ecowatch/Insects_Invertebrates/ephemeroptera.htm (accessed on September 3, 2004).

"Mayfly Central." Department of Entomology, Purdue University. http://www.entm.purdue.edu/entomology/research/mayfly/mayfly.html (accessed on September 3, 2004).

Class: Insecta

Order: Odonata

Number of families: 23 families

order

CHAPTER

PHYSICAL CHARACTERISTICS

phylum

class

subclass

● **order**

monotypic order

suborder

family

Odonates (OH-duh-nayts) have large eyes with ten thousand to thirty thousand individual lenses in each eye. The eyes of dragonflies meet, or almost meet, on the top of the head, while those of damselflies are widely separated, giving them a "barbell" look when viewed head on. The adults have four wings. The wingspans range from 0.8 to 6.5 inches (20.3 to 165 millimeters). Dragonfly wings are very strong and provide these insects with amazing flight maneuverability. The spiny legs are well developed for perching and seizing prey, animals that are hunted for food, but are of little or no use for walking. Instead, dragonflies rely on their four powerful wings for getting around. The large, strong wings are mostly transparent, see-through, and are supported by a network of veins. Some species have distinctly colored or patterned wings.

The ten-segmented abdomen of the dragonfly is long and slender. Males have a unique reproductive system with a special second set of structures on the underside, at the base of the abdomen. Damselfly and some dragonfly females have well-developed egg-laying structures for inserting their eggs into plant tissue. In most other dragonflies this structure is not very well developed, and their eggs are simply dropped into water. Both sexes have appendages (uh-PEN-dih-jehz), fingerlike structures, on the tips of their abdomens. The males use them like claspers to grab the female during mating.

Dragonfly larvae (LAR-vee) do not look like adults. Their bodies are thick and squat. They breathe with the aid of gills inside the abdomen. The bodies of damselflies are long and slender. Their abdomens are tipped with three leaflike gills used for breathing underwater. The long lower lips of all odonates are hinged at the base and extend forward like an arm. At the end of the lip are two jawlike structures armed with sharp teeth. Larvae capture their prey by thrusting the lower lip forward with blazing speed to grab them. When not in use, the lip is folded underneath the body, leaving the jawlike structures covering the face like a mask.

GEOGRAPHIC RANGE

Dragonflies are found worldwide, except in frozen polar areas. They are especially abundant in the tropics.

HABITAT

The larvae are found in most standing and running freshwater habitats, where they live on the bottom, under stones, clinging to vegetation, or buried in mud or detritus (dih-TRY-tuhs), loose, tiny bits of plant and animal remains. A few species live in small air pockets inside the stems of plants, while others occupy wet burrows in the ground in forests and marshy areas. Adults live near all bodies of freshwater, where they search for food, mates, and places to lay their eggs.

DIET

Larvae are ambush predators (PREH-duh-ters), meaning that they sit and wait for a food animal to come within their reach. Adults actively hunt and capture and eat insects on the wing, using their spiny legs as a basket for scooping up mosquitoes, gnats, midges, and other small airborne insects. The larvae capture insects, worms, and even small fish and tadpoles with their lower lips.

BEHAVIOR AND REPRODUCTION

Dragonflies always perch with their wings flat and spread apart, while damselflies usually hold their wings together over the body when they are at rest. The exceptions to this rule are the damselflies known as spreadwings, which keep their wings angled away from their bodies at rest.

Dragonflies regulate body temperature by assuming different postures, ways of holding their bodies, and selecting specific perching sites. In cool weather they create a whir with their wings and land on sun-facing perches. In hot weather they avoid overheating by sticking the abdomen almost straight up in the air to expose the least possible body surface area to the hot sun.

Dragonflies are among the world's most agile (A-juhl), nimble, flying animals. Some species have been clocked at speeds up to 35 miles (56.3 kilometers) per hour. They can hover effortlessly or fly short distances backward. Their bristly antennae (an-TEH-nee) and wing hairs track changes in wind speed and direction. The U.S. Navy and Air Force have studied their aerial acrobatics and learned that dragonflies twist their wings on the downward stroke, creating miniature whirlwinds to reduce the air pressure above the wing, so that they remain in the air.

Many males are territorial, meaning that they protect their living areas. They patrol their areas of water, chasing away all other males. In some species, males make threatening displays for other males or courtship displays for females, by exposing color patches on the head, legs, abdomen, or wings. Females cruise through these territories in search of possible egg-laying sites.

Mating in dragonflies and damselflies is unique among all animals. Before mating, the male bends the abdomen forward underneath his body to transfer sperm from the tip of his abdomen to a second set of reproductive structures, near the base of the abdomen. When he finds a mate, he uses the appendages at the end of his abdomen to grasp the female. Dragonfly males hold the female at the back of the head, while damselflies grab the front part of the thorax, or midsection of the body. The female responds by bending her abdomen forward to bring her reproductive structures in contact with those of the male near the base of his abdomen. Coupled together in this position, males and females resemble a wheel. After mating, the female lays her eggs by herself or is guarded by the male, who continues to hold her. She lays her eggs in the water, either simply dropping them off or placing them in mud or plant tissues.

The larvae, which lack wings, develop in the water. Depending on water temperatures and food supplies, they take six months to five years to reach adulthood and will molt, shed their external skeleton, several times. Mature larvae leave the water at night to avoid predators and to molt for the last time. They crawl onshore and climb up nearby plants, rocks, or tree trunks. The external skeleton splits open along the back of the thorax. This opening forms an escape hatch through which the newly formed adult can leave its old body. The new adult is

THE LARGEST DRAGONFLY EVER!

The largest wingspan for a living odonate belongs to an Australian dragonfly, *Petalura ingentissima*, measuring 6.5 inches (165.1 millimeters). The largest living damselfly, the forest giant (*Megaloprepus caerulatus*), has a wingspan measuring 6.4 inches (162.5 millimeters). The largest odonate in the United States is the giant darner (*Anax walsinghami*), from the American Southwest. Its wingspan is more than 3 inches (50 centimeters), and it has a body length of 4 inches (101.6 millimeters) or more. But the largest dragonfly that ever lived was *Meganeuropsis permiana*, an extinct species known only from fossils (FAH-suhls), ancient impressions of the insect's body left in mud that eventually turned to stone. It flew across the swamps of North America nearly 250 million years ago with wings measuring 28 inches (711.2 millimeters) across!

pale and soft at first, and its wings are crumpled. It hangs upside down until the abdomen is completely withdrawn from the old larval skin. The new adult then turns around and hangs head upward until the wings have fully expanded and stiffened. By morning it is ready to take its first flight. After reaching adulthood, some species will undertake long-distance migrations (my-GRAY-shuns), sometimes flying hundreds or thousands of miles. Adults live one to two months in cooler climates, but some tropical species may live for a year.

DRAGONFLIES AND DAMSELFLIES AND PEOPLE

Despite the menacing common names given to them, such as "devil's darning needles" or "horse stingers," odonates are harmless and are unable to sting. They eat large numbers of harmful insects, especially disease-carrying mosquitoes. Their presence or absence in bodies of freshwater is used as a measure of water quality. In fact, the Navaho Indians use dragonflies as a symbol to signify pure water.

Dragonflies are revered in East Asia, where they have been worshipped by people for centuries and used in medicines. Traditionally known as the "invincible insect," the dragonfly was a favorite symbol of strength among Japanese warriors. The ancient Chinese and Japanese used concoctions made from dragonflies or damselflies to treat a variety of illnesses, among them, eye diseases, sore throats, and fevers. Even the old name for the island of Japan, Akitsushima, means Island of the Dragonfly.

The Japanese have established more than twenty dragonfly sanctuaries across Japan. Images of dragonflies are found on tunnels, sidewalks, and city buildings of Nakamura City. The Yamma Bashi, or large dragonfly bridge, spanning the nearby Ikeda River, is supported by giant sculptures of dragonflies. Even the public transportation system pays tribute to these insects, with the Tosa Kuroshio Train, or Red Dragonfly, linking Nakamura City to Kubokawacho.

Large adult dragonflies are eaten by humans and are considered delicacies in many parts of the world. In Thailand they are roasted, mixed with shrimp, or eaten raw. In Indonesia odonates are mixed with other small animals in a thick, spicy soup. The Balinese fry dragonflies in coconut oil and serve them with vegetables. They also remove their wings and boil them in coconut milk seasoned with ginger, garlic, shallots, and chili pepper. Sometimes coconut meat is substituted for coconut milk, and the entire mixture is wrapped in a banana leaf and cooked together.

CONSERVATION STATUS

The World Conservation Union (IUCN) lists two species as Extinct, meaning that no member of either species is alive. Thirteen species are Critically Endangered, meaning that they face an extremely high risk of extinction in the wild in the near future, and fifty-five species are Endangered, meaning that they face a very high risk of extinction. Thirty-nine species are classed as Vulnerable, or facing a high risk of extinction, and seventeen are Near Threatened, or at risk of becoming threatened with extinction. For most species, very little is known about their distribution, or geographic range, and habitat preferences. Habitat destruction often prevents scientists from gathering important information that could help conserve species that are threatened by extinction. Programs to preserve dragonfly habitats are under way in Australia, India, Japan, Europe, South Africa, and the United States. Japanese conservation programs, which include the creation of artificial habitats to encourage dragonfly reproduction, are some of the best examples of efforts to conserve dragonflies and their habitats.

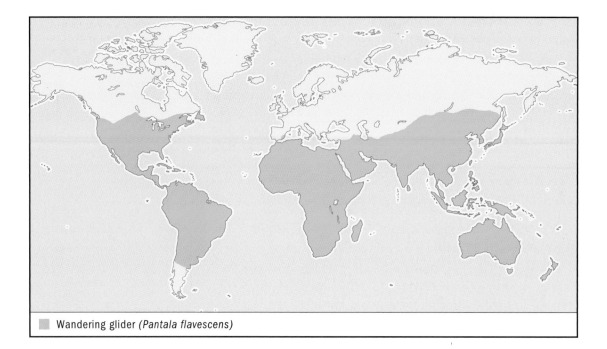

Wandering glider (*Pantala flavescens*)

SPECIES ACCOUNTS

WANDERING GLIDER
Pantala flavescens

Physical characteristics: The body of the wandering glider is yellowish red in color. The base of the back wing is distinctly widened, with a faint yellowish patch. The abdomen narrows toward the tip and has a black strip along the back.

Geographic range: This species is found worldwide but is more common in the tropics.

Habitat: The wandering glider breeds in small, shallow pools, often in puddles left by thunderstorms. Adults are commonly found far away from water.

Diet: The species eats small flying insects, especially gnats, mosquitoes, and midges.

Behavior and reproduction: These insects are strong fliers and seldom land. They sometimes form large feeding and migratory swarms.

The feeding flights may continue into the early evening. They are often seen far out at sea and are attracted to the lights of ships at night.

Males patrol territories about 30 to 150 feet (9 to 45.7 meters) in length. After mating, the male remains with the female while she lays her eggs. Females lay their eggs by tapping the surface of the water with the tip of the abdomen. The larvae live in temporary pools, including swimming pools, and develop rapidly.

Wandering gliders and people: This species is not known to affect people or their activities.

Conservation status: This species is not threatened or endangered. ◼

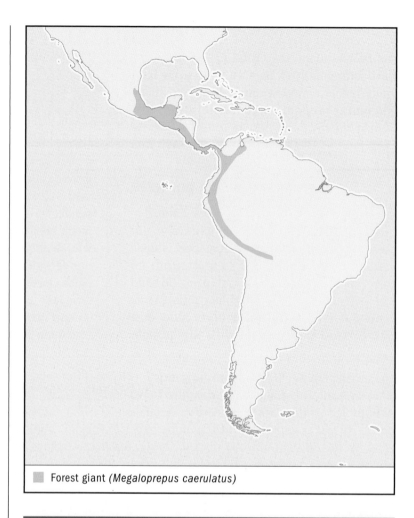

Forest giant (*Megaloprepus caerulatus*)

FOREST GIANT
Megaloprepus caerulatus

Physical characteristics: This is the largest damselfly in the world, with a wingspan of 6.4 inches (162.6 millimeters) and a body length of 4 inches (101.6 millimeters). Their wings have a wide, dark blue band. The males are larger than the females and have a white patch before the blue band and the glassy wingtip. The females are shorter, with only white patches on their wingtips.

Geographic range: The forest giant lives in the rainforests of Central and South America, from Mexico to Bolivia.

Habitat: The larvae breed in water that collects at the bases of plants growing on the limbs of rainforest trees. Adults prefer sunlit gaps or clearings in the forest.

Diet: The adults are specialist hunters. They search for spiders and pluck them from their webs. Occasionally, they feed on the spider's own prey, which is wrapped in silk. The larvae feed on mosquito and fly larvae and small crustaceans (krus-TAY-shuns), animals that live in water and have soft, segmented bodies covered by a hard shell. They also eat tadpoles and the larvae of other species of damselflies.

Behavior and reproduction: Because their special breeding sites are scattered throughout the forest, these insects are never abundant at any given place or time. In an open forest gap, a territorial male uses a slow wing beat to appear as a pulsating, rhythmically beating, blue-and-white beacon to possible mates and to competing males. The male aggressively defends a particular tree hole for up to three months. After mating, the female uses her long abdomen to lay her eggs inside tree holes filled with water.

Forest giants and people: This species is not known to affect people or their activities.

Conservation status: This species is not endangered or threatened. ∎

FOR MORE INFORMATION

Books:

Biggs, K. *Common Dragonflies of the Southwest: A Beginner's Pocket Guide.* Sebastopol, CA: Azalea Publishing, 2004.

Dunkle, S. W. *Damselflies of Florida, Bermuda, and the Bahamas.* Gainesville, FL: Scientific Publishers Nature Guide, 1990.

Dunkle, S. W. *Dragonflies through Binoculars: A Field Guide to Dragonflies of North America.* New York: Oxford University Press, 2000.

Lam, E. *Damselflies of the Northeast.* Forest Hills, NY: Biodiversity Books, 2004.

Nikula, Blair, Jackie Sones, Don Stokes, and Lillian Stokes. *Stokes Beginner's Guide to Dragonflies.* Boston: Little, Brown, 2002.

Silsby, J. *Dragonflies of the World.* Washington, DC: Smithsonain Institution Press, 2001.

Web sites:

"Critter Catalog: Dragonflies." BioKids. http://www.biokids.umich.edu/critters/information/Anisoptera.html (accessed on September 7 2004).

"Dragonflies and Damselflies." Odonata Information Network. http://www.afn.org/iori/ (accessed on September 7, 2004).

"Odonata: Dragonflies, Damselflies." Ecowatch. http://www.ento.csiro.au/Ecowatch/Insects_Invertebrates/odonata.htm (accessed on September 7, 2004).

"Resources for Learning More about Dragonflies." Ode News. http://www.odenews.net/resources.htm (accessed on September 7, 2004).

Other sources:

Walton, R. K., and R. A. Forster. *Common Dragonflies of the Northeast.* Concord, MA: Natural History Services, 1997. Videotape.

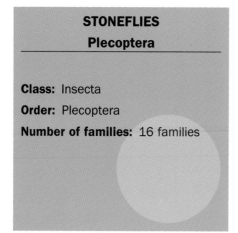

STONEFLIES

Plecoptera

Class: Insecta

Order: Plecoptera

Number of families: 16 families

order

PHYSICAL CHARACTERISTICS

Adult stoneflies are brown, black, green, or yellow and are usually marked with distinctive light or dark patterns. Their bodies are somewhat flattened with legs outstretched to the sides. They range in length from 0.19 to 1.97 inches (5 to 50 millimeters). The broad head is equipped with compound eyes that have more than one lens each, with simple eyes with only one lens, and with chewing mouthparts that are directed forward. The antennae (an-TEH-nee), or sense organs, are long and threadlike. Nearly all species have four fully developed wings that are held flat over the back. At rest the wings are usually as long or longer than the abdomen. A few species of stoneflies are completely wingless or have short wings that are not capable of flight. The hind wings are folded lengthwise when held at rest under the forewings. The abdomen is ten-segmented and is tipped with a pair of short to long, thread-like projections.

The larvae (LAR-vee), or young form of the animal, may or may not closely resemble the adults. Like the adults, their bodies are flattened, with short, sometimes pointed wing pads and outstretched legs. Plant feeders and scavengers (SKAE-vihn-jers), or animals that eat decaying matter, have specialized mouthparts that allow then to scrape algae off rocks, collect fine bits of plant food, shred living and dead leaves into smaller pieces, or chew chunks from leaves. Predatory larvae have sharpened mouthparts that help them to grasp and hold their prey, or animals hunted for food. The larvae may have simple or feathery gills located on their head, thorax or midsection, and abdomen. They always have a pair of segmented projections on the tip of their abdomen.

GEOGRAPHIC RANGE

Stoneflies live on all continents, except Antarctica. They are also found on most larger islands except Cuba, Fiji, Hawaii, and New Caledonia. There are approximately two thousand species of stoneflies worldwide, with about six hundred in the United States and Canada.

HABITAT

Both adults and larvae live primarily in cold, running streams and rivers. The larvae live on the bottom of streams and rivers. A few species prefer the gravelly shores of mountain lakes where there is a lot of wave action. Each species of stonefly lives in its own special habitat, including rocky bottoms, in spaces among loose gravel, piles of waterlogged leaves and debris, or on submerged logs. Adults are found during the day resting on vegetation, rocks, and debris along running waters. They are sometimes attracted to lights at night.

DIET

The adults of some species feed on algae (AL-jee), lichen (LIE-kuhn), pollen, or nectar, but the food preferences of most species are still unknown. Some adults apparently do not feed at all. The larvae feed on living and dead plant or animal materials. Some species shift their food preferences from one food group to another as they mature.

BEHAVIOR AND REPRODUCTION

In North America and Europe male and female stoneflies usually find one another by joining in mating swarms near streams and rivers. Males and females locate one another through a complex series of vibration signals known as drumming. These signals are attractive only to individuals of the same species. Stoneflies drum by tapping, rubbing, or scraping their abdomens on a rock or log. Other species produce signals by doing pushups or rocking back and forth. Males typically drum as they search for females. If interested, a female perched nearby will drum back. Both the male and female continue to communicate this way until they locate one another and mate.

Males will attempt to mate many times, but females will mate only once. Mated females will not answer male drumming calls.

Males transfer sperm directly to the female's reproductive organs during mating. The eggs are laid in pellets or masses containing many eggs. The female then flies over the water, either dipping her abdomen in the water to deposit the eggs, or simply dropping them from the air. In some species the female runs along the shore to lay her eggs directly in shallow water. Other females submerge themselves completely to place their eggs directly on the stream bottom. The eggs either hatch within three to four weeks or enter diapause (DIE-uh-pawz), a period of rest that lasts three months to one or more years.

Stonefly larvae somewhat or closely resemble the adults and develop gradually. They molt, or shed their exoskeletons or hard outer coverings, ten to twenty-five times before reaching adulthood. Their life cycle may take months or years depending on species and local conditions, such as water temperature. When mature the larvae crawl out of the water and molt for the last time. Their shed exoskeletons are commonly found on rocks and vegetation near streams and rivers in spring and summer. The adults live only briefly and do not provide any care for the larvae.

STONEFLIES AND PEOPLE

Stoneflies are a very important part of stream food webs. Since nearly all species require clean water to reproduce, their presence in a stream or river is used as an indication of good water quality. Both the adults and larvae are an important food source for fish. Fishermen make lures called flies that imitate the forms of both adult and larval stoneflies and use them instead of living bait to catch fish.

CONSERVATION STATUS

Four species of stoneflies are listed by the World Conservation Union (IUCN). One is listed as Extinct, or no longer living; two are listed as Vulnerable, or facing a high risk of extinction in the wild. The fourth species lacks sufficient information to determine the chances of it becoming extinct. Habitat destruction caused by development, logging, and other manmade or natural events that change water quality are the greatest threat to stonefly populations.

Stonefly species are sometimes found only in a particular stream system or are considered rare and restricted to a small geographic region. This has resulted in the development of local, regional, and state lists that identify these species and their need for special consideration and further study. Stonefly larvae have similar space and clean water requirements to small trout and other fish of similar size. Techniques used to maintain healthy native fish populations might work equally well to manage populations of stonefly larvae. However, these practices are rarely used to protect stonefly habitats.

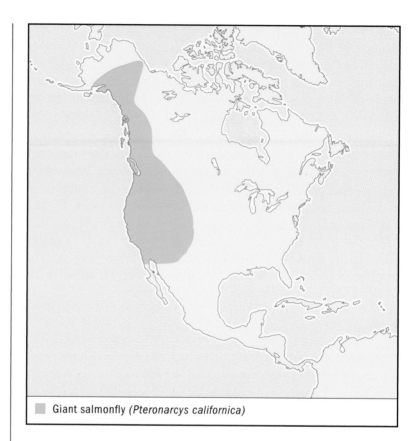

Giant salmonfly (*Pteronarcys californica*)

GIANT SALMONFLY
Pteronarcys californica

Physical characteristics: The giant salmonfly is a large stonefly measuring 1.18 to 1.97 inches (30 to 50 millimeters) in length, with a wingspan of 2.25 to 3.25 inches (58 to 84 millimeters). They are dark brown, with a reddish line down the middle of their midsection. The larvae have branched gills under the first two abdominal segments. These gills are reduced to small stubs in the adults.

Geographic range: The giant salmonfly is widespread in western North America.

Habitat: Adults and larvae are associated with fast-moving mountain streams.

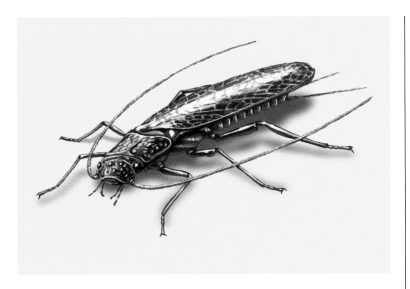

Diet: The larvae feed on algae and shred plant materials. The adults do not feed.

Behavior and reproduction: Adult males and females emerge in spring and gather along streams and rivers on vegetation for drumming and mating. Males produce heavy six-beat signals, and females answer with similar signals. The larvae require two to three years to reach adulthood.

Giant salmonflies and people: The giant salmonfly is an important food source for trout. Both the larvae and adults are used as models by fly fishermen to create artificial lures.

Conservation status: This species is not endangered or threatened. ■

FOR MORE INFORMATION

Books:

Resh, V. H., and D. M. Rosenberg. *The Ecology of Aquatic Insects.* New York: Praeger Publishers, 1984.

Stark, B. P., S. W. Szczytko, and C. R. Nelson. *American Stoneflies: A Photographic Guide to the Plecoptera.* Columbus, OH: Caddis Press, 1998.

Stewart, K. W., and B. P. Stark. *Nymphs of North American Stonefly Genera (Plecoptera),* 2nd ed. Columbus, OH: Caddis Press, 2002.

Periodicals:

Amos, W. H. "Unseen Life of a Mountain Stream." *National Geographic* 151, No. 4 (April, 1977): 562–580.

Web sites:

Gordon's Plecoptera (Stonefly) Page. http://www.earthlife.net/insects/plecopt.html (accessed on September 29, 2004).

"Plecoptera. Stoneflies," *Ecowatch.* http://www.ento.csiro.au/Ecowatch/Insects_Invertebrates/plecoptera.htm (accessed on September 29, 2004).

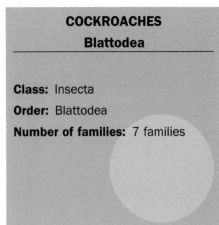

COCKROACHES

Blattodea

Class: Insecta

Order: Blattodea

Number of families: 7 families

order

CHAPTER

PHYSICAL CHARACTERISTICS

Cockroaches are related closely to termites and mantids (such as the praying mantis) and are sometimes grouped with them. Adult cockroaches range in length from 0.8 to 3.1 inches (20.3 to 78.7 millimeters). They are flat and oval in shape, and they usually have four wings. Most species are uniformly dark in color and are typically black, brown, or reddish brown. Some species have unique markings, warning possible predators (PREH-duh-ters), or animals that hunt them for food, that they might be poisonous or taste bad. The larvae (LAR-vee), or cockroach young, look very similar to the adults. While many cockroaches have body chemicals that make them taste bad, most do not. Brightly colored species are mostly mimics, pretending to look like some other kind of insect that predators associate with a bad taste, painful bites, or stings. Some cockroaches that live in the tropics look like fireflies, ladybird beetles, or wasps. Almost nothing is known about the relationship of these cockroaches to the insects they mimic.

Cockroaches have strong, chewing mouthparts that point downward. The threadlike antennae (an-TEH-nee), feelers, are usually longer than the body. Their bodies are made up of many small segments too numerous to count easily. They have compound eyes, eyes with many lenses, but in some species, especially those that live in caves, they may be small or absent. The first part of the thorax is often shieldlike, and the edge often covers most of the head. The forewings, if there are any, are slightly thickened membranes with a network of supporting

phylum

class

subclass

● **order**

monotypic order

suborder

family

veins. These wings may be short, exposing part of the abdomen, or long, covering the abdomen entirely. The hind wings, if present, are sometimes fanlike, but they may also be very small. They, too, are somewhat like membranes and thinner, and they have a network of supporting veins. The cockroaches' long and spiny legs are especially suited for running, although some species rely on them for digging.

GEOGRAPHIC RANGE

Cockroaches are found around the world, with most species living in the tropics. Species are found wherever humans live and work.

HABITAT

Wild cockroaches do not live with humans and are not considered pests. They live almost everywhere in the world, except in very cold habitats. However, one species of cockroach, *Eupolyphaga everestinia*, is found on the slopes of Mount Everest at 18,500 feet (5,639 meters). German cockroaches and other pest species can survive indoors in extremely cold climates. Cockroaches live in caves, mines, animal burrows, bird nests, ant and termite nests, deserts, and even around water. Most species live outdoors and spend their days near the ground, hiding under bark, dead leaves, soil, logs, or stones. About twenty species of cockroaches worldwide have the same temperature and moisture requirements as humans do. They prefer to live in homes, restaurants, food stores, hospitals, and sewers. Living in these stable climates protects them from extremely high or low temperatures and assures them of plenty of water.

Many species live on plants, but it is not clear whether the plants are essential to their survival. Most cockroaches found on plants are simply taking advantage of a place to hide and find food. Some species damage plants by feeding on them, but others transport pollen from one tropical plant to another. Several species prefer to live on land at the edges of streams or pools, and they sometimes spend brief periods of time in the water.

In the western United States, desert cockroaches live on plants during the day and avoid the blistering sun of spring, summer, and fall. From November through March, when the nighttime temperatures are cooler, they burrow into the sand at the bases of plants. They come up to the surface just after dark to feed, taking advantage of the warmest nighttime temperatures.

DIET

Cockroaches eat almost any plant or animal. Some pest species can survive days or weeks without food or water and can live up to three months on just water. Cave-dwelling species will eat bat droppings, while those living in sewers will feed on human waste. Many species that live underground or in dead trees burrow into soil or wood and form a chamber from which they emerge to forage (FOR-ihj), or search, for food. They collect dead leaves and carry them back to the chamber, where they can feed in safety. Species that feed on dead wood depend on microscopic animals or bacteria in their stomachs to help them digest their food.

BEHAVIOR AND REPRODUCTION

Most species are active at night, but some wild cockroaches are active during the day.

Many cockroaches burrow under the ground, beneath dead leaves, or in rotten wood to avoid danger or to rest. Cave-dwelling species burrow into piles of bat waste or slip into narrow cracks in rock walls. Some species run quickly or fly away to avoid danger. Others simply freeze with the approach of a predator. Many cockroaches have special organs in their bodies that make a variety of irritating chemicals that they spray from the tip of the abdomen at their attackers. Many larval cockroaches and some adults produce a glue from the abdomen, which sticks to the legs of ants and beetles, preventing them from attacking the cockroach.

When disturbed, many cockroaches can make sounds. Madagascan hissing cockroaches hiss by quickly blowing air out of breathing holes along the sides of their abdomens. In other species there is a rasp on the edge of the midsection. Next to the rasp is a thickened vein, or file, on the forewing. By rubbing these two structures together, the cockroach can make a faint rasping or squeaking sound.

Some cockroaches live in groups and provide care for their larvae. The rhino cockroach of Queensland, Australia, digs its burrow in sandy soil and builds an underground nest for its young, lining it with leaves, grass, and roots. Other species live in groups but do not care for their young. Still other cockroaches are loners, living mostly by themselves until it is time to mate.

Mates locate each other through pheromones (FEHR-uh-mohns), special chemicals released from the body that are especially attractive to members of the opposite sex of the same species. Eyesight plays little or no part in finding a mate or in courtship, despite the fact that most species have well-developed compound eyes. Many cockroaches engage in complex courtship dances. Females "call" males by raising their wings to expose special glands on the abdomen that release a pheromone to attract the male. Males have their own special organs on their backs that the female either eats or licks during mating. Other species show little or no courting activity before mating. During mating the male transfers his sperm packet directly into the reproductive organs of the female.

Nearly all female cockroaches put their eggs in a pillow-like capsule. Each capsule may have just a few to nearly 250 eggs, aligned in two rows. In some species the female carries the egg capsule on the tip of her abdomen for several days or weeks and then later leaves or buries them near a good supply of food and water. Some species can draw the capsule into the abdomen for short periods of time, to protect it. In other species, the capsule is kept in the abdomen until the eggs hatch inside the mother. The larvae are then "born" as they leave the mother's body. A few Australian cockroaches do not produce an egg capsule, but the eggs are kept inside the body. Only one species, *Diploptera punctata*, gives birth to live young. Its eggs are kept inside the body without a capsule and are nourished, or fed, by the mother's body until they are born. Most cockroaches never see their young. But in some species the larvae gather in a group under the mother, where they remain for a short period of time. Among some cockroaches the larvae spend their first days in a special chamber under the mother's wings.

COCKROACHES AND PEOPLE

If they are not controlled, some species may build up huge populations not only in homes and businesses but also in sewers. They are known to carry funguses; bacteria; parasitic worms, worms that infest the cockroaches' internal organs; and other microscopic organisms on and in their bodies that cause diseases in humans. They have the potential for spreading harmful organisms indirectly, through contact with foods and utensils used in home and commercial food preparation areas. There is still no solid evidence that cockroaches spread diseases to humans, but they can trigger allergic reactions among people who are especially sensitive to them. Researchers regularly working with cockroaches in laboratories may eventually become sensitive to them. In time they may experience allergy attacks, asthma, or skin irritations when exposed to cockroaches or the materials with which cockroaches have come into contact.

Pest species are often used for experiments and research in university and government laboratories, studying how their bodies work. Researchers are developing tiny "robotic" cockroaches using the Madagascan hissing cockroach as a model. Equipped with wristwatch-sized sensors and a video camera to help start and steer, the "Biobot" cockroach is able to "see" and take measurements in faraway places that are not safe for humans, such as buildings that have been destroyed by bombs or earthquakes.

Most cockroaches do not live with humans and are not considered pests. Instead, these species live in tropical rainforests, mountains, and deserts. They break down plant materials, recycling them into food that can be used by other plants and animals. In parts of Asia, humans eat cockroaches as food. In southern China and in other parts of the world, dried specimens of *Opisthoplatia orientalis* are sold for medicinal purposes. And many large cockroaches, such as the Madagascan hissing cockroach, are bred and kept in captivity as pets.

CONSERVATION STATUS

No species of cockroaches are officially endangered. The greatest threat to wild cockroaches is the destruction of their habitats, especially tropical species that have a very limited geographic range or live in small, specialized habitats. At least one species, the Russian steppe cockroach (*Ectobius duskei*), has become extinct because the continual expansion of cultivated wheat completely replaced its habitat.

TAKE A COCKROACH TO LUNCH!

Despite their reputation as disgusting pests, cockroaches are used as food by humans. Those daring enough to try adult cockroaches have said that they taste like shrimp. The Aborigines of Australia and the Lao Hill tribe of Thailand eat them raw, while children throughout Laos collect the egg capsules for frying. In the United States cockroaches are never on the menu, but they still occasionally wind up on our plates, accidentally served up from kitchens that have fallen behind in their pest control efforts.

Madeira cockroach (*Rhyparobia maderae*)

MADEIRA COCKROACH
Rhyparobia maderae

Physical characteristics: Adults range in length from 1.57 to 1.97 inches (39.9 to 50 millimeters). Males and females are very similar in appearance. Their bodies are pale brown to tan. The forewings are fully developed and cover the entire body. Each forewing has two black lines at the base, while the rest of the wings have small spots.

Geographic range: This species is native to West Africa but is now found throughout the tropical regions of the world and is especially common on the islands of the Caribbean. In 1950 it became established in basements of some buildings in New York City but has spread little since then.

Habitat: The Madeira cockroach infests food stores indoors, but outdoors it prefers to live in sugarcane fields, as well as palms, guava, and bananas growing next to the fields.

Diet: This cockroach probably eats both plant and animal tissues. It is especially fond of bananas and grapes.

Behavior and reproduction: The Madeira cockroach lives in groups and may form large colonies. The male sometimes taps the ground or tree trunk with his midsection, possibly to attract females. During courtship the female feeds on special fluids from the male's second abdominal segment. The pair remain together for twenty to thirty minutes.

At temperatures ranging between 86 and 97°F (30 and 36°C), mated females produce their first egg capsule about twenty days after reaching maturity. Each egg capsule contains about forty eggs. The eggs take about two months to develop inside the body of the mother. The young larvae forage for food with their mother. They molt, shed their external skeletons, seven or eight times before reaching maturity. Males mature in 121 days; females require 150 days. The total life span, from egg to adult, is about two and a half years.

 Madeira cockroaches and people: This species is a pest in some tropical regions, where it eats fruits intended for humans. It is also used as an experimental laboratory animal.

Conservation status: This species is not endangered or threatened. ∎

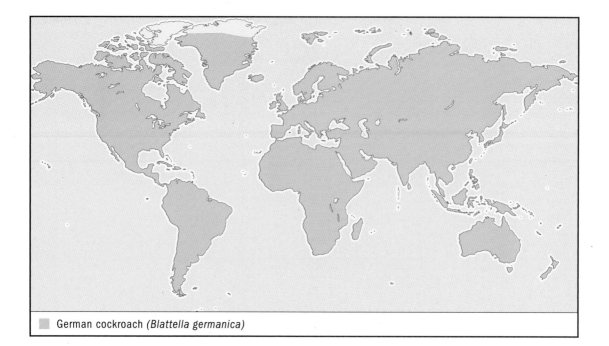

German cockroach (*Blattella germanica*)

GERMAN COCKROACH
Blattella germanica

Physical characteristics: This species measures 0.4 to 0.5 inches (10.2 to 12.7 millimeters) in length. Males and females are fully winged and similar in appearance. Their bodies are pale yellowish brown to tan. The midsection has dark parallel stripes.

Geographic range: The German cockroach is found in association with humans around the world. It is even found in cold climates, such Greenland, Iceland, and the Canadian Arctic, where it lives indoors in homes and businesses.

Habitat: This species is a common pest in kitchens, food-storage areas, and restaurants. They are also widespread in the galleys and storerooms of ships and jetliners. In warmer climates they are found outdoors, living under houses, in trash piles, on date palms, and in city dumps. They also occur in gold mines and caves in South Africa.

Diet: German cockroaches eat almost anything that is plant or animal in origin.

Behavior: German cockroaches lives in groups and may build up large colonies if they are not controlled. For example, a four-room apartment in Texas had an infestation of mostly German cockroaches numbering between fifty thousand and one hundred thousand individuals. Despite their well-developed wings, they are poor fliers. They usually just glide down to the floor. Mature females "call" males by raising their wings to release a pheromone from a special gland near the tip of the abdomen. During courtship the female climbs on the back of the male and feeds on a fluid coming out of glands on the male's abdomen. Eventually, the male deposits a sperm packet directly into the body of the female.

German cockroaches and people: This species can be a household pest and is known to cause asthma attacks in people. It is also suspected to carry bacteria that cause disease in humans.

Conservation status: This species is not endangered or threatened. ■

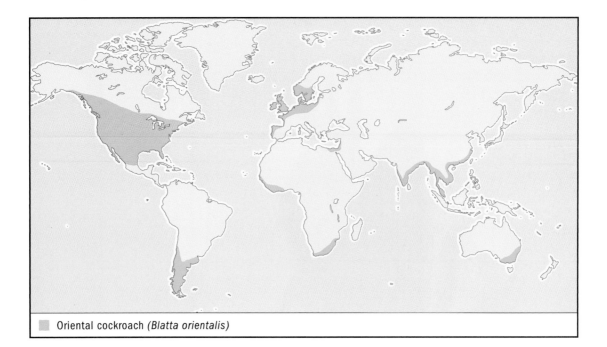

Oriental cockroach *(Blatta orientalis)*

ORIENTAL COCKROACH
Blatta orientalis

Physical characteristics: This shiny blackish brown species measures 0.7 to 0.94 inches (18 to 23.9 millimeters) in length. The forewings of the male are short, covering only about two-thirds of the abdomen. The female's forewings form small pads that barely cover the rear of the thorax, or midsection. There are no hind wings.

Geographic range: This species is found in port cities around the world. It also is found throughout the United States, England, northern Europe, Israel, southern Australia, and southern South America.

Habitat: In buildings, oriental cockroaches are usually found on the ground floor or in the basement, but small numbers may be found up to the fifth floor. They prefer basements and cellars, service ducts, crawl spaces, and toilets and areas behind baths, sinks, radiators, ovens, and hot-water pipes. Large numbers can be seen around storm drains and other sources of water. In warmer parts of the United

The Oriental cockroach is a household pest. It often comes up through drains, only to become trapped in sinks and tubs. (Adrian Davies/Bruce Coleman Inc. Reproduced by permission.)

States, they often are seen outdoors around homes. During warm summer nights they commonly walk on sidewalks, in alleys, and along walls. They live in hollow trees and in garbage and trash dumps.

Diet: The oriental cockroach eats almost anything that is plant or animal in origin.

Behavior and reproduction: The life cycle of this species is seasonal. Although adults in some areas are seen throughout the year, they usually appear in May and June. They are very tolerant of cold conditions and are known to breed outdoors in England and southern Russia.

At temperatures between 86 and 97°F (30 and 36°C), mated females produce their first egg capsule twelve days after they reach maturity. Females produce two or three capsules in a lifetime. Each capsule contains, on average, sixteen eggs, which take forty-four days to hatch. The larvae molt eight to ten times before reaching adulthood. Raised in captivity, males require 146 days to reach maturity, while females take 165 days.

Oriental cockroaches and people: This species is considered a household pest. It often comes up through drains, and becomes trapped in sinks and tubs.

Conservation status: This species is not endangered or threatened. ■

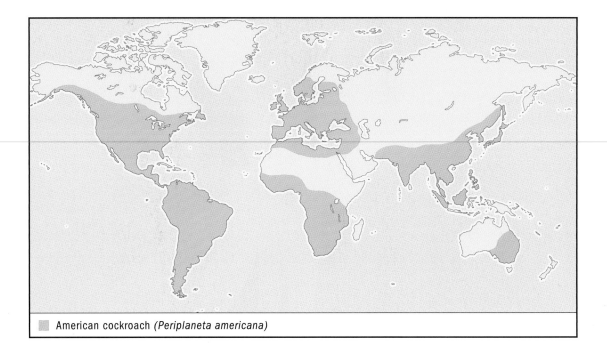

American cockroach *(Periplaneta americana)*

AMERICAN COCKROACH
Periplaneta americana

Physical characteristics: Adult American cockroaches measure 1.1 to 1.7 inches (28 to 43.2 millimeters) in length. The wings are fully developed in both males and females. Their bodies are reddish brown, with pale yellow margins around the edge of the midsection.

Geographic range: Originally from tropical Africa, this species is now found throughout the warmer regions of the world, accidentally distributed by sailing ships carrying goods and slaves.

Habitat: This species is seen both inside and outside human dwellings. American cockroaches prefer warm, moist habitats and are the most common species of cockroach in sewers in the United States. In tropical and subtropical areas they are found outdoors and in dumps, woodpiles, sewers, and cesspools.

Diet: The American cockroach feeds on almost all plant and animal materials and eats human waste in sewers.

Adult female American cockroaches live up to two years, producing as many as ninety egg capsules. (Kim Taylor/Bruce Coleman Inc. Reproduced by permission.)

Behavior and reproduction: American cockroaches live in groups and may form large colonies numbering in the millions. When threatened, they can fly short distances. Females produce a pheromone that attracts males from as far away as 98 feet (30 meters).

Under laboratory conditions, with temperatures ranging from 64 to 81°F (18 to 27°C) during winter and a maximum summer temperature of 95°F (35°C), female larvae need fifteen to sixteen months to reach adulthood, while males take about eighteen months. At higher temperatures the development time is shorter. Adult females live up to two years, producing as many as ninety egg capsules. Each capsule contains about sixteen eggs that take almost two months to hatch. The larvae molt nine to thirteen times before reaching adulthood.

American cockroaches and people: The American cockroach, along with the German cockroach, is the most common cockroach pest. American cockroaches have many kinds of microscopic organisms on and in their bodies that can cause disease in humans.

Conservation status: This species is not endangered or threatened. ■

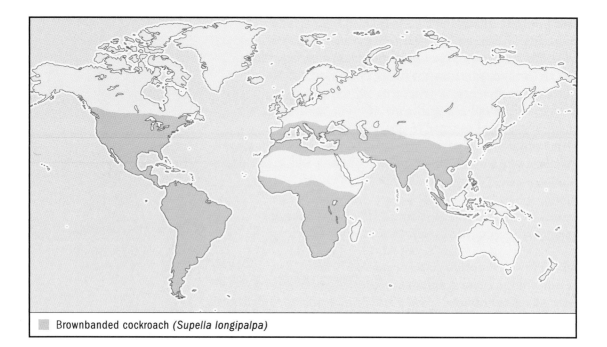

Brownbanded cockroach (*Supella longipalpa*)

BROWNBANDED COCKROACH
Supella longipalpa

Physical characteristics: This small cockroach measures only 0.39 to 0.57 inches (9.9 to 14.5 millimeters) in length. In males the forewings completely cover the body, while those of the female seldom reach the tip of the abdomen. The forewings are reddish brown, with pale areas at the base and in the middle. The body color varies: the dark midsection often has a pale area in the center.

Geographic range: The brownbanded cockroach is probably native to Africa. It has now become widespread around the warmer, wetter regions of the world. It is usually found in association with homes and businesses.

Habitat: The brownbanded cockroach is found throughout homes: behind pictures, under picture frames, on and under furniture, in cupboards and closets, on bookshelves, inside televisions, and in showers.

Diet: Brownbanded cockroaches feed on all kinds of foods in kitchens. They often eat the glues of book bindings, wallpaper paste, and the adhesives on the backs of stamps and gummed labels.

Behavior and reproduction: This species tends to fly when it is disturbed. The female releases a pheromone that attracts the male from a distance.

At a temperature of about 86°F (30°C), larvae molt six to eight times before reaching adulthood. Both males and females take about fifty-five days to become adults. Males live for about 115 days, while females live about ninety days. The female produces her first egg capsule about ten days after reaching maturity and produces, on average, eleven capsules in six-day intervals during her lifetime. Each capsule contains about sixteen eggs, which take about forty days to hatch. The egg capsules are found throughout the home on walls and ceilings and on or near kitchen sinks, desks, tables, and bedding.

Brownbanded cockroaches and people: These cockroaches are household pests that can spread throughout homes.

Conservation status: This species is not endangered or threatened. ■

The brownbanded cockroach is found throughout homes: behind pictures, under picture frames, on and under furniture, in cupboards and closets, on bookshelves, inside televisions, and in showers. (Illustration by Amanda Smith. Reproduced by permission.)

FOR MORE INFORMATION

Books:

Gordon, David George. *The Compleat Cockroach: A Comprehensive Guide to the Most Despised (and Least Understood) Creature on Earth.* Berkeley, CA: Ten Speed Press, 1996.

Taylor, R. L. *Butterflies in My Stomach; or, Insects in Human Nutrition.* Santa Barbara, CA: Woodridge Press, 1975.

Periodicals:

Boraiko, A. A. "The Indomitable Cockroach." *National Geographic* 159, no. 1 (January 1981): 130–142.

Park, A. "Guess Who's Coming to Tea? Cockroaches!" *Australian Geographic* 18 (April–June 1990): 30–45.

Web sites:

"The Blattodea or Cockroaches." The Earthlife Web. http://www.earthlife. net/insects/blatodea.html (accessed on September 8, 2004).

"Blattodea: Cockroaches." Ecowatch. http://www.ento.csiro.au/Ecowatch/Insects_Invertebrates/blattodea.htm (accessed on September 8, 2004).

"Critter Catalog: Cockroaches." BioKids. http://www.biokids.umich.edu/critters/information/Blattaria.html (accessed on September 8, 2004).

"Madagascar Hissing Cockroaches." University of Kentucky Entomology. http://www.uky.edu/Agriculture/Entomology/entfacts/misc/ef014.htm (accessed on September 2004).

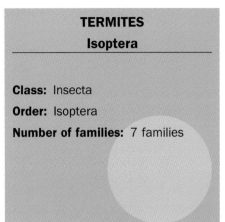

order

PHYSICAL CHARACTERISTICS

Termites are the most primitive group of living winged insects that lay their eggs on land. Some scientific studies suggest that termites are most closely related to cockroaches. The most primitive cockroaches, wingless wood cockroaches from North America, closely resemble termites in their appearance and behavior. Similarly, the most primitive termites, *Mastotermes darwiniensis* from Queensland, Australia, look and act like cockroaches. The similarities between termites and cockroaches suggest that termites could be called "social cockroaches" and cockroaches could be called "solitary termites." However, there are major differences in overall body plan and wing structure. Still, it is very likely that termites and cockroaches had a common ancestor but then branched off into their own distinct groups a very long time ago.

Termites have a caste system, meaning that each member of a group has a different function within the group. Each "caste" is told apart from another by its size, form, and the ability or lack of ability to reproduce. The castes usually consist of workers, soldiers, and kings and queens. Only the kings and queens reproduce. Termite workers and soldiers are unable to reproduce. Termites are usually pale and soft-bodied. Their thorax, or midsection, is broadly attached to the abdomen, giving them a thick waist. They have short antennae (an-TEH-nee) with beadlike segments. The workers and soldiers might be either male or female. Worker termites have powerful jaws for chewing wood or other plant materials. Depending on the species, soldiers may have big heads with sharp, scissorlike jaws or smaller, pointed heads. They tend to be larger and darker and have heavier bodies than the workers.

Only the insects that reproduce have wings, mate, and lay eggs. The forewings and hind wings of these termites are the same size. Termites hold their wings flat over the body when resting. The wings of king and queen termites break off just before the point where they are attached to the thorax. Queens among the mound-building termites often have bloated, sausage-shaped abdomens and are basically egg-laying machines. They range in length from 2 to 4 inches (5.1 to 10.2 centimeters). Larvae (LAR-vee), or young termites, look like the adults.

GEOGRAPHIC RANGE

Termites are found in warmer regions of the world, especially in the tropics and subtropics, or regions that border on the tropics.

HABITAT

Most termites prefer to live in warm, humid climates, especially at low altitudes along river valleys and in coastal areas. Other species are found in mountain forests, deserts, and grasslands.

DIET

Although the best-known termites eat dead wood, others eat a wide variety of foods, including small bits of decomposed, or disintegrated, plants; leaf litter; dead grass; dung, or the waste material of animals; funguses, and lichens, or certain plantlike organisms that live together, as one. Some of these termite species are considered pests when their food-gathering activities include crops, such as corn.

Unable to digest plant materials on their own, wood-eating and plant-feeding termites must rely on tiny organisms in their stomachs to help them digest their food. This organism, a protozoan (proh-toh-ZOH-uhn), whose body is made up of only one cell, and the termite depend on each other for food. Some termites lack these microscopic partners and instead must grow their own fungus for food, or else they have special chambers in their stomachs populated with different kinds of bacteria, another type of tiny single-celled organism, that help with digestion.

BEHAVIOR AND REPRODUCTION

Termites lead secretive lives hidden in wood, underground, or in specially constructed tubes or nests. They seldom come out in the open, except to mate, but some species routinely search for food above ground. They are social insects that live in colonies with thousands to millions of individuals. Most colonies are made up of different castes (workers, soldiers, kings, and queens) that work together to expand and repair the nest, defend the colony, reproduce, and care for and feed the young.

A long-lived king and queen are usually at the head of each colony. The queen is the only member of the colony capable of laying eggs. Workers make up the majority of the colony's population. They build and repair the nest, hunt for food, and feed and groom other members of the colony. However, among primitive termites, there is no true worker caste. Instead, their wingless young perform the tasks of workers. Soldiers defend the colony from ants and other invaders by snapping their scissorlike jaws at the intruders, chopping them up into little bits. Others have very small mouthparts, but their heads are packed with special glands that produce sticky and poisonous fluids. Some of these termite soldiers have pointed heads that are used as spray nozzles to direct a foul smelling, sticky glue at their attackers, gumming up their legs and antennae.

Termites rely on pheromones (FEHR-uh-mohns), special chemicals released from their bodies, to find one another and to communicate. For example, workers and soldiers have glands underneath the thorax that produce pheromones that compel others nearby to help repair damages nest walls. Species that tunnel through the soil create chemical trails underground so that their nest mates can follow them to food.

Termites spend a lot of time grooming, nibbling, and licking each other with their mouthparts. They also drink fluids from the tip of one another's abdomens, so they can pass along the microscopic organisms they need to help digest plant materials. Primitive termites live in or near their food source. The most familiar wood-feeding species nest in tunnels chewed in dead logs, stumps, and timbers. Some desert species live in the soil or under a protective papery coating that they build on the outside of the dead branches and trunks of desert plants. Other termites build their nests away from any food source. Their nests are constructed entirely underground, beneath rocks, partially above ground, or completely on the surface. Underground nests are usually made up of chambers or layers of tunnels, called galleries. The walls of the chambers and galleries are plastered with the hardened waste material of termites.

Species living in the open grasslands of Africa, Australia, and South America build cathedrallike mound nests on the surface, using mostly clay and their own waste droppings mixed with saliva as building materials. Some of these mounds are truly the skyscrapers of the insect world, reaching a height of 36 feet (10.9 meters) or more. The inside of these towering structures are filled with chambers, chimneys, and ventilation shafts that function as air conditioning to maintain fairly constant temperatures inside, no matter what the temperature is outside. With their walls almost as hard as concrete, these mounds are truly monuments, lasting for decades or even centuries.

In the tropics termites sometimes attach their lumpy or mushroom-shaped nests to tree trunks or high up on tree limbs. These nests are often linked to the ground by a series of tubelike runways. The materials used to make these mounds and tubes depend on the diet of the particular termite. Typically, they are made from chewed-up bits of plants, soil, and termite droppings, all mixed with saliva. Once dried, the nest walls feel and look like very coarse paper.

Each spring and summer thousands of winged kings and queens take to the air. They soon land, shed their wings, and begin the search for a mate from another colony. Some queens produce a pheromone to attract males. In some species, a pair of termites runs rapidly over the ground in a zigzag pattern during courtship, with the queen leading the way and the king following close behind. After courtship, the king and queen search together for a nesting site, usually in the soil or in a crevice (KREH-vuhs) or hole in wood. After clearing a small chamber and sealing themselves inside, they mate. All termites, whether they are male or female, develop from fertilized (FUR-teh-lyzed) eggs.

In other termite species, new colonies form by a process known as budding. Their sprawling colonies simply keep expanding into new territory, with new kings and queens moving to the edges of the continually expanding nest to start their own colonies. Their workers and soldiers mix freely with those of the original colony.

The king and queen tend to the first batch of young and actively join in nest building and other duties, but these tasks are taken over by the young termites as they mature. Young termites look like the adults when they hatch. They molt, or shed their external skeletons, several times before reaching adulthood, and they may or may not develop wings. Eventually, they and future generations take over all of the duties of the nest. Soon the queen's only job is to lay eggs. Some queens live as long as twenty years and lay millions of eggs during their lifetimes. In mature colonies, if the king or queen should die, he or she is quickly replaced by another king or queen already developing in the nest.

TERMITES AND PEOPLE

Most people think of termites as pests, and with good reason. Their feeding and nesting activities damage or destroy wood and wood products used in books, furniture, buildings, telephone poles, and fence posts, causing millions of dollars of damage every year. Millions of dollars more are spent trying to control their populations or get rid of them. Termite control methods include applying heat to infested areas, freezing them with liquid nitrogen, and zapping them with microwaves or electrical shocks. Each method is used for a particular kind of infestation. Lumber yards now treat much of the wood used in the construction of buildings with chemicals designed to repel termite attacks.

Because of their ability to convert plant materials into animal protein, termites could be used to turn large amounts of raw plant waste into food for humans. The feeding activities of termites could be applied to breaking down sawdust and scrap lumber piling up in sawmills or eliminating straws, bean pods, and sugarcane pulp from food and sugar-processing plants. They might even be used to break down dried dung gathering in cattle feed lots and dairy farms. Raised on these waste products, the termites could then be fed to chickens and fish raised for human consumption. Raising large amounts of termites on

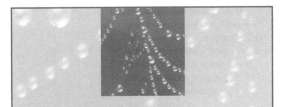

GOING FOR THE GOLD

A Canadian geologist, a scientist who studies rocks, visited Niger to look for the best sites to find gold. He had read that ancient African civilizations used termite mounds, sometimes 6 feet (1.8 meters) high and 6 feet across at the base, to locate deposits of the precious metal. Some termites dig down 250 feet (76 meters) below the surface and use gold-bearing soil to build their mounds. He managed to find a few mounds with gold, suggesting possible sites for further exploration.

these and other waste products is challenging and requires more termite research.

CONSERVATION STATUS

No termites are officially listed as endangered or threatened. With so much time and money invested in killing them, little consideration has been given to their conservation. In the tropics, termites are estimated to make up as much as 75 percent of the total weight of insects found in the forests and 10 percent of the total weight of all animals. Next to earthworms, termites represent one of the most important parts of any tropical habitat. They recycle vast amounts of plant material, making it available again as food for other plants and animals.

The widespread clearing and destruction of tropical forests for timber and farming have probably greatly cut down the populations of some termite species. The loss of termites affects not only the amount of plant materials converted into food for other organisms but also the numbers of birds, mammals, reptiles, insects, and spiders that depend on them for food and on their nests for shelter.

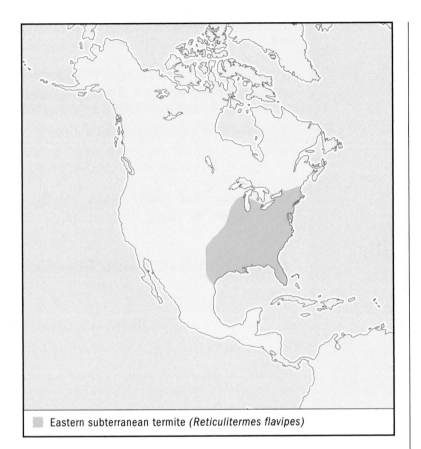

Eastern subterranean termite *(Reticulitermes flavipes)*

EASTERN SUBTERRANEAN TERMITE
Reticulitermes flavipes

Physical characteristics: Kings and queens measure 0.4 inches (10.2 millimeters) from head to wingtips. Their bodies are black, except for their yellow leg segments. Soldiers have a long, straight-sided, almost rectangular yellow head with a pale spot on top. Their thick, black, toothless jaws are strongly curved inward at the tips. Workers are about 0.2 inches (5.1 millimeters) long, with creamy white bodies.

Geographic range: These termites are native to the forests of the eastern United States, from Maine south to Florida and west to Minnesota and Texas; they were introduced into Canada in southern Ontario and Quebec.

Eastern subterranean termites eat the wood of many kinds of trees, preferring the outer portion of the trunk. (©James H. Robinson/Photo Researchers, Inc. Reproduced by permission.)

Habitat: This species is found in deciduous (di-SID-joo-wus) hardwood forests, meaning forests of hardwood trees that loose their leaves in cold or dry weather.

Diet: Eastern subterranean termites eat the wood of many kinds of trees, preferring the outer portion of the trunk. Small, paper-thin layers of a dried paste made from their droppings divide their galleries. When working above ground in buildings and trees, they build protected tubes or shelters made from small bits of soil and saliva, lined inside with a paste made from their droppings.

Behavior and reproduction: Workers forage (FOR-ihj), or search, for food in shallow, narrow tunnels in the ground that connect stumps, logs, and roots. They also climb living trees to reach dead limbs or other areas with dead or rotten wood, and they attack landscaping items made of wood, such as fence posts, firewood piles, wood-chip mulch, scrap lumber, and flower planter boxes. From these items they invade nearby homes, sheds, and other structures. Since they feed inside exposed timbers or concealed wood frames, they can cause considerable damage over the years before they are found.

These termites do not build a nest structure. Instead, large, mature colonies consist of loosely connected galleries occupied by an extended family, with several kings and queens producing broods that contribute to the overall colony. Colonies expand, shrink, and move as foraging areas run out of food and new sources are found. The termites make their egg and nursery chambers inside logs, stumps, and other large items of wood that have plenty of moisture. Timbers in homes and other buildings are usually dry, and termites seldom use them as sites for their egg laying or for raising their broods. In winter they move down into the soil, beneath the frost line.

Eastern subterranean termites and people: This is one of the most important and destructive termite pests in eastern North America. Hundreds of millions of dollars are spent every year to control them and repair the damage they do. Shelter tubes crossing over the foundation of a structure are the clearest signs of their presence in homes and other buildings.

Conservation status: This species is not endangered or threatened.

■

Black macrotermes (*Macrotermes carbonarius*)

BLACK MACROTERMES
Macrotermes carbonarius

Physical characteristics: This is the largest termite in Southeast Asia. Winged kings and queens are about 1.2 inches (30.5 millimeters) from head to wingtips, with a wingspan of at least 2 inches (50.8 millimeters). The bodies of both workers and soldiers are very dark, nearly black. Male workers are larger than female workers. The soldiers are all females, large or small, and have very sharp, swordlike jaws.

Geographic range: Black macrotermes live in Borneo and Southeast Asia, including Thailand, Cambodia, and Malaysia.

Habitat: Black macrotermes are found in flat lowlands and are seen less often in hilly areas. They are especially common in coastal forests, but they also live on coconut and rubber plantations.

Diet: These termites collect mostly dead grass, twigs, and other plant debris (duh-BREE). These plant materials are hauled below ground into the nest. Small workers chew up the material, eat it, and then deposit their droppings as fertilizer on masses of spongelike fungus. The spores, or reproductive bodies that sprout on the outer surface of the fungus, are then fed to the younger termites in the colony. Older termites eat the remains of old fungus.

Behavior and reproduction: Colonies build large mounds up to 13 feet (4 meters) high and 16 feet (5 meters) wide at the base. The fungus is usually grown in large chambers around the edges of the mound.

Smaller workers spend all their time in the nest, caring for the king and queen, feeding the young, and repairing the nest. Larger workers and some soldiers hunt for plant materials on the ground at night. Foraging parties visit a new area every night. Major workers build paved tracks from the mound to the foraging area. Workers follow the track and then fan out to collect dead grass and twigs, with both large and small soldiers standing guard nearby.

The king and queen live in a special thick-walled cell inside the mound. The abdomen of the queen grows to extremely large proportions as it fills up with eggs. When the king and queen die, the colony may also die, unless there are other winged kings and queens already present in the colony to act as replacements.

Black macrotermes and people: This species does not have an impact on people or their activities.

Conservation status: This species is not endangered or threatened. ■

Black macrotermes are found in flat lowlands and are seen less often in hilly areas. They are especially common in coastal forests, but they also live on coconut and rubber plantations. (Illustration by Barbara Duperron. Reproduced by permission.)

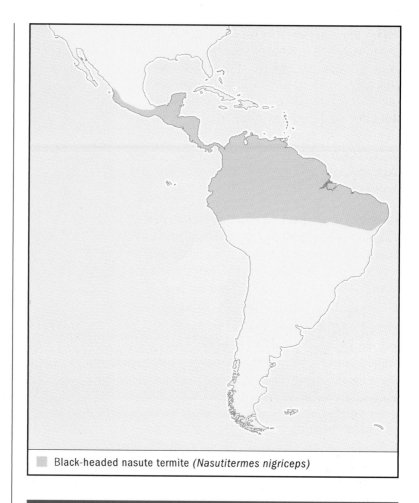

Black-headed nasute termite (*Nasutitermes nigriceps*)

BLACK-HEADED NASUTE TERMITE
Nasutitermes nigriceps

Physical characteristics: The queen is 0.7 inches (17.8 millimeters) in length, without wings. Her body is mostly reddish yellow, and the abdomen is very large. Soldiers have very dark heads covered with short, bristling hairs. Workers come in two sizes. Both large and small workers have dark bodies and rectangular heads.

Geographic range: These termites range from Mazatlán in western Mexico south to Panama and northern South America.

Habitat: Black-headed nasute termites are found along coastal plains, from sea level to about 3,280 feet (1,000 meters).

Diet: This species feeds on wood, mainly above the ground. The termites build extensive networks of broad tubes along the lower sides of tree branches.

Behavior and reproduction: Colonies live in large paperlike nests that are visible on trees, fence posts, and poles. A single colony may have more than one nest. Each colony is headed by a king and queen.

Black-headed nasute termites and people: This species occasionally attacks homes and other buildings.

Conservation status: This species is not endangered or threatened. ■

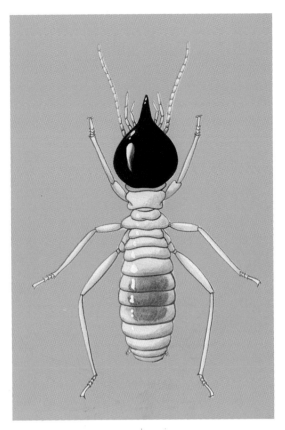

Colonies of black-headed nasute termites live in large paperlike nests that are visible on trees, fence posts, and poles. A single colony may have more than one nest. (Illustration by Barbara Duperron. Reproduced by permission.)

Linnaeus's snapping termite (*Termes fatalis*)

LINNAEUS'S SNAPPING TERMITE
Termes fatalis

Physical characteristics: Kings and queens are brown and measure about 0.3 inches (8.5 millimeters), including wings. The soldiers are long and pale yellow. Their heads are straight-sided and have a small hornlike bump toward the front. They have long and slender jaws.

Geographic range: This species is found in northeastern South America, including Guyana, Suriname, Trinidad, and Brazil.

Habitat: This species lives in tropical forests.

Diet: The structure of their jaws suggests that they eat bits of decaying plants and soft, rotten wood.

Behavior and reproduction: The soldiers are thought to use their long jaws to anchor their bodies in the tunnel to block invasions by ants and other predators. Very little is known about their nesting behavior. They use their own waste to build their turret-like nests. This building material dries to form a dark, hard wall.

Nothing is known about their reproductive behavior.

Linnaeus's snapping termites and people: This species is the first termite ever to receive a formal scientific name.

Conservation status: This species is not endangered or threatened. ■

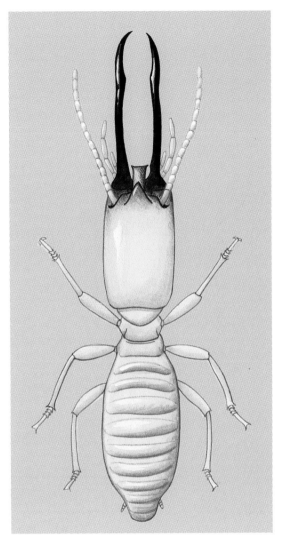

Linnaeus's snapping termites use their own waste to build their turret-like nests. This building material dries to form a dark, hard wall. (Illustration by Barbara Duperron. Reproduced by permission.)

WIDE-HEADED ROTTENWOOD TERMITE
Zootermopsis laticeps

Physical characteristics: This is the largest and most primitive termite in North America. Winged kings and queens measure 1.0 to 1.2 inches (25.4 to 30.5 millimeters) from head to wingtips, with a wingspan up to 1.9 inches (48.3 millimeters). Their bodies are dark yellowish. Soldiers measure 0.6 to 0.9 inches (15.2 to 22.9 millimeters) in length. The flattened head is widest at the back, and they have very long and roughly toothed jaws. Workers, soldiers, and other castes are whitish yellow or cream in color.

Geographic range: In the United States these termites are found from central and southeastern Arizona to southern New Mexico and western Texas; they also live in Chihuahua and Sonora, Mexico.

Habitat: This species lives in dry habitats between 1,500 and 5,500 feet (457 and 1,676 meters) along canyons and river valleys. The termites are found inside the rotten cores of logs and large branches of living willows, cottonwoods, sycamores, oaks, alders, ash, walnuts, hackberries, and other hardwoods.

Diet: Wide-headed rottenwood termites feed only on rotten hardwoods. Unlike many other termites, this termite is not known to feed on completely dead and rotten logs or on pines, firs, and their relatives.

Behavior and reproduction: Colonies are found in galleries and open chambers in rotten wood. The chambers eventually become filled with masses of termite waste. The termites sometimes gain access to a rotten tree core through a knothole. These and other knotholes are plugged with termite waste in the form of hardened pellets. Inside, the galleries are usually quite damp. Soldiers with powerful jaws defend the colony against ants and other predators.

Kings and queens fly in the middle of the night from late June through early August. Mated pairs look for tree scars, knotholes, or small pockets of rot or other wounds in trees, where they can gain access to the rotten core. A single king and queen usually head each colony, but there may be additional termites that can reproduce and contribute broods to the colony. Colonies are small and rarely have more than one thousand individuals.

Wide-headed rottenwood termites and people: This species attacks living trees, quickening their collapse and death from rot on the inside. However, they are not considered pests because the trees they attack are not used for lumber.

Conservation status: This species is not endangered or threatened. ∎

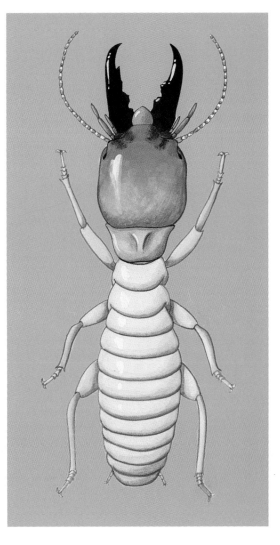

Wide-headed rottenwood termite are found inside the rotten cores of logs and large branches of living willows, cottonwoods, sycamores, oaks, alders, ash, walnuts, hackberries, and other hardwoods. (Illustration by Barbara Duperron. Reproduced by permission.)

FOR MORE INFORMATION

Periodicals:

"Geographica: African Termites Guide Way to Gold." *National Geographic* 190, no. 6 (December 1996).

"Geographica: Glow-in-the-Dark Colors Expose Termite Secrets." *National Geographic* 184, no. 5 (November 1993).

Prestwich, G. D. "Dweller in the Dark: Termites." *National Geographic* 153, no. 4 (April 1978): 532–547.

Web sites:

"Critter Catalog: Termites." BioKids. http://www.biokids.umich.edu/critters/information/Isoptera.html (accessed on September 9, 2004).

"Isoptera: Termites." Ecowatch. http://www.ento.csiro.au/Ecowatch/Insects_Invertebrates/isoptera.htm (accessed on September 9, 2004).

MANTIDS
Mantodea

Class: Hexapoda

Order: Mantodea

Number of families: 15 families

PHYSICAL CHARACTERISTICS

Mantids are fairly large insects, ranging in length from 0.4 to 6.7 inches (1 to 17 centimeters). The green, brown, or gray body color of mantids serves as camouflage to protect them from predators that hunt them for food. Species living in grasslands and meadows are usually pale yellowish brown or light green. Mantids found in leaf litter tend to be dark brown, while those found on or near flowers are yellow, white, pink, or light green.

Mantids are easily recognized by their large and spiny front legs held out in front of their bodies as if they were in prayer. The head is usually distinctive and triangular in shape. A few species have a single horn on the head. They have both well-developed compound eyes, each with hundreds of lenses, and three simple eyes, each with only one lens. The chewing mouthparts are usually directed downward. The antennae (an-TEH-nee), or sense organs, are long and threadlike. The head is attached to a very thin, flexible neck and is capable of turning nearly all the way around.

The first part of the midsection, or thorax, is usually long and slender and bears the raptorial (rap-TOR-ee-all), or grasping, front legs. The front legs are armed with one or two rows of short, sharp spines used to stab and hold prey, or food animals, securely. The remaining four legs are mostly long and slender. Mantids usually have four wings. The front wings, or forewings, are slightly thickened and have very fine veins. The hind wings are fanlike in shape and are carefully folded beneath the forewings. Most adult mantids have a single "ear" located

phylum

class

subclass

● **order**

monotypic order

suborder

family

on their underside, in the middle of the thorax near the abdomen. The ten-segmented abdomen is tipped with a pair of short, segmented projections.

Males are typically smaller than females, sometimes only half their size. They generally have larger simple eyes and longer and thicker antennae than females, and their bodies are lighter and more slender. Their abdomens are completely covered by the folded wings. In females the abdomen is not quite covered by the wings. Mantids' closest relatives are cockroaches and, to a lesser degree, termites. Mantids are sometimes grouped together in another order with these insects.

GEOGRAPHIC RANGE

Mantids are found worldwide in warm and tropical climates. There are twenty-three hundred species worldwide, mostly in the tropical rainforests of South America, Africa, and Southeast Asia. Many species are restricted to small areas, but others are found on more than one continent, having been accidentally introduced by humans to continents outside their range. Twenty species live in the United States and Canada.

HABITAT

Mantids are found only on land in rainforests, dry forests, undisturbed and second-growth forests, or forests that grow naturally after cutting or a fire, grasslands, and deserts.

DIET

Mantids will eat any small animal they can catch, including other mantids. They usually attack bees, butterflies, grasshoppers, and other insects, as well as spiders. On rare occasion they will attack small mice, lizards, frogs, and birds. They generally choose prey their own size or smaller. Right after hatching, mantid larvae (LAR-vee), or young, spend their first few weeks eating their brothers and sisters, aphids, and other small insects.

BEHAVIOR AND REPRODUCTION

Most mantids sit quietly and wait for prey to come within reach, but a few species actually chase down their victims. They have excellent vision and extremely quick reflexes and so are able to strike at and successfully capture insect prey in as little as one-twentieth of a second. After feeding, they always spend a great deal of time grooming. They use their forelegs to wipe their eyes and heads, while their legs and antennae are cleaned with the mouth.

Males spend much of their time searching for mates, while females spend most of their time hunting for food and looking for suitable egg-laying sites. In some species adult females use pheromones (FEHR-uh-moans), special chemicals that attract males as mates. Females require a large food supply so their eggs will develop properly. Therefore, they are usually found on or near flowers that attract large numbers of wasps, bees, butterflies, and other insect prey.

Mating may last for up to one hour. During this time the male deposits his sperm packet directly into the body of the female. It is a well-known myth that the female always bites off the head of the male while they are mating. Occasionally, a female may attack and eat a male as he approaches her or during or just after they mate, but this does not happen all the time. Hungry females are more likely to eat their mates.

Ten to two hundred eggs are deposited inside a foamy egg case that soon hardens into a protective, papery coating. The egg cases are attached to branches, walls, and other objects, and the adults die soon afterward. The young mantids hatch the following spring. They will molt, or shed their hard outer coverings, six to nine times before reaching adulthood. In cooler regions only one generation of mantids is produced each season, but in the tropics several generations may overlap every year.

MAGICAL MANTIDS

Mantids have captured the imaginations of people for thousands of years. They often appear in illustrations, paintings, and stories. It was once thought that, with their front legs held as if to pray, they could help direct travelers to find their way home. The Chinese staged fighting contests between mantids to bet on which insect would survive the battle. And there is a style of kung fu, a type of martial art, that mimics the movements of mantids.

MANTIDS AND PEOPLE

Some mantids are sold as pets and have become popular display animals in insect zoos. Another species is used extensively as a means of controlling plant pests without the use of harmful poisons. Throughout the United States people buy egg cases in the winter at nurseries and place them in their gardens to hatch in spring. However, young mantids will eat anything they can catch, including helpful insects as well as garden pests.

CONSERVATION STATUS

One species of mantid is listed by the World Conservation Union (IUCN) as Near Threatened, or likely to become threatened in the near future. There is very little information on most mantid populations; the greatest threats to them are habitat destruction and misuse of pesticides.

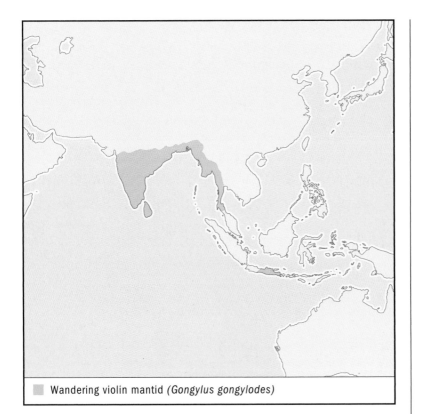

Wandering violin mantid (*Gongylus gongylodes*)

WANDERING VIOLIN MANTID
Gongylus gongylodes

Physical characteristics: Males measure 2.8 to 3.1 inches (7 to 8 centimeters) in length, while females are 3.1 to 3.5 inches (8 to 9 centimeters). They vary from light to dark brown in color. The head has a cone-shaped horn on top. The first section of the thorax is extremely thin and expanded into a diamond shape just before the head. All of the legs have leafy structures. The antennae of the females are threadlike, while those of the males appear feathery.

Geographic range: This mantid is found in southern India, Sri Lanka, Thailand, and eastern Java.

Habitat: This species lives on land in undisturbed and second-growth rainforests.

Diet: This species eats any insect that it can catch.

Behavior and reproduction: Their color and the leaflike extensions on their legs camouflage them against backgrounds of leaf litter and shrubbery.

Their egg cases contain from fifty to one hundred eggs. The egg cases are deposited on woody stems and hatch after several weeks.

Wandering violin mantids and people: This species does not have any effect on people or their activities.

Conservation status: This species is not listed by the World Conservation Union (IUCN). However, its habitat is threatened with destruction due to human overpopulation. ■

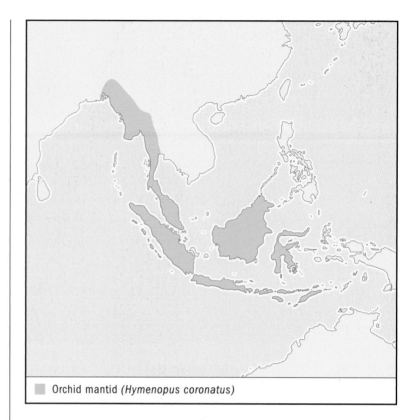

Orchid mantid *(Hymenopus coronatus)*

ORCHID MANTID
Hymenopus coronatus

Physical characteristics: Adults are white with pink patches on the head, forewings, and legs. Females average 2 inches (5 centimeters) in length, while males are only half the size at 1 inch (2.5 centimeters). The eyes are cone-shaped and stick out beyond the outline of the head. Their legs have leaflike projections.

Geographic range: This mantid is found in Southeast Asia.

Habitat: This species lives on land in undisturbed and second-growth rainforests.

Diet: They eat any small insect or spider they can catch.

Orchid mantids eat any small insect or spider they can catch. (©Ray Coleman/Photo Researchers, Inc. Reproduced by permission.)

Behavior and reproduction: This species is typically found on or near flowers, waiting to ambush prey. During courtship, males tap their antennae against the forewings of the females, probably as a way to show they are ready to mate.

The long, narrow egg cases are 2 inches (5 centimeters) long and are attached to the stems and branches of plants and shrubs. The larvae have red bodies and black heads when they first hatch and mimic, or look like, ants because ants defend themselves with bites, stings, or bad-tasting chemicals and are usually not eaten by predators.

Orchid mantids and people: This is a popular species among insect hobbyists, people who enjoy the challenge of raising interesting and unusual insects.

Conservation status: This species is not endangered or threatened. ■

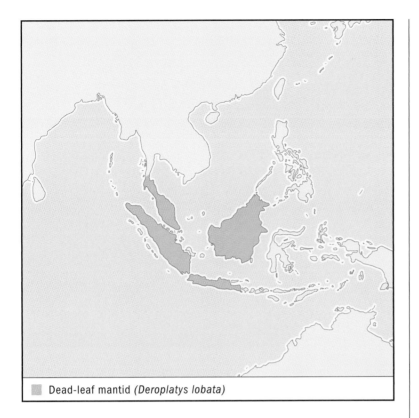

Dead-leaf mantid (*Deroplatys lobata*)

DEAD-LEAF MANTID
Deroplatys lobata

Physical characteristics: Adult males are 2.5 inches (6 centimeters) long, while the females are about 2.8 inches (7 centimeters). They use a special kind of camouflage called crypsis (KRIP-sis), with bodies that resemble not only the color of dead, dry leaves but also their shape and texture. Their bodies are light gray to dark brown with faint spots. The midsection is expanded to the sides and shaped like a leaf. Their middle and hind legs have leaflike expansions, giving them an even more leafy appearance.

Geographic range: This species is found in Southeast Asia.

Habitat: This species lives on land in undisturbed and second-growth rainforests.

Diet: They eat small insects and their relatives.

Dead-leaf mantids use a special kind of camouflage called crypsis. This makes their bodies resemble not only the color of dead, dry leaves but also their shape and texture. (©Art Wolfe/Photo Researchers, Inc. Reproduced by permission.)

Behavior and reproduction: This species lives in leaf litter and on shrubs. When threatened, they flash the bright colors on the insides of their front legs and expose the eyespots underneath their forewings, all in an effort to startle predators.

Females lay egg cases on twigs, which take about thirty to fifty days to hatch.

Dead-leaf mantids and people: This is a popular species among insect hobbyists. They are sometimes featured in insect zoos as examples of unusual coloring.

Conservation status: This species is not now endangered or threatened. However, the destruction of their habitat remains a threat to their widespread populations. ■

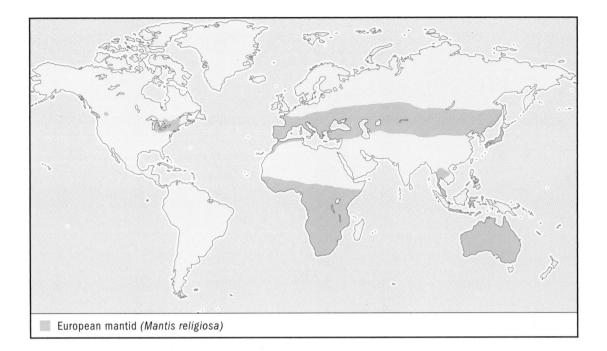

European mantid (*Mantis religiosa*)

EUROPEAN MANTID
Mantis religiosa

Physical characteristics: Adult European mantid males range in length from 2 to 2.5 inches (5 to 6 centimeters), while the females are 2.5 to 3.2 inches (6 to 8 centimeters). They vary in color from light green to brown. The inside of each foreleg has a distinctive bull's-eye-like spot.

Geographic range: This species is distributed throughout southern Europe, sub-Saharan Africa, temperate Asia, Australia, the northeastern United States, and Canada.

Habitat: The species prefers living in open fields and meadows.

Diet: They eat small insects.

Behavior and reproduction: European mantids are usually well hidden among low shrubs. They are strong flyers and are attracted to bright lights at night.

European mantids are usually well hidden among low shrubs. They are strong flyers and are attracted to bright lights at night. (©Michael Lustbader/Photo Researchers, Inc. Reproduced by permisson.)

Each egg case contains from fifty to one hundred eggs. The cases are laid in fall and are attached to low grasses and on rocks or buildings. The larvae hatch the following spring.

European mantids and people: This species does not have any effect on people or their activities.

Conservation status: This widespread species is not endangered or threatened. They are slowly expanding their range in North America.   ∎

Chinese mantid (*Tenodera aridifolia sinensis*)

CHINESE MANTID
Tenodera aridifolia sinensis

Physical characteristics: The Chinese mantid is the largest species in North America, with adult females reaching 4 inches (10 centimeters) in length or more. They are green, brown, or gray, with a distinct pale green border along the edges of their forewings.

Geographic range: This species is found in temperate eastern Asia, eastern United States, and California. They were deliberately introduced into the United States in 1896 to control insect pests.

Habitat: They prefer living in open fields and meadows.

Diet: They will eat any insect or spider that they can catch.

Behavior and reproduction: They are typically found on green, leafy plants and shrubs. Adult females are especially fond of perching near flowers, where they wait to ambush prey.

Each egg case contains one hundred to two hundred eggs. The egg cases are attached in the fall to almost any surface, including leaves, stems, branches, fences, buildings, lawn furniture, and automobiles. The larvae hatch the following spring.

Chinese mantids and people: Gardeners buy their egg cases in an effort to control garden insect pests. They are also kept as pets.

Conservation status: This species is not threatened or endangered. ■

FOR MORE INFORMATION

Books:

Helfer, J. R. *How to Know the Grasshoppers, Crickets, Cockroaches, and Their Allies.* New York: Dover Publications, 1987.

Preston-Mafham, K. *Grasshoppers and Mantids of the World.* London: Blandford, 1990.

Tavoloacci, J., ed. *Insects and Spiders of the World.* New York: Marshall Cavendish, 2003.

Periodicals:

Ross, E. S. "Mantids: The Praying Predators." *National Geographic* 165, no. 2 (February 1984): 268–280.

Tomasinelli, F. "Praying Mantids: An Introduction to Their Lifestyle and Biology." *Reptilia* 16 (June 2001): 16–28.

Web sites:

Mantis Study Group Home Page. http://www.earthlife.net/insects/msg.html (accessed on September 13, 2004).

"Mantodea: Praying Mantids." Ecowatch. http://www.ento.csiro.au/Ecowatch/Insects_Invertebrates/mantodea.htm (accessed on October 24, 2004).

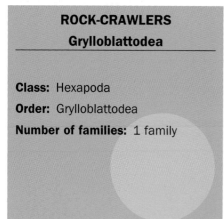

ROCK-CRAWLERS

Grylloblattodea

Class: Hexapoda
Order: Grylloblattodea
Number of families: 1 family

PHYSICAL CHARACTERISTICS

Rock-crawlers are slender, flattened, soft-bodied insects. Adults range from 0.6 to 1.4 inches (15 to 35 millimeters) in length. They are mostly brown, while the legs and underside are light brown. The larvae (LAR-vee), or young, form of the animal, which must go through changes in form before becoming an adult, are white, yellowish, or sometimes black. The head is short, with small compound eyes present or absent, depending on species. Their chewing mouthparts point forward. The antennae (an-TEH-nee), or sense organs, are threadlike and made up of twenty-eight to fifty segments. Rock-crawlers never have wings, and all of their legs are long and thin. The abdomen has ten segments, with a pair of long, segmented structures at the tip.

GEOGRAPHIC RANGE

All twenty-seven species of rock-crawlers live in the Northern Hemisphere; they are found in Siberia, northeastern China, Korea, and Japan. Eleven species are known to live in the United States and Canada.

HABITAT

Rock-crawlers are secretive animals that live at elevations between 656 and 10,499 feet (between 200 and 3,200 meters) in mixed forests or in mountains above the highest point where trees can grow, usually near snowfields. They prefer cooler temperatures, of about 38.7°F to 60°F (3.7°C to 15.5°C), and are found in moist habitats beneath rocks and in crevices (KREH-vuh-ses) in rocky snowfields or inside subterranean lava tubes.

DIET

Both adults and young eat the soft tissues of captured and dead insects and spiders. The larvae also eat parts of plants and other bits of plant or animal tissues in the soil.

BEHAVIOR AND REPRODUCTION

Rock-crawlers are typically found singly or in sexual pairs and are active at night.

Some North American species look for food on the surface of the snow. They detect prey and other food items with their mouthparts. The larvae can survive without food for three to six months. Although they are adapted for survival at cooler temperatures, rock-crawlers will die if they are caught in extended periods of freezing temperatures. They will also die if temperatures rise to 82°F (28°C).

Courtship takes place under stones and includes lots of leg nibbling and touching with the antennae. Occasionally, the female may suddenly eat the male. Females lay sixty to 150 eggs in or on the soil, in decayed wood, or under leaves and stones. The eggs hatch in about 150 days but may take as long as three years. The larvae strongly resemble the adults when they hatch and gradually get larger as they mature. They molt, or shed their outer covering, or exoskeleton, three times during the first year and once a year for the next four or more years before reaching adulthood.

ROCK-CRAWLERS AND PEOPLE

Rock-crawlers are important research animals for scientists studying how animals survive in cold temperatures. The distribution of rock-crawlers may also provide clues about where ancient animals lived during the Ice Ages over the past two million years.

ONE OF NATURE'S CHIMERAS

In Greek mythology the Chimera (ki-MER-a) was a fire-breathing monster, part lion, part goat, and part snake. When first discovered high in the mountains of Canada in 1914, rock-crawlers were recognized as the chimeras of the insect world. The first-known species, *Grylloblatta campodeiformis*, was named after three other kinds of insects: crickets, cockroaches, and diplurans. It was not until 1932 that these puzzling animals were placed in their very own order, the Grylloblattodea.

CONSERVATION STATUS

Only one species of rock-crawler is listed by the World Conservation Union (IUCN). The Mount Saint Helens rock-crawler is listed as Vulnerable, or facing a high risk of extinction in the wild. It is found in the U.S. Pacific Northwest.

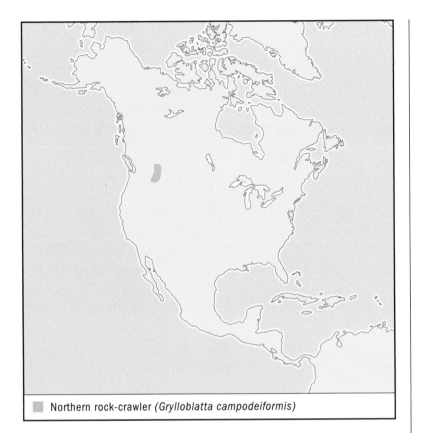

Northern rock-crawler (*Grylloblatta campodeiformis*)

NORTHERN ROCK-CRAWLER
Grylloblatta campodeiformis

Physical characteristics: The adults measure 0.98 to 1.06 inches (25 to 27 millimeters) in length. Their bodies are yellowish brown. The antennae have fewer than thirty segments.

Geographic range: Northern rock-crawlers are found in southeastern British Columbia, southwestern Alberta, eastern Washington, northern Idaho, western and southern Montana.

Habitat: Northern rock-crawlers live in the mountains above the highest point where trees can grow. They prefer habitats where there is plenty of moisture and the temperatures range between 38°F and

Northern rock-crawlers live alone or in pairs. They avoid light and forage for food at night on and around snowfields. (Illustration by Marguette Dongvillo. Reproduced by permission.)

60°F (3°C and 15°C), such as the edges of glacial bogs in moss, decaying wood, or damp areas deep under rocks. They are sometimes buried up to 3.3 feet (1 meter) in piles of pebbles, small stones, and other rocky debris.

Diet: Adults find and eat mostly small, dead insects, especially wingless crane flies. The larvae scavenge dead insects but also feed on some plant tissues.

Behavior and reproduction: Northern rock-crawlers live alone or in pairs. They avoid light and forage for food at night on and around snowfields. Although they prefer to live at cooler temperatures, they will die if exposed to long periods of freezing temperatures. The larvae may take up to seven years to reach adulthood.

Northern rock-crawlers and people: This insect is an important research animal for scientists studying how organisms survive at low temperatures. They are used as the official symbol of a scientific organization that studies insects, the Entomological Society of Canada, as well as of the Department of Entomology at Montana State University in Bozeman.

Conservation status: This species is not endangered or threatened. ∎

FOR MORE INFORMATION

Books:

Tavoloacci, J., ed. *Insects and Spiders of the World.* New York: Marshall Cavendish, 2003.

Web sites:

"Grylloblattodea." Tree of Life Web Project. http://tolweb.org/tree ?group=Grylloblattidae&contgroup=Neoptera (accessed on October 25, 2004).

"Ice Bugs (Grylloblattodea)." Gordon's Insect World. http://www.earthlife .net/insects/gryllobl.html (accessed on September 14, 2004).

Meyer, John R. "Grylloblattodea." http://www.cals.ncsu.edu/course/ ent425/compendium/rockcrwl.html#pix (accessed on October 25, 2004).

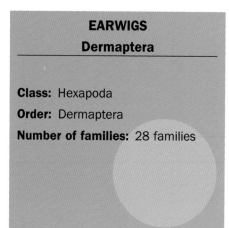

EARWIGS
Dermaptera

Class: Hexapoda
Order: Dermaptera
Number of families: 28 families

order

PHYSICAL CHARACTERISTICS

Earwigs are related to crickets, grasshoppers, and stick insects. They are long, slender, flattened insects that come in various shades of brown or black, sometimes with patterns of light brown or yellow. A few species are metallic green. Most earwigs measure between 0.16 to 3.2 inches (4 to 78 millimeters) in length, without the pinchers (PIN-churs), or grasping claws. The head is distinctive and has chewing mouthparts that are directed toward the front. The antennae (an-TEH-nee), or sense organs, are long, thin, and threadlike. The compound eyes, eyes with many lenses, are usually well developed. However, simple eyes, those that have only single lenses, are absent. Most adult earwigs have four wings. When present, the forewings, or front wings, are short, thick, and leathery and cover a pair of tightly folded, fanlike flight wings that are shaped like the human ear. Their long, flexible abdomen ends in a pair of strong pinchers. The pinchers of the adult male are larger and thicker than those of the females and young earwigs or larvae (LAR-vee).

The young earwig, or larva, resembles the adult except that the larva may not have wings. Larvae of wingless species are distinguished from the adults by their smaller size. Their pinchers are nearly straight and are similar to those of the female.

GEOGRAPHIC RANGE

There are approximately 1,800 species of earwigs found throughout the world, except in the Arctic and Antarctic. They are especially common in the tropics and subtropics. Twenty-two species live in the United States and Canada.

HABITAT

Most earwigs live in moist crevices (KREH-vuh-ses) of all kinds, including under bark, between leaves, and under stones. Some species live on the furry bodies of giant rats or bats as parasites, or animals that live on another organism or host and obtain food from it.

DIET

Most earwigs are scavengers (SKAE-vihn-jers) and predators (PREH-duh-ters), feeding both on living and dead insects and plants. Some species eat mainly plants, while others eat mostly insects, such as chinch bugs, mole crickets, mites, scales, aphids, and caterpillars. Parasitic species scavenge bits of dead skin or fungi growing on the bodies of giant rats or feed on skin secretions of bats.

A LIFE OF RATS AND BATS

Parasitic earwigs spend their entire lives on the bodies of their host animals. These small (0.4 inches or 10 millimeters) insects are blind and have short, bristlelike pinchers. They cling to the fur of their hosts with special claws. They feed only on bits of skin and fungus growing on the bodies of African giant rats or on the skin secretions of just one species of Asian bat. Unlike all other earwigs, parasitic earwigs do not lay eggs but bear live young.

BEHAVIOR AND REPRODUCTION

Earwigs are active at night. They hide during the day in moist, dark, tight-fitting places under stones, logs, and bark. They also seek shelter inside cracks in the soil or deep inside flowers. Other species live in caves or actively burrow through the soil. Earwigs often live in groups of dozens or hundreds of individuals. Both males and females use their pinchers for grooming, capturing prey, and courtship. The pinchers are also used to help fold and unfold the wings.

Earwigs will defend themselves by using their powerful pinchers as a weapon. Other species have glands in their abdomens that spray a foul-smelling fluid at attackers up to 2.9 to 3.9 inches (75 to 100 millimeters) away.

After mating, females dig a chamber in the soil or leaf litter to lay their eggs. Some earwigs guard the eggs and will frequently turn and lick them to keep them moist and free of mold. After hatching, the young larvae may remain with their mother. She will swallow food and then spit it up to offer it to the larvae. Earwig larvae closely resemble the adults but lack wings. They will molt, or shed their exoskeletons or hard outer coverings, four to six times before reaching adulthood. Earwigs produce one or two generations every year.

EARWIGS AND PEOPLE

The name "earwig" is thought to come from the mistaken belief that this insect likes to crawl into and hide in the ears of sleeping people. Earwigs are harmless and do not bite people, although some larger species can pinch. Most earwigs are not considered important pests. Earwigs— like cockroaches—have been transported throughout the world by ships and in cargo. They will cause damage in gardens by feeding on flowers and leaves. Sometimes earwigs are helpful because they eat other insects and mites that are harmful to plants. Occasionally, large numbers of earwigs may invade homes, but they cause little harm. Still, many people waste time and money trying to control earwigs.

CONSERVATION STATUS

One species, the St. Helena earwig (*Labidura herculeana*), is listed as Endangered by the World Conservation Union (IUCN). It may even be extinct and no longer exist.

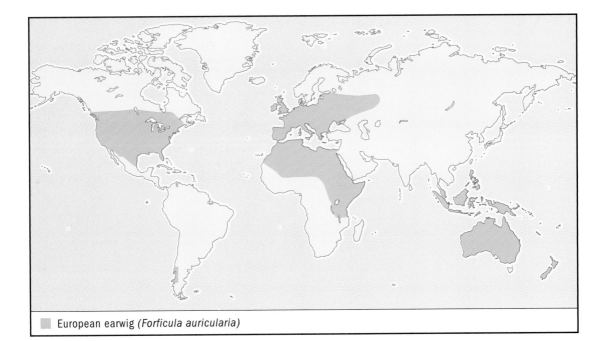

European earwig (*Forficula auricularia*)

EUROPEAN EARWIG
Forficula auricularia

Physical characteristics: The European earwig is reddish brown to nearly black with yellowish brown wing covers, legs, and antennae. The pinchers are reddish brown. Adults are fully winged and measure 0.47 to 0.59 inches (12 to 15 millimeters) in length, without the pinchers. The male's pinchers are broad with tiny notches at the bases and are sometimes as long as the abdomen and curved. They vary in size from 0.16 to 0.31 inches (4 to 8 millimeters) long. The pinchers of the female are thinner and crossed, measuring 0.12 inches (3 millimeters). The larvae look just like the adults but are smaller and lack wings.

Geographic range: The European earwig was originally known from Europe, western Asia, and North Africa. It now lives in East Africa, North America, the East Indies, Australia, New Zealand, Chile, and Argentina.

Habitat: The European earwig hides among petals or leaves of garden plants or inside damaged fruit, shrubs, along fences, in woodpiles, around bases of trees, and behind loose boards on buildings.

Diet: They feed on plants, ripe fruit, lichens, fungi, and other insects.

Behavior and reproduction: Adults are fully winged but seldom fly. They remain hidden during the day and forage at night for food and water.

In North America females lay batches of fifty to ninety eggs in chambers dug in moist soil from November to January. Another clutch with fewer eggs is laid in March or April. Depending on temperature the eggs will hatch in forty to fifty days. Females guard the eggs until they hatch. The larvae take about forty to fifty days to reach adulthood. They molt four times during this period. There is only one generation produced each year. Both larvae and adults are found throughout most the year, but adults are usually found in fall.

European earwigs and people: This species is not considered to be much of a pest in Europe, but in the United States they will attack flower crops, butterfly bushes, hollyhocks, lettuce, strawberries, celery, potatoes, sweet corn, roses, seedling beans and beets, and grasses. They are considered helpful when they eat aphids and other plant pests.

Conservation status: This species is not endangered or threatened. ■

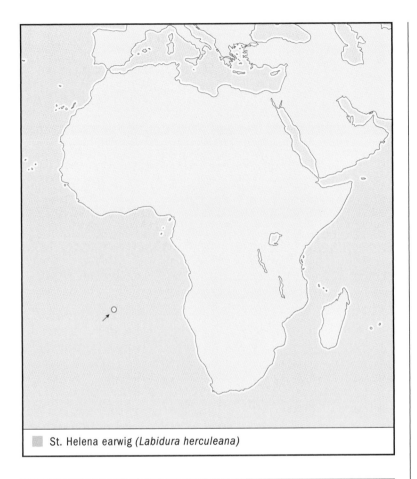

St. Helena earwig (*Labidura herculeana*)

ST. HELENA EARWIG
Labidura herculeana

Physical characteristics: This species is the largest earwig in the world. They are black with reddish legs and wing covers, with no hind wings. Their bodies measure between 1.44 to 2.13 inches (36 to 54 millimeters). Their pinchers add an additional 0.6 to 0.96 inches (15 to 24 millimeters). The largest known specimen is a male measuring 3.1 inches (78 mm).

Geographic range: The species is found on Horse Point Plain in the extreme northeastern portion of the island of St. Helena. St. Helena is located in the Atlantic Ocean, almost midway between the continents of Africa and South America.

This species is of scientific interest because it is the largest earwig in the world. However, the St. Helena earwig was last seen in 1967 and may no longer exist today. (Illustration by Marguette Dongvillo. Reproduced by permission.)

Habitat: The St. Helena earwig lives in a dry and barren habitat, with stony soil, bushes, and tufts of grass.

Diet: Nothing is known.

Behavior and reproduction: Living specimens have been found under stones or near burrows in the soil. St. Helena earwigs are nocturnal and active during summer rains. During the dry season they remain underground.

St. Helena earwigs and people: This species is of scientific interest because it is the largest earwig in the world.

Conservation status: The St. Helena earwig is listed as Endangered by the World Conservation Union (IUCN). Endangered means it faces a very high risk of extinction in the wild. It is in danger because it is found only on one part of a very small and remote island. This species was last seen in 1967 and may not still be alive today. More study is needed to determine whether or not this species still exists and, if so, how to protect it from becoming extinct. ■

FOR MORE INFORMATION

Books:

Helfer, J. R. *How to Know the Grasshoppers, Crickets, Cockroaches, and Their Allies.* New York: Dover Publications, 1987.

Holm, E., and C. H. Scholtz. *Insects of Southern Africa.* Durban, South Africa: Butterworths, 1985.

Rights, M. *Beastly Neighbors: All about Wild Things in the City, or Why Earwigs Make Good Mothers.* Boston: Little, Brown, 1981.

Tavoloacci, J., ed. *Insects and Spiders of the World.* New York: Marshall Cavendish, 2003.

Periodicals:

Hoffman, K. M. "Earwigs (Dermaptera) of South Carolina, with a Key to the Eastern North American Species and a Checklist of the North American Fauna." *Proceedings of the Entomological Society of Washington* (1987) 89: 1–14.

Web sites:

"Dermaptera." North Carolina State University. http://www.cals.ncsu.edu/course/ent425/compendium/earwigs.html (accessed on September 20, 2004).

"Dermaptera. Earwigs." Ecowatch. http://www.ento.csiro.au/Ecowatch/Insects_Invertebrates/dermaptera.htm (accessed on September 21, 2004).

"Dermaptera. Earwigs." Tree of Life Web Project. http://tolweb.org/tree?group=Dermaptera&contgroup=Neoptera#refs (accessed on September 21, 2004).

"Earwigs. Dermaptera." Biokids. *Critter Catalog.* http://www.biokids.umich.edu/critters/information/Dermaptera.html (accessed on September 20, 2004).

"Gordon's Earwig Page." Earthlife. http://www.earthlife.net/insects/dermapta.html (accessed on September 21, 2004).

order

phylum

class

subclass

● **order**

monotypic order

suborder

family

PHYSICAL CHARACTERISTICS

The Orthoptera include grasshoppers, crickets, katydids, and their relatives. Most orthopterans are medium to large in size, ranging in length from 0.4 to 3.9 inches (10 to 100 millimeters). The smallest species are crickets that live with ants; they are rarely more than 0.08 inches (2 millimeters) in length. The largest species are the katydids, each with wingspans of 7.9 inches (200 millimeters) or more. The heaviest orthopteran, which also happens to be the heaviest insect in the world, is the New Zealand giant weta that weighs in at a hefty 0.16 lb (71 g).

The head is distinct and has powerful chewing mouthparts that are usually pointed downward. The antennae (an-TEH-nee) are relatively short and thick, with 30 or fewer segments (as on grasshoppers), or long and threadlike, with more than 30 segments (as for crickets and katydids).

The midsection of the body is only the first part of a three-part thorax. This section of the body is sometimes enlarged and extends back over part or all of the body. The wings, if present, number four and cover the rest of the thorax. The forewings are slightly thickened and are supported by a network of veins. In most katydids and crickets, the bases of the forewings have special structures that resemble a scraper and a file. These structures are rubbed against one another to produce buzzes, chirps, and clicks. The hindwings, if present, are folded fanlike under the forewings when the animal is at rest. They are sometimes longer and stick out just beyond the tips of the forewings. Larvae (LAR-vee), or young form of the animal, closely resemble the adults but lack fully developed wings and reproductive organs. The developing wings are positioned so that the second pair of wings partially cover the first. In adults the forewings always cover the hindwings, even in species that never fully develop wings.

The wings of many grasshoppers are colored and textured so that they blend in with leaves, sticks, rocks, gravel, or sand in their habitat. Katydids mimic living and dead plants with leaflike wings and colors. A few grasshoppers have bright and distinctive patterns, or aposematic (APO-se-ma-tik) coloration, on their wings and bodies that warns predators that their bodies are filled with bad-tasting chemicals.

The front and middle legs are usually slender and are used for walking. In mole crickets and other species that like to dig, both the front and middle legs are rakelike for moving soil. The legs of katydids that eat other insects are spiny and used to capture and hold on to their prey. In crickets and katydids, each front leg has an ear. Grasshopper ears are located on the sides of the abdomen just behind the thorax. The hind legs are usually large, muscular, and used for jumping. Digging species no longer have the need to jump, so their hind legs more closely resemble the other legs.

The abdomens of most female crickets and katydids have a distinctive egg-laying device, or ovipositor (O-vih-pa-zih-ter). The ovipositor is either hooked, swordlike, or needlelike and is used to place eggs inside rotten wood or deep in the soil. Grasshoppers lack this kind of egg-laying device.

GEOGRAPHIC RANGE

Grasshoppers, crickets, and katydids are found on all continents and islands, except Antarctica. There are about 21,400 species of orthopterans worldwide, with about 3,000 species in the United States and Canada.

HABITAT

Grasshoppers, crickets, and katydids inhabit virtually all terrestrial habitats, from rocky coastlines, underground burrows, and caves, to the tops of trees in rainforests and high mountain peaks. Others prefer wetlands, with some species living right on the shores of ponds, streams, lakes, and rivers. A few species actually live in water. Many species live in meadows and deserts. Still other species are very particular about where they live; some specialists take shelter in ant nests, while others are at home in greenhouses and basements.

DIET

Most orthopterans eat plants, but a few species will supplement their diets with living or dead insects. Nearly all grasshoppers are plant feeders, or herbivores (URH-bi-vorz). However, when there is a lack of water, or too many individuals in a small area, some grasshoppers may begin to eat each other and scavenge their dead. Herbivores will eat all parts of grasses, weeds, shrubs, and trees. Some species living in trees will also eat lichens (LIE-kuhns) and mosses. Most species will eat whatever plants are available, but a few will eat only one kind of plant or a few closely related species.

Many species of crickets, katydids, and their relatives are also herbivores. At least one Australian katydid feeds only on the pollen and nectar of flowers. Others prefer grass seeds or just leaves. Very few katydid species feed on the needles of pines and other cone-bearing trees. Some species are omnivores (AM-ni-vorz), animals that eat both plant and animal foods, and will eat whatever is available to them. Although crickets and cave crickets tend to be omnivorous, they seem to prefer feeding on live insects. Tree crickets will eat aphids. Omnivorous mole crickets are the only insects that gather and store seeds in underground chambers. They will then use the young sprouts as food. The Central American rhinoceros katydid will eat flowers, fruits, and seeds, as well as caterpillars, other katydids, snails, and frog eggs. They have even been known to attack small lizards.

A few orthopterans are strictly meat-eaters, or carnivores (KAR-ni-vorz), and eat the flesh of other insects. These katydids either use a "sit-and-wait" strategy to ambush their prey or actively hunt for food. Prey is captured and held with the aid of sharp spines on their front and middle legs.

BEHAVIOR AND REPRODUCTION

Most grasshoppers feed and mate during the day but molt and lay their eggs at night. The majority of katydids and crickets tend to be active at night, especially in the tropics. However, a wasp-mimicking katydid from Central America is active during the day. These katydids are black and orange and strongly resemble the large tarantula hawk wasps. These harmless katydids not only look like wasps, they act like them too. They are found in sunny openings in lowland rainforests, where they move in a jerky, wasplike fashion, constantly twitching their orange-tipped antennae. At night their behavior changes. Unable to rely on their wasplike appearance to fool their enemies in the dark, their movements become slow and deliberate, just like the katydids that resemble leaves.

Most orthopterans tend to live by themselves, except during the mating season. However, many crickets are often found in small groups. Locusts sometimes form massive swarms made up of hundreds of thousands, even billions, of individuals. Locusts are grasshoppers that show a definite change in their behavior, shape, and vital body functions as they go from living alone to joining other individuals in swarms. Other groups of orthopterans also form swarms. The North American Mormon cricket is actually a large, wingless katydid that regularly forms large groups that can totally destroy any crops in their paths. African conehead katydids also form large flying swarms.

One of the most common features associated with many orthopterans is their ability to produce sounds. There are few places during the warmer months where the daytime rasps and snaps of grasshoppers or the nocturnal chirps, clicks, and buzzes of katydids and crickets cannot be heard. These calls are produced to claim territory, attract mates, or to sound an alarm. The volume and pitch of the calls, usually produced by males, are unique to each species and helps them to recognize one another.

Contrary to popular belief, none of these insects produces sounds by rubbing its legs together. Males produce sounds by rubbing the bases of their wings together or their hind legs against the edges of the wings. Crickets and katydids generally rub a set of tiny pegs, or file, located at the base of one wing against a strong ridge, or scraper, on the other wing to produce buzzes, chirps, and clicks. A few species grind their jaws together to produce sounds, while others rub the bases of their legs against the underside of the thorax. The sound produced is amplified by a smooth membrane located on the base of the wings.

Grasshoppers "sing" by rubbing the inside surface of their jumping legs against the edges of their forewings. They can amplify the sound by expanding their wings. Some grasshoppers also make a crackling sound when they fly. The sound is produced by rapidly bending their hind wings while in the air. The crackling sound is common among band-winged grasshoppers and is used in courtship and territorial displays.

Courtship and mating behaviors involve sight, sound, smell, and touch. Grasshoppers use mostly visual communication. Males often have bright markings on different parts of their bodies and wings that are unique to their species. They instinctively display these features as if they were in a highly practiced dance routine. Male crickets and katydids sometimes produce two different kinds of calls. The first is used as long-range advertising to attract a female. The second is quieter and is used in courtship when the female is nearby. In a few species, the females may respond with a call of their own. Courtship in katydids and crickets depends not only on sounds but also on smells. Odors, or chemical signals, make sense since they are mostly active at night and cannot see each other, but their use of smells is not very well known. A few species, such as female giant wetas in New Zealand, produce pheromones (FEH-re-moans) and other odors to attract males.

Males place the sperm packet directly into the body of the female. The sperm packet may weigh as much as 60% of the total body weight of the male. In some species the males have special organs that are eaten by the female while they are mating. In other species males have special projections on their abdomens that are used to hold the female while they mate.

Most female crickets and katydids use their hooked, needle-like, or swordlike ovipositors to place eggs out of harm's way deep into soil or rotting wood. Female grasshoppers lack external ovipositors, but have thickened valves on the tips of their abdomen. They drill through the soil using hardened plates on the tip of their abdomens and deposit them deep in the soil or rotten wood by stretching the entire length of their abdomen into the hole. Sometimes the eggs are placed in a foamy mass that helps to keep them from drying out.

The larvae usually hatch within a few weeks or months, sometimes longer. They strongly resemble the adults when they hatch but lack developed wings and reproductive organs. Most orthopterans do not care for their young, although in some species the mother will guard her eggs. Mole crickets lay their eggs in special chambers and lick them to prevent them from becoming spoiled by fungus. After hatching, the young mole cricket larvae remain with their mother for a few weeks before going out on their own. Larvae develop gradually, molting six to ten times before reaching adulthood.

ORTHOPTERANS AND PEOPLE

Plagues of crickets and grasshoppers have invaded homes and ravaged crops for centuries.

In Africa and Asia locusts are still a serious threat to crops, but the problem has decreased over the years as scientists now have a better understanding of reasons for their population explosions and have developed various control measures. However, once the swarms become airborne, there is little that can be done to stop them. A promising fungal disease in locusts has proven to provide yet another way of controlling them without using dangerous and expensive chemicals. Other species of locusts, Mormon crickets, and some katydids are sometimes serious agricultural pests in the western United States.

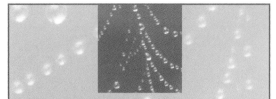

A PLAGUE OF LOCUSTS

A single swarm of desert locusts might contain up to ten billion insects and weigh up to 77,161 tons (70,000 metric tons). In 1794 a massive swarm that spread over 1,930.5 square miles (5,000 square kilometers) was blown out to sea and drowned off the western coast of South Africa. A 4-foot (1.2 meters) deep wall of dead insects soon washed up along 50 miles (80 kilometers) of coastline.

In many parts of the world orthopterans are important in the human diet and are sometimes considered to be a real treat. Tribal people in southern Africa eat locusts boiled or roasted, and grilled locusts are often consumed in Cambodia. Mole crickets and some armored katydids are also eaten in some parts of Africa.

Katydids and crickets are very popular in poetry and other arts of China and Japan. Both Chinese and Japanese families vacation in summer to areas with lots singing insects. The Japanese have long appreciated their calls in the wild and often keep them indoors in special cages as pets. Today, selling caged singing crickets and katydids is a thriving business in China, and the Japanese have even designed a digital replica of the katydid's call.

CONSERVATION STATUS

Seventy-four species of orthopterans are listed by the World Conservation Union (IUCN).

Two of these species, the central valley grasshopper and Antioch dunes shieldback, are listed as Extinct, or no longer alive. The Oahu deceptor bush cricket is listed as Extinct in the Wild, or alive only in an artificial environment. Eight species are listed as Critically Endangered, another eight as Endangered, and 50 more species are listed as Vulnerable. Critically Endangered means facing an extremely high risk of extinction in the wild. Endangered means facing a very high risk of extinction in the wild, and Vulnerable means facing a high risk of extinction in the wild.

The single most important threat to all orthoptrans is habitat destruction. This is especially true for species that are found only in small geographic areas. The introduction of ants, cats, and rats, especially on islands such as New Zealand, is a serious threat to many orthopteran species.

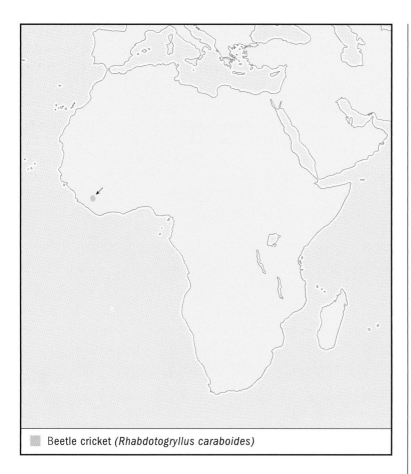

Beetle cricket (*Rhabdotogryllus caraboides*)

BEETLE CRICKET
Rhabdotogryllus caraboides

Physical characteristics: Beetle crickets are small, black, shiny, and beetlelike. Males and females have short, thick forewings covering only half of the abdomen. The veins on these wings are made up of many straight, parallel veins. Males lack the ability to produce sound with their wings.

Geographic range: Guinea (West Africa).

Habitat: Beetle crickets are found in leaf litter of the lowland and middle elevation rainforests, as well as in termite mounds.

Diet: Nothing is known.

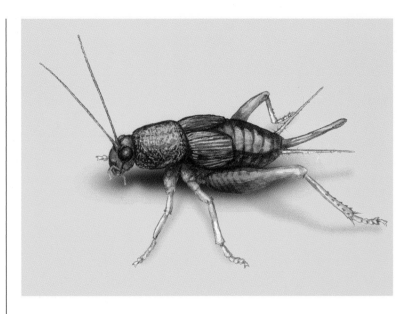

Behavior and reproduction: Almost nothing is known about its behavior or reproduction. It may be associated with termites, but the nature of this relationship is unknown.

Beetle crickets and people: Beetle crickets are not known to impact people or their activities.

Conservation status: This species is likely to be threatened by habitat loss but is not now endangered or threatened. ∎

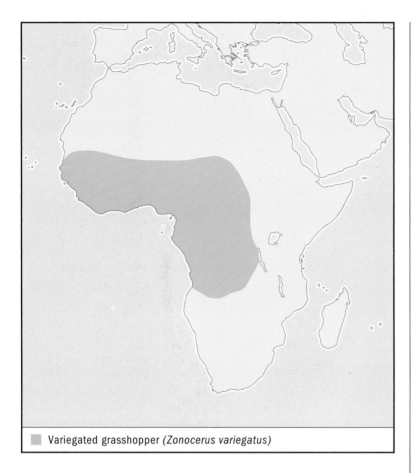

Variegated grasshopper (*Zonocerus variegatus*)

VARIEGATED GRASSHOPPER
Zonocerus variegatus

Physical characteristics: The variegated grasshopper has a yellow-green body 1.4 to 2.2 inches (35 to 55 millimeters) in length, with yellow, orange, white, and black markings. The wings are usually very short, covering only half of the abdomen, but long-winged individuals are also known. Larvae are black with bright yellow speckles.

Geographic range: Variegated grasshoppers are found in sub-Saharan Africa.

Habitat: They live in savannahs, pastures, and agricultural fields.

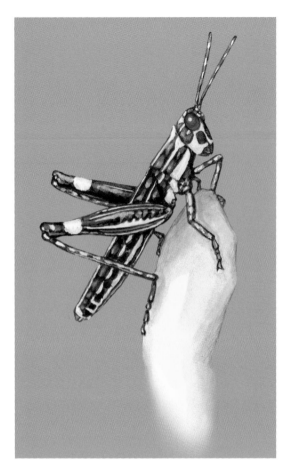

Variegated grasshoppers are serious pests of cassava, maize, and other crops in Africa south of the Sahara Desert. (Illustration by Bruce Worden. Reproduced by permission.)

Diet: They feed on a variety of plants, especially relatives of peas. They take bad-tasting chemicals from these plants and use them in their own body tissues as part of their own defense strategy. The bright colors of these grasshoppers advertise the fact that they taste bad. Because they eat many kinds of plants with little or no bad-tasting chemicals, some grasshoppers may not taste bad at all. For example, they are commonly roasted and eaten by people living in southern Nigeria.

Behavior and reproduction: The larvae feed in groups, forming clusters of tens or hundreds of individuals on a single plant. Both the larvae and adults are slow moving. Even the fully winged adults are reluctant to fly, apparently relying on their bright warning colors to discourage most predators.

Females lay their eggs in foamy egg pods and bury them in the soil.

Variegated grasshoppers and people: They are serious pests of cassava, maize, and other crops in Africa south of the Sahara Desert.

Conservation status: This species is not endangered or threatened. ■

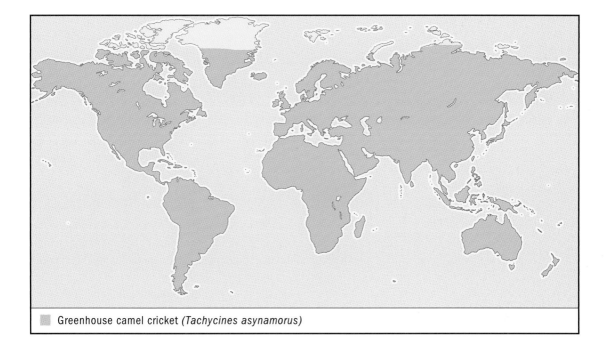

Greenhouse camel cricket *(Tachycines asynamorus)*

GREENHOUSE CAMEL CRICKET
Tachycines asynamorus

Physical characteristics: The wingless bodies of greenhouse camel crickets are yellow-brown, spotted, and measure 0.5 to 0.7 inches (13 to 19 millimeters) in length. The legs and antennae are long and slender, giving them the appearance of a long-legged spider. They are very quick and capable of jumping long distances. Females have a long swordlike ovipositor.

Geographic range: Originally from the Far East (probably China), they are now found throughout the world, except in the polar regions.

Habitat: Wild populations once lived in caves, but now most are found in greenhouses and in homes in warm, humid cellars and basements.

Diet: They are omnivorous, feeding on a variety of plant and animal foods, including other insects and plants.

Greenhouse camel crickets are only active at night and spend their days hidden in crevices and under large objects. They are always found in groups. (Arthur V. Evans. Reproduced by permission.)

Behavior and reproduction: They are active only at night and spend their days hidden in crevices and under large objects. They are always found in groups.

Females lay their eggs in soil. When the larvae hatch they will join groups of older individuals.

Greenhouse camel crickets and people: They are sometimes a pest in greenhouses, eating young plants. They are a nuisance to people because they are quick, jump unpredictably, and resemble spiders.

Conservation status: This species is not endangered or threatened. ■

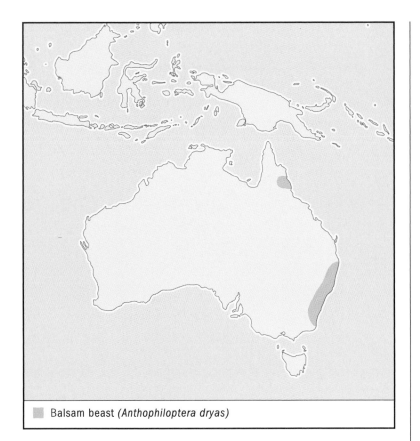

Balsam beast (*Anthophiloptera dryas*)

BALSAM BEAST
Anthophiloptera dryas

Physical characteristics: The body is green or brown, leaflike, and measures 2 to 2.75 inches (50 to 70 millimeters) in length. Their mouthparts point forward, instead of downward. The legs, antennae, and wings are long and slender.

Geographic range: Balsam beasts are found in New South Wales and Queensland (Australia).

Habitat: They live in coastal wooded suburbs and gardens.

Diet: This species feeds on a wide variety of flowers and trees and is especially fond of garden balsam (*Impatiens* sp.).

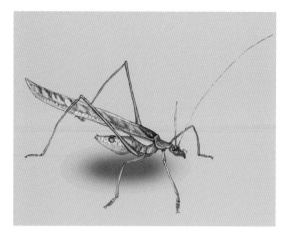

Balsam beasts are found in New South Wales and Queensland, Australia. (Illustration by Bruce Worden. Reproduced by permission.)

Behavior and reproduction: They are active at night in the tree tops.

Females lay their eggs one at a time in the cracks found on bark, especially near the base of the tree.

Balsam beasts and people: They are sometimes considered garden pests.

Conservation status: This species is not endangered or threatened.   ■

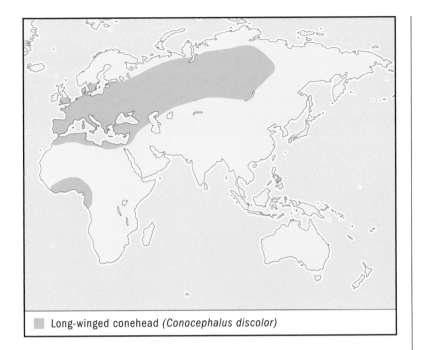

Long-winged conehead (*Conocephalus discolor*)

LONG-WINGED CONEHEAD
Conocephalus discolor

Physical characteristics: The body of a long-winged conehead is light green, with a distinctive dark brown stripe down the back, and measures 0.5 to 0.7 inches (12 to 17 millimeters) in length. The wings are longer than the body, with the hind wings extending beyond the tips of the forewings. The ovipositor is straight and is nearly as long as the body.

Geographic range: They are widespread in Europe and western Asia.

Habitat: Long-winged coneheads live in meadows, marshes, reed beds, and near water.

Diet: This species eats grasses and other plants but will also catch small insects, such as aphids, and caterpillars.

Behavior and reproduction: This day-active species has very good vision. They are very alert and are quick to the other side of a stem

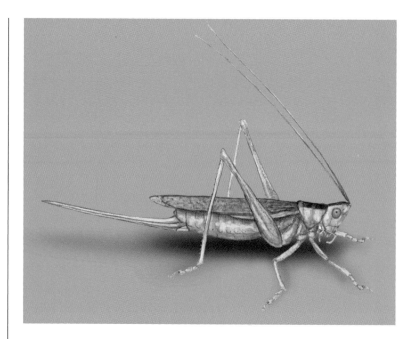

or jump when threatened. The call of the male is a soft, continuous buzz.

Females lay their eggs in grass or reed stems. Sometimes they will chew small holes in stems through which they insert their ovipositor. Like the adults, the larvae are light green with a black stripe down the back.

Long-winged coneheads and people: This species does not impact humans or their activities.

Conservation status: This species is not endangered or threatened. ■

Dead leaf mimetica (*Mimetica mortuifolia*)

DEAD LEAF MIMETICA
Mimetica mortuifolia

Physical characteristics: Dead leaf mimeticas are excellent mimics of living and dead leaves. Their bodies and wings are green, brown, or a combination of both. The forewings resemble the shape of a leaf and have leaflike veins. They also have small notches cut out of them as if they were leaves that had been nibbled by another herbivorous insect. Hind wings are very small. The female's ovipositor is strongly curved, with a thick, sawlike tip.

Geographic range: They are found in Costa Rica and Panama.

Habitat: The dead leaf mimetica lives in lowlands and middle elevations, from low shrubs to high up in trees.

Diet: This species eats the leaves of various trees.

Remaining motionless in the trees, the dead leaf mimetica is nearly impossible to find during the day. It feeds on leaves at night. (Arthur V. Evans. Reproduced by permission.)

Behavior and reproduction: Remaining motionless in the trees, this species is impossible to find during the day. It feeds on leaves at night. The males make short, buzzing calls.

The strongly curved ovipositor of females is shaped to penetrate tissues of plant stems where eggs are laid. To lay eggs, the female bends abdomen down and forward until her ovipositor faces forward between her front legs. She then uses her legs to guide the ovipositor and insert it into plant tissue. Eggs are laid individually, left partially protruding from the plant to allow for easy exchange of oxygen for developing embryo.

Dead leaf mimeticas and people: This species is not known to impact humans or their activities.

Conservation status: This species is not now endangered or threatened. They are abundant but could easily be threatened by habitat destruction. ■

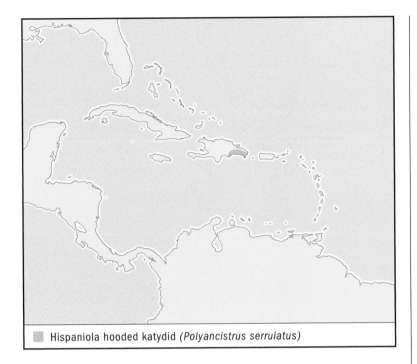

Hispaniola hooded katydid (*Polyancistrus serrulatus*)

HISPANIOLA HOODED KATYDID
Polyancistrus serrulatus

Physical characteristics: The body is usually brown, sometimes green, and measures 1.4 to 2.5 inches (35 to 65 millimeters) in length. Both males and females have a hoodlike plate on top of their midsection. The female's ovipositor is long and sword-shaped.

Geographic range: This species is found in the Dominican Republic (Hispaniola).

Habitat: They live in trees and tall bushes.

Diet: They eat the leaves, fruits, and flowers of a wide variety of plants.

Behavior and reproduction: These hooded katydids are active at night. Both males and females produce loud calls. They spend their days in rolled-up leaves or under loose strips of tree bark.

Females most likely lay their eggs in soil.

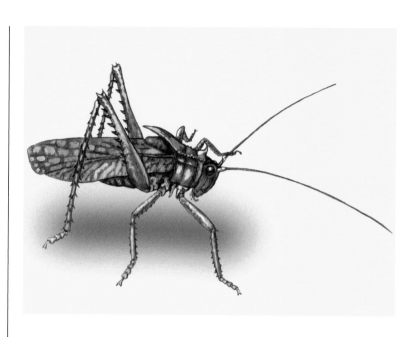

Hispaniola hooded katydids and people: This species does not impact people or their activities.

Conservation status: This species is not endangered or threatened. As with most species living in tropical rainforests, they may become threatened by the destruction of their habitat. ∎

FOR MORE INFORMATION

Books:

Capinera, J. L., C. W. Scherer, and J. M. Squitier. *Grasshoppers of Florida.* Gainesville: University Press of Florida, 2001.

Helfer, J. R. *How to Know the Grasshoppers, Crickets, Cockroaches, and Their Allies.* New York: Dover Publications, 1987.

Meads, M. *Forgotten Fauna: The Rare, Endangered, and Protected Invertebrates of New Zealand.* Wellington: DSIR Publications, 1990.

Preston-Mafham, K. *Grasshoppers and Mantids of the World.* London: Blandford, 1990.

Tavoloacci, J., ed. *Insects and Spiders of the World.* New York: Marshall Cavendish, 2003.

Periodicals:

Moffett, M. W. "Wetas-New Zeland's Insect Giants." *National Geographic* 180, no. 5 (November 1991): 101–105.

Web sites:

"Chinese Cricket Culture." *Cultural Entomology Digest 3* http://www.insects.org/ced3/chinese_crcul.html (accessed on September 21, 2004).

"Grasshoppers and crickets (Orthoptera)." Gordon's Orthoptera Page. http://www.earthlife.net/insects/orthopta.html (accessed on September 21, 2004).

"Grasshoppers and Relatives." Biokids Critter Catalog. http://www.biokids.umich.edu/critters/information/Orthoptera.html (accessed on September 21, 2004).

"Orthoptera. Grasshoppers, crickets, locusts, katydids." Ecowatch. http://www.ento.csiro.au/Ecowatch/Orthoptera/orthoptera.htm (accessed on September 21, 2004).

Compact discs:

Songs of Crickets and Katydids of the Mid-Atlantic States. An Identification Guide. Hershey, PA: Will Hershberger and Steve Rannels, 1998.

Videos:

"*Crickets, Grasshoppers and Friends.*" Bug City. Wynnewood, PA: Schlessinger Media, 1998.

**HEEL-WALKERS
OR GLADIATORS**
Mantophasmatodea

Class: Hexapoda

Order: Mantophasmatodea

Number of families: 3 families

phylum

class

subclass

● **order**

monotypic order

suborder

family

PHYSICAL CHARACTERISTICS

Heel-walkers are brown, gray, green, or yellow and are sometimes marked with darker dots or stripes. The sides of their midsection, or thorax, are sometimes spiny. They measure 0.35 to 0.94 inches (9 to 24 millimeters) in length. The males are usually smaller than the females. Both sexes are wingless and resemble young mantids or stick insects. The larvae (LAR-vee), or young form of the animal that must change form before becoming an adult, strongly resemble the adults.

The head is distinct and has chewing mouthparts with sharp jaws that are directed downward. The antennae (an-TEH-nee), or sense organs, are long, threadlike, and have many segments. The compound eyes, each with many individual lenses, are well developed, but simple eyes, those with only a single lens each, are absent. The front and middle legs are slightly enlarged and have two rows of short, sharp spines. The hind legs are slender and lack rows of spines. All of the feet have five segments, but the first three are fused, or joined together.

The abdomen consists of ten well-developed segments and a much smaller eleventh segment. In the females, the eighth and ninth segments have three structures that together form a short egg-laying device, or ovipositor. The tip of the abdomen has a pair of projections. In females these projections are short, but in males they are much longer and curved.

GEOGRAPHIC RANGE

All thirteen living species are found in Africa in Namibia, South Africa, and Tanzania. Two fossil species preserved in amber were found in Russia.

HABITAT

They are found in dry, scrubby habitats that receive little rain. Heel-walkers live down inside tufts of grass or grasslike plants, where they blend in perfectly thanks to their spotted and striped bodies.

DIET

They eat various kinds of insects, including each other, grasping and holding their prey with their strong and spiny front and middle legs. Heel-walkers will eat all but the wings and legs.

BEHAVIOR AND REPRODUCTION

Heel-walkers usually live alone, but pairs of males and females are often found together in the same tuft of grass. Populations are usually concentrated in small patches within a much larger area of suitable habitat. They appear to be active day and night, moving very slowly through the grass. However, they can move quickly to capture prey or while mating. The common name "heel-walker" comes from the fact that as they walk, the clawed tips of their feet are always held up in the air. The males use the projections on special plates located on their abdomens to tap on the ground, possibly as a means of communicating with other heel-walkers.

Courtship among heel-walkers is unknown. Males climb up on the female's back to mate, a process that may take up to three days. Females produce several sausage-shaped egg pods, each containing ten to twenty long, oval eggs. The egg pods are covered by a coating of sand mixed with special fluids produced by the female. The coating is shaped by the female's ovipositor and eventually becomes hard. The larvae hatch at the beginning of the rainfall period and strongly resemble the adults. They will molt, or shed their hard outer coverings, several times before reaching adulthood near the end of the winter wet season and

IN A LEAGUE OF THEIR OWN

Thousands of new insect species are discovered every year. But the last time a new order of insects was discovered was back in 1914. Heel-walkers had been known for more than one hundred years but were ignored by scientists because they closely resembled young praying mantids. In 2001, forgotten specimens of heel-walkers collected in Namibia and Tanzania were discovered in museum collections. In 2002, after careful examination, researchers placed them in their own order, the Mantophasmatodea.

die during the following summer dry season. Their life span varies considerably, depending on how much rain falls in the summer and winter.

HEEL-WALKERS AND PEOPLE

Each species of heel-walker lives in a very small area, and their populations are widely separated. The fact that they are distributed this way makes them especially interesting to scientists that study the distributions of animals in southern Africa.

CONSERVATION STATUS

No species of Mantophasmatodea is endangered or threatened. Since very little is known about the species, it is not clear which are threatened by development or habitat destruction. It is very possible that populations, even entire species, living in only a few places could become extinct (ihk-STINKT), or no longer exist, if their habitats were damaged or destroyed. However, some populations appear to be able to survive human activities and have been found right alongside of roads.

Gladiator (*Praedatophasma maraisi*)

GLADIATOR
Praedatophasma maraisi

Physical characteristics: The gray bodies of gladiators measure 0.8 to 1.2 inches (20 to 30 millimeters) in length. They have round heads and large eyes. The antennae are threadlike and nearly as long as the body. The front and middle legs, as well as the sides of the thorax, are spiny.

Geographic range: They are found in the Karasburg Region, southern Namibia.

Habitat: Gladiators are found near the Orange River, in the Nama Karoo.

Heel-walkers live down inside tufts of grass or grasslike plants, where they blend in perfectly thanks to their spotted and striped bodies. (Illustration by Bruce Worden. Reproduced by permission.)

Diet: Gladiators probably eat other insects.

Behavior and reproduction: Nothing is known about the behavior and reproduction of this species.

Gladiators and people: This species does not impact people or their activities.

Conservation status: This species is not endangered or threatened. ∎

FOR MORE INFORMATION

Periodicals:

Adis, J., O. Zompro, E. Moombolah-Goagoses, and E. Marais. "Gladiators: A New Order of Insect." *Scientific American* 287, no. 5 (November 2002): 60–65.

Klass, K., O. Zompro, N. P. Kristensen, and J. Adis. "Mantophasmatodea: A New Insect Order with Extant Members in the Afrotropics." *Science* 296, no. 5572 (May 24, 2002): 1456–1459.

Picker, Mike D., Jonathan F. Colville, and Simon van Noort. "Mantophasmatodea Now in South Africa." *Science* 297, no. 5586 (August 30, 2002): 1475.

Web sites:

"Mantophasmatodea (Gladiator) Fossil Insect Gallery." http://www.fossilmuseum.net/Fossil_Galleries/Insect_Galleries_by_Order/Mantophasmatodea/Mantophasmatodea.htm (accessed September 24, 2004).

New Insect Order Discovered for First Time Since 1915. http://www.conservation.org/xp/news/press_releases/2002/041702.xml (accessed on September 24, 2004).

"Order: Mantophasmatodea (Heelwalkers)." http://www.museums.org.za/bio/insects/mantophasmatodea/ (accessed on September 21, 2004).

Trevidi, B. P. "New Insect Found in Southern Africa." *National Geographic News.* http://news.nationalgeographic.com/news/2002/03/0328_0328_TVstickinsect.html (accessed on September 24, 2004).

PHYSICAL CHARACTERISTICS

Most phasmids are long, smooth bodied, and are colored green or brown to better match the surrounding vegetation. A few species are brightly marked with bold stripes. Their bodies are usually smooth, but some vary from slightly to very rough. A few species are covered with short, sharp spines. The head is distinct. Compound eyes are present, with each eye having multiple lenses. There are no simple eyes, or eyes with a single lens. Their chewing mouthparts are directed forward. Stick insects may have fully developed or small wings or lack wings altogether, except for one species with small, rounded wings in southern Florida. All six legs are similar to one another in size and shape and are not designed for jumping. The fingerlike appendages on the tip of the abdomen are very short. Some males have claspers on the tips of their abdomens used to grasp the female while mating. Females have longer and heavier bodies than males.

Stick insects are mostly long, slender insects resembling twigs. They are sometimes two-toned, with lighter colors underneath and darker colors above. Some species have fully developed wings, while those of others are very small or absent altogether. Several stick insects have beautifully colored hind wings and rival the color of butterflies. Unlike grasshoppers, the back legs are not enlarged for jumping. Instead, all of their legs are about the same size and length. They range in length from 1.2 to 12.9 inches (30 to 328 millimeters). Several species of tropical phasmids are among the world's longest insects. For

phylum

class

subclass

● **order**

monotypic order

suborder

family

example, the body of Australia's *Phobaeticus kirbyi* reaches up to 12.9 inches (328 millimeters) in length, but with its front legs outstretched in front of its body, its total length jumps to 21.5 inches (546 millimeters).

Leaf insects have broad, flattened, leaflike bodies and legs. The wings are long and slender in males, shorter and wider in females, but they do not cover the edges of the abdomen. They measure 1.1 to 4.4 inches (28 to 112 millimeters) in length. The largest leaf insect is from Malaysia.

Timemas are not typical of stick or leaf insects. They are smaller (0.5 to 1.2 inches or 13 to 30 millimeters), somewhat flattened insects with thicker bodies and never have wings. Unlike most other phasmids, timemas are able to jump when threatened.

GEOGRAPHIC RANGE

Phasmids live on all continents, except Antarctica. They are also found on many islands. There are approximately three thousand species of phasmids worldwide, with about forty-four species in Canada and the United States.

HABITAT

Phasmids are found in a wide variety of habitats in warmer and tropical climates, including gardens, woodlands, pine and fir forests, chaparral, desert scrub, and grasslands. They are most common in moist, tropical forests. Phasmids spend their days resting on shrubs and trees or hiding in nearby leaf litter or crevices (KREH-vuh-ses).

DIET

Phasmids eat many different kinds of plants, chewing large, circular bites along the edges of leaves. A few species also eat bark and flowers. Most species eat a wide variety of plants, but a few are specialists and prefer feeding on only a few closely related species. Insect zoos and hobbyists, people that raise phasmids in captivity for fun, have successfully kept many tropical species on plants other than what they would normally eat in the wild. These plants include oak, pyracantha, bramble, Australian gum, and guava.

BEHAVIOR AND REPRODUCTION

Phasmids spend most of their time hidden among their food plants, remaining absolutely motionless. They become active at night to feed and locate mates. Stick insects are sometimes found perching on walls and window screens with their fore legs extended forward. Since most species are colored in various shades of greens and browns, camouflage and remaining still are their first lines of defense. Some species are able to change their colors to better match their backgrounds. Many pretend to be dead when threatened and fall to the ground, where they become lost among the leaves, grasses, and other vegetation. They might even voluntarily break off a leg to distract a predator (PREH-duh-ter) or animal that hunts other animals for food. Several species have bright, contrasting colors to warn predators that they will spray a foul-smelling, milky defensive fluid from glands in the thorax or midsection. This fluid can cause temporary blindness if it gets in the eyes. Winged species will suddenly open their colorful wings and begin to rattle them in an attempt to startle a potential predator.

Males transfer the sperm packet directly into the reproductive organs of the females during mating. After mating the male will remain clinging to the female for several hours or days. In fact, male timemas spend most of their adult lives riding around on the back of adult females. This behavior prevents other males from mating with her. If males are not available, some species of phasmids can reproduce by parthenogenesis (PAR-thuh-no-JEH-nuh-sihs). Parthenogenesis does not require sperm from a male to produce healthy eggs. All parthenogenetic eggs hatch into females. In a few species, males are completely unknown, and reproduction is entirely by parthenogenesis.

Females lay between one hundred and two thousand eggs. Some species drop or flick their eggs to the ground, while others glue them singly or in batches to leaves and branches. A few actually place them inside leaf tissues. Phasmid eggs are very distinctive in shape, size, and color. Seedlike eggs often have a caplike handle that makes it easy for ants to carry them back to their nests. This actually benefits the eggs by keeping them out of reach of other predators. The ants eat only the cap, leaving the rest of the egg intact.

Depending on the species, the eggs will hatch anywhere from about a month to more than a year. The larvae (LAR-vee), or young of the animal that must change form before they become adults, strongly resemble the adults but lack wings (if present) and are not able to reproduce. Phasmid larvae usually molt, or shed their exoskeleton or hard outer covering, six to seven

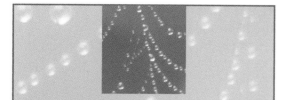

Many species of insects mimic ants, and with good reason. Ants are well known for their defensive behaviors. Many predators avoid them because they will not hesitate to bite, sting, or spray stinging chemicals at their attackers. The young larvae of some stick insects are thought to mimic the movement of ants by running frantically over the ground.

times and can replace lost or damaged limbs as they grow. Adults may live for several months, although some species may live up to three years.

STICK INSECTS AND PEOPLE

Natives of Goodenough Island, New Guinea, used the large hooks found on the back legs of male *Eurycantha*, a large spiny species common in the region, as fishhooks. Large and spectacularly colored species are commonly collected, preserved, and mounted in decorative frames for sale to tourists. Living phasmids are popular with hobbyists, but the importation of exotic stick insects is strictly regulated in many countries, especially in the United States. Authorities are concerned that the accidentally or purposefully introduced foreign species may become plant pests. Exotic species can also crowd out native species or introduce harmful diseases to their populations. Exotic species are often displayed, under special permits, in insect zoos and other institutions with living arthropod exhibits. Nearly all phasmids are harmless, but some species can deliver a painful pinch with sharp spines on their legs or squirt bad-smelling sprays that are known to cause temporary blindness in humans. A few stick insects are occasionally regarded as pests when they devour nearly all of the leaves of individual trees.

CONSERVATION STATUS

Only one species of phasmid is listed by the World Conservation Union (IUCN). The Australian Lord Howe Island stick insect, sometimes called the "land lobster," is listed as Critically Endangered, or facing an extremely high risk of extinction in the wild. It was thought that they had been wiped out, pushed to extinction by introduction of insect-eating rats to the island in 1918. Fortunately, a living population of this spectacular insect was discovered in 2001 on Balls Pyramid, a rugged and bare volcanic rock formation. The Australian authorities are now trying to breed them in the laboratory for later release back into rat-free habitats.

Insect zoos and hobbyists rely mainly on phasmids reared from captive stock and not specimens caught in the wild. However, some large and showy species, such as the jungle nymph from the Cameron Highlands of Malaysia, are sometimes collected in large numbers in the wild and exported around the world.

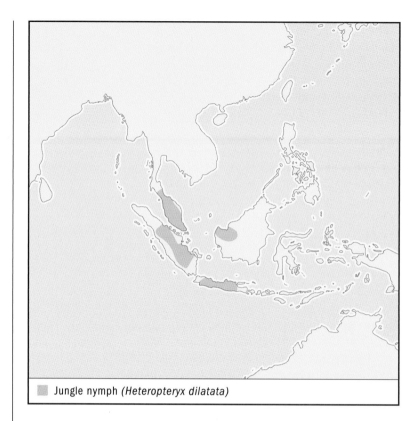

Jungle nymph (*Heteropteryx dilatata*)

JUNGLE NYMPH
Heteropteryx dilatata

Physical characteristics: The large, broad, spiny, apple green females measure 5.4 to 6.3 inches (140 to 160 millimeters) in length and weigh up to 2.3 ounces (65 grams). The short green forewings of the adult completely cover the hind wings underneath. Males are smaller, ranging in length from 3.1 to 3.5 inches (80 to 90 millimeters) and are mottled brown with slender wings that cover the entire length of the abdomen. The legs of both males and females are very spiny.

Geographic range: The jungle nymph is found in Java, Malaysia, Sarawak, Singapore, Sumatra, and Thailand.

Habitat: The jungle nymph lives on shrubs and trees in tropical forests.

Diet: This species eats the leaves of many kinds of bushes and trees in the wild and in captivity, including eugenia, guava, and bramble.

Behavior and reproduction: When threatened both males and females arch their bodies forward and strike out with their spiny hind legs. They also produce a hissing sound by rubbing their forewings and hind wings together. They will also bite if none of the previous strategies work. Gynandromorphs (GAI-nan-druh-morfs), individuals that show the characteristics of both males and females, are sometimes found in the wild and in captive-bred colonies.

Females bury their eggs in soil. The eggs take eight to eighteen months to hatch.

Jungle nymphs and people: The droppings of jungle nymphs are dried and mixed with herbs in China as a cure for numerous ailments, such as asthma. Chinese families often rear them on guava leaves to keep a steady supply of droppings handy. This is also a popular species for live displays in zoos and butterfly houses around the world.

Conservation status: This species is not endangered or threatened. However, specimens are routinely collected in large numbers, mounted and framed, and sold to tourists. ■

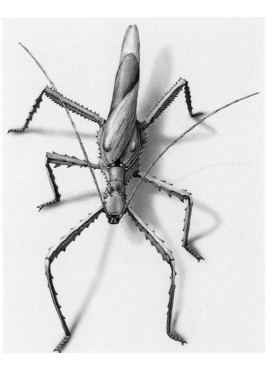

When threatened both the male (pictured here) and female jungle nymphs arch their bodies forward and strike out with their spiny hind legs. They also produce a hissing sound by rubbing their forewings and hind wings together. (Illustration by Emily Damstra. Reproduced by permission.)

Indian stick insect *(Carausius morosus)*

INDIAN STICK INSECT
Carausius morosus

Physical characteristics: This species is somewhat smooth, plain, wingless, with antennae about one-third the length of the body. Adult males are thin, brown, and reach 1.9 to 2.4 inches (48 to 61 millimeters) in length. The bodies of the females are somewhat knobby and measure 2.8 to 3.3 inches (70 to 84 millimeters) in length. They are variously colored dull green or brown. The inner base of each foreleg is bright red.

Geographic range: Indian stick insects are native to Shembagonor and Trichinopoly in Madura Province, southern India. They now also live in Madagascar and the Cape Town suburbs of South Africa. Released individuals and escapes are occasionally found in the United

States, United Kingdom, and other countries of Europe. In these cooler climates they generally die out within a few years.

Habitat: These insects live on many species of bushes and trees in India. In other parts of the world they are found on garden plants and natural vegetation.

Diet: This species eats a wide variety of plants in the wild and in captivity. Captive colonies are often kept on hedges.

Behavior and reproduction: Indian stick insects play dead when disturbed and will remain motionless for hours.

Males are rare, and reproduction is mainly by parthenogenesis. Females drop several hundred eggs to the ground. The life cycle usually is completed in twelve to sixteen months. Gynandromorphs also are reared occasionally.

Indian stick insects and people: This species is very easy to raise and is regularly used as a study animal by scientists.

Conservation status: This species is not endangered or threatened. ■

Both female (pictured here) and male Indian stick insects play dead when disturbed and will remain motionless for hours. (Illustration by Emily Damstra. Reproduced by permission.)

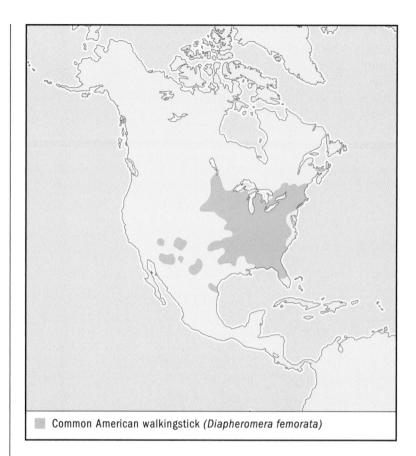

Common American walkingstick *(Diapheromera femorata)*

COMMON AMERICAN WALKINGSTICK
Diapheromera femorata

Physical characteristics: This species is long, slender, and shiny, with long antennae. Males measure 2.2 to 3.3 inches (55 to 84 millimeters) in length. The females are 2.8 to 4.0 inches (70 to 101 millimeters) long. The middle legs of the male are banded, and the appendages on the tip of their abdomen are distinctive and curved. Adult females are green, gray, or brown, and males are brownish with stripes.

Geographic range: The common American walkingstick is found in North America, from southern Canada, from Manitoba to Quebec, south to Arizona and Florida, and also in northern Mexico.

Habitat: This species is found in woodlands populated with broadleaf trees.

Diet: The adults prefer eating oak leaves, while the larvae will also feed on various plants and shrubs under the oaks.

Behavior and reproduction: The common American walkingstick relies on its camouflage to hide among vegetation. Eggs are dropped to the ground in fall and hatch in spring.

Common American walkingsticks and people: This species is sometimes regarded as a pest when large numbers eat most of the leaves on a tree.

Conservation status: This species is not endangered or threatened. ■

Macleay's spectre (*Extatosoma tiaratum tiaratum*)

MACLEAY'S SPECTRE
Extatosoma tiaratum

Physical characteristics: Macleay's spectre is a large, winged leaf-mimic. The plump, heavy females have short wings and weigh 0.7 to 1.1 ounces (20 to 30 grams) and measure 3.9 to 6.3 inches (100 to 160 mm) in length. The smaller, lighter males have fully developed wings covering the length of the abdomen and range from 3.2 to 4.5 inches (81 to 115 millimeters). The legs and bodies of both males and females have leaflike expansions. Females are brown, sometimes green, and very spiny.

Geographic range: They are found in parts of New South Wales and southeast and north Queensland, Australia.

Habitat: This species is found in suitable bush or gardens.

The Macleay's spectre is popular as a display animal in insect zoos worldwide. In parts of Papua, New Guinea, one of its relatives is sometimes cooked and eaten by local people. (©Richard R. Hansen/Photo Researchers, Inc. Reproduced by permission.)

Diet: Their natural food plants include eucalyptus, but they will also accept oak and pyracantha in captivity.

Behavior and reproduction: In response to a perceived threat, the spiny hind legs are spread and strike out. Forelegs are waved, and sometimes the body sways from side to side. Females curl their abdomens up over the rest of their bodies, a posture suggesting that of a scorpion.

It is possible that females attract males by flashes of ultraviolet light. Reproduction is usually by mating, but females are capable of reproducing by parthenogenesis. Adults live for several months. Females lay several hundred eggs, which are flicked to the ground. The eggs take five to eight months to hatch. The larvae take anywhere from three to six months to reach adulthood.

Macleay's spectres and people: This species is popular as a display animal in insect zoos worldwide. In parts of Papua, New Guinea, one of its relatives is sometimes cooked and eaten by local people.

Conservation status: This species is not endangered or threatened. ■

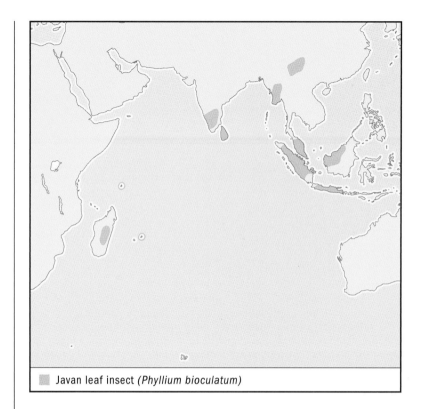

Javan leaf insect (Phyllium bioculatum)

JAVAN LEAF INSECT
Phyllium bioculatum

Physical characteristics: The Javan leaf insect is a supreme leaf-mimic. Their broad green bodies and legs, with or without spots, are quite flattened. The antennae of the females are very short, while those of the male are longer. Adult males are 1.8 to 2.7 inches (46 to 68 millimeters) in length. Females range from 2.6 to 3.7 inches (67 to 94 millimeters).

Geographic range: This species is widespread in Southeast Asia, including Borneo, China, India, Java, Malaysia, Singapore, and Sumatra. They are also found in Madagascar, Mauritius, and the Seychelles.

Habitat: They live on tropical rainforest vegetation.

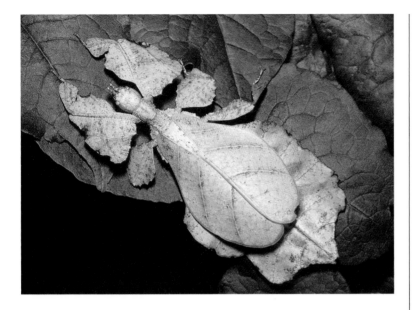

Javan leaf insects eat the leaves of guava and rambutan. In captivity they will also eat oak and bramble. (Arthur V. Evans. Reproduced by permission.)

Diet: Javan leaf insects eat the leaves of guava and rambutan. In captivity they will also eat oak and bramble.

Behavior and reproduction: Males can fly well and are usually short-lived, while the longer-lived females are flightless. Both males and females rely on their excellent camouflage to avoid predators.

Females drop their oddly shaped, seedlike eggs to the ground. The larvae may take several months to reach adulthood.

Javan leaf insects and people: This species is popular with hobbyists and as a display animal in insect zoos, although they can sometimes be difficult to maintain.

Conservation status: This species is not endangered or threatened. ■

FOR MORE INFORMATION

Books:

Brock, P. D. *The Amazing World of Stick and Leaf Insects.* Orpington, U.K.: Amateur Entomologists' Society, 1999.

Brock, P. D. *A Complete Guide to Breeding Stick and Leaf Insects.* Havant, U.K.: T.F.H. Kingdom Books, 2000.

Brock, P. D. *Stick and Leaf Insects of Peninsular Malaysia and Singapore.* Kuala Lumpur: Malaysian Nature Society, 1999.

Periodicals:

Sivinski, J. "When Is a Stick Not a Stick?" *Natural History* no. 1012 (June 1992): 30–35.

Vallés, S. R. "Phasmids." *Reptilia* no. 13 (October 2000): 16–25.

Web sites:

Gordon's Phasmida Page. http://www.earthlife.net/insects/phasmida .html (accessed on September 26, 2004).

Phasmatodea. http://www.cals.ncsu.edu:8050/course/ent425/ compendium/stick.html (accessed on September 26, 2004).

"Phasmatodea. Stick Insects, Leaf Insects." Ecowatch. http://www.ento .csiro.au/Ecowatch/Insects_Invertebrates/phasmatodea.htm (accessed September on 26, 2004).

Species List by Biome

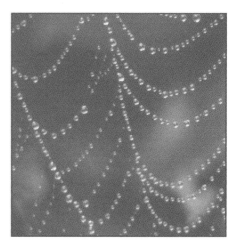

CONIFEROUS FOREST
American cockroach
Bed bug
Book louse
Book scorpion
Brown mayfly
European earwig
German cockroach
Giant salmonfly
Giant whip scorpion
Greenhouse camel cricket
Hair follicle mite
Holijapyx diversiuguis
Honeybee
Human head/body louse
Indian mealmoth
Long-bodied cellar spider
Megarhyssa nortoni
Oriental cockroach
Rock-crawler
Rocky Mountain wood tick
Schummel's inocelliid snakefly
Silverfish
Slender pigeon louse
Wandering glider
Zebra jumping spider

CONTINENTAL MARGIN
Colossendeis megalonyx
Horseshoe crab

DECIDUOUS FOREST
Allopauropus carolinensis
American burying beetle
American cockroach
Bed bug
Big black horse fly
Book louse
Book scorpion
Brownbanded cockroach
Brown mayfly
Chigoe
Chiloporter eatoni
Chinese mantid
Common American
  walkingstick
Common harvestman
Devil's coach-horse
Eastern dobsonfly
Eastern subterranean
  termite
European earwig
European mantid
European marsh crane fly
European stag beetle
Flat-backed millipede
Garden symphylan
German cockroach
Giant whip scorpion
Greenhouse camel cricket
Gypsy moth

Hair follicle mite
Halictophagus naulti
Holijapyx diversiuguis
House centipede
Honeybee
Hubbard's angel insect
Human head/body louse
Indian mealmoth
Long-bodied cellar spider
Macleay's spectre
Mediterranean fruit fly
Megarhyssa nortoni
Moth lacewing
Oriental cockroach
Panorpa nuptialis
Pea aphid
Pill millipede
Rock-crawler
Potter wasp
Rocky Mountain wood
  tick
Saunders embiid
Scolopender
Seventeen-year cicada
Silkworm
Silverfish
Sinetomon yoroi
Slender pigeon louse
Spider bat fly
Spoonwing lacewing

Tarantula hawk
Triaenodes bicolor
Trissolcus basalis
Velvet ant
Wandering glider
Western flower thrips
Zebra jumping spider

DESERT
American cockroach
Antlion
Bed bug
Big black horse fly
Book louse
Brownbanded cockroach
Camel spider
European earwig
Hair follicle mite
Honeybee
House centipede
Indian mealmoth
German cockroach
Giant whip scorpion
Greenhouse camel cricket
Long-bodied cellar spider
Oriental cockroach
Sacred scarab
Scolopender
Silverfish
Slender pigeon louse
Spider bat fly
Tarantula hawk
Wandering glider
Western flower thrips
Wide-headed rottenwood
  termite
Zebra jumping spider

GRASSLAND
American burying beetle
American cockroach
Antlion
Backswimmer
Big black horse fly
Bed bug
Book louse
Book scorpion

Brownbanded cockroach
Common harvestman
Death's head hawk moth
Emperor scorpion
European earwig
European marsh crane fly
European mantid
Garden symphylan
German cockroach
Giant whip scorpion
Gladiator
Hair follicle mite
Honeybee
House centipede
Human head/body louse
Indian mealmoth
Indian stick insect
Large blue
Long-bodied cellar spider
Lucerne flea
Oriental cockroach
Pea aphid
Sacred scarab
St. Helena earwig
Scolopender
Sheep and goat flea
Silverfish
Slender pigeon louse
Spider bat fly
Spoonwing lacewing
Tarantula hawk
Trissolcus basalis
Tsetse fly
Variegated grasshopper
Velvet ant
Wandering glider
Western flower thrips
Wide-headed rottenwood
  termite
Yellow fever mosquito
Zebra jumping spider

LAKE AND POND
American cockroach
Brownbanded cockroach
German cockroach
Great water beetle
Hair follicle mite

Honeybee
Oriental cockroach
Wandering glider

OCEAN
Colossendeis megalonyx
Sea skater

RAINFOREST
American cockroach
Atlas moth
Bed bug
Balsam beast
Beetle cricket
Black macrotermes
Black-headed nasute termite
Blue morpho
Book louse
Brownbanded cockroach
Chigoe
Cubacubana spelaea
Dead-leaf mantid
Dead leaf mimetica
Emperor scorpion
European earwig
Forest giant
German cockroach
Giant water bug
Giraffe-necked weevil
Green lacewing
Greenhouse camel cricket
Greenhouse whitefly
Hair follicle mite
Hercules beetle
Hispaniola hooded katydid
Honeybee
House centipede
Human head/body louse
Indian mealmoth
Javan leaf insect
Jungle nymph
Leaf-cutter ant
Linnaeus's snapping termite
Madeira cockroach
Mantid lacewing
Mediterranean fruit fly

Orchid mantid
Oriental cockroach
Pea aphid
Saunders embiid
Scolopender
Silverfish
Slender pigeon louse
Spider bat fly
Stalk-eyed fly
Tailless whip scorpion
Tarantula hawk
Tsetse fly
Wandering glider
Wandering violin mantid
Yellow fever mosquito

RIVER AND STREAM
American cockroach
Brownbanded cockroach

Forest giant
German cockroach
Hair follicle mite
Honeybee
Oriental cockroach
Rocky Mountain wood tick
Triaenodes bicolor
Wandering glider

SEASHORE
Hair follicle mite
Honeybee
Horseshoe crab
Petrobius brevistylis
Wandering glider

TUNDRA
Book louse
Hair follicle mite

Human head/body louse
Slender pigeon louse

WETLAND
American cockroach
Big black horse fly
Brownbanded cockroach
European earwig
German cockroach
Greenhouse camel cricket
Hair follicle mite
Human head/body louse
Long-winged conehead
Oriental cockroach
Rocky Mountain wood
 tick
Slender pigeon louse
Wandering glider

Species List by Geographic Range

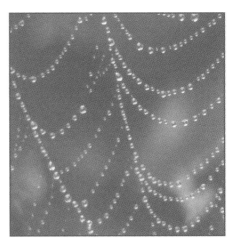

AFGHANISTAN
American cockroach
Bed bug
Brownbanded cockroach
German cockroach
Greenhouse camel cricket
Greenhouse whitefly
Hair follicle mite
Honeybee
Human head/body louse
Indian mealmoth
Liposcelis bostrychophila
Long-bodied cellar spider
Lucerne flea
Pea aphid
Silverfish
Wandering glider
Western flower thrips

ALBANIA
American cockroach
Bed bug
Book scorpion
Brown mayfly
Brownbanded cockroach
Common harvestman
Death's head hawk moth
Devil's coach-horse
European earwig
European mantid

European stag beetle
German cockroach
Great water beetle
Greenhouse camel cricket
Greenhouse whitefly
Gypsy moth
Hair follicle mite
Honeybee
Human head/body louse
Indian mealmoth
Large blue
Liposcelis bostrychophila
Long-bodied cellar spider
Long-winged conehead
Lucerne flea
Mediterranean fruitfly
Pea aphid
Sacred scarab
Silverfish
Slender pigeon louse
Spoonwing lacewing
Triaenodes bicolor
Velvet ant
Western flower thrips
Zebra jumping spider

ALGERIA
American cockroach
Bed bug
Brownbanded cockroach

Camel spider
Death's head hawk moth
Devil's coach-horse
European mantid
German cockroach
Greenhouse camel cricket
Gypsy moth
Hair follicle mite
Honeybee
House centipede
Human head/body louse
Indian mealmoth
Liposcelis bostrychophila
Long-bodied cellar spider
Long-winged conehead
Lucerne flea
Mediterranean fruitfly
Sacred scarab
Scolopender
Silverfish
Slender pigeon louse
Spoonwing lacewing
Wandering glider
Western flower thrips
Yellow fever mosquito

ANDORRA
American cockroach
Antlion
Bed bug

Book scorpion
Brown mayfly
Brownbanded cockroach
Common harvestman
Death's head hawk moth
Devil's coach-horse
European earwig
European mantid
European stag beetle
German cockroach
Great water beetle
Greenhouse camel cricket
Greenhouse whitefly
Gypsy moth
Hair follicle mite
Honeybee
House centipede
Human head/body louse
Indian mealmoth
Large blue
Liposcelis bostrychophila
Long-bodied cellar spider
Long-winged conehead
Lucerne flea
Mediterranean fruitfly
Pea aphid
Sacred scarab
Silverfish
Slender pigeon louse
Spoonwing lacewing
Velvet ant
Western flower thrips
Yellow fever mosquito
Zebra jumping spider

ANGOLA
American cockroach
Bed bug
Brownbanded cockroach
Chigoe
Death's head hawk moth
European mantid
German cockroach
Greenhouse camel cricket
Greenhouse whitefly
Hair follicle mite

Honeybee
Human head/body louse
Indian mealmoth
Liposcelis bostrychophila
Long-bodied cellar spider
Lucerne flea
Madeira cockroach
Scolopender
Silverfish
Tsetse fly
Variegated grasshopper
Wandering glider
Yellow fever mosquito

ANTIGUA AND BARBUDA
Bed bug
German cockroach
Greenhouse camel cricket
Hair follicle mite
Honeybee
Human head/body louse
Indian mealmoth
Liposcelis bostrychophila
Long-bodied cellar spider
Lucerne flea
Silverfish
Wandering glider

ARCTIC
German cockroach

ARGENTINA
American cockroach
Backswimmer
Bed bug
Brownbanded cockroach
Chiloporter eatoni
German cockroach
Greenhouse camel cricket
Greenhouse whitefly
Hair follicle mite
Honeybee
Human head/body louse
Indian mealmoth

Leaf-cutter ant
Liposcelis bostrychophila
Long-bodied cellar spider
Lucerne flea
Oriental cockroach
Pea aphid
Silverfish
Wandering glider

ARMENIA
American cockroach
Bed bug
Brown mayfly
Death's head hawk moth
Devil's coach-horse
European mantid
German cockroach
Greenhouse camel cricket
Greenhouse whitefly
Hair follicle mite
Honeybee
Human head/body louse
Indian mealmoth
Liposcelis bostrychophila
Long-bodied cellar spider
Lucerne flea
Pea aphid
Silverfish
Slender pigeon louse
Yellow fever mosquito

ATLANTIC OCEAN
Colossendeis megalonyx
Sea skater

AUSTRALIA
American cockroach
Balsam beast
Bed bug
European earwig
European mantid
German cockroach
Green lacewing
Greenhouse camel cricket
Greenhouse whitefly

Gypsy moth
Hair follicle mite
House centipede
Human head/body louse
Indian mealmoth
Liposcelis bostrychophila
Long-bodied cellar spider
Lucerne flea
Macleay's specter
Mantid lacewing
Mediterranean fruitfly
Moth lacewing
Oriental cockroach
Pea aphid
Scolopender
Silverfish
Spider bat fly
Trissolcus basalis
Wandering glider
Western flower thrips
Yellow fever mosquito

AUSTRIA

American cockroach
Bed bug
Book scorpion
Brown mayfly
Common harvestman
Devil's coach-horse
European earwig
European mantid
European marsh crane fly
European stag beetle
Flat-backed millipede
German cockroach
Great water beetle
Greenhouse camel cricket
Greenhouse whitefly
Hair follicle mite
Honeybee
House centipede
Human head/body louse
Indian mealmoth
Large blue
Liposcelis bostrychophila
Long-bodied cellar spider

Long-winged conehead
Lucerne flea
Pea aphid
Silverfish
Slender pigeon louse
Spoonwing lacewing
Triaenodes bicolor
Velvet ant
Western flower thrips
Zebra jumping spider

AZERBAIJAN

American cockroach
Bed bug
Brown mayfly
Common harvestman
Death's head hawk moth
Devil's coach-horse
European mantid
German cockroach
Greenhouse camel cricket
Greenhouse whitefly
Hair follicle mite
Honeybee
Human head/body louse
Indian mealmoth
Liposcelis bostrychophila
Long-bodied cellar spider
Lucerne flea
Pea aphid
Silverfish
Slender pigeon louse
Yellow fever mosquito
Zebra jumping spider

BAHAMAS

Bed bug
German cockroach
Greenhouse camel cricket
Hair follicle mite
Honeybee
Human head/body louse
Indian mealmoth
Liposcelis bostrychophila
Long-bodied cellar spider

Lucerne flea
Silverfish
Wandering glider

BAHRAIN

Bed bug
Camel spider
German cockroach
Greenhouse camel cricket
Hair follicle mite
Honeybee
Human head/body louse
Indian mealmoth
Liposcelis bostrychophila
Long-bodied cellar spider
Lucerne flea
Silverfish
Slender pigeon louse
Wandering glider
Yellow fever mosquito

BANGLADESH

American cockroach
Atlas moth
Bed bug
Brownbanded cockroach
German cockroach
Greenhouse camel cricket
Greenhouse whitefly
Hair follicle mite
Honeybee
Human head/body louse
Indian mealmoth
Liposcelis bostrychophila
Long-bodied cellar spider
Lucerne flea
Orchid mantid
Oriental cockroach
Pea aphid
Scolopender
Silkworm
Silverfish
Slender pigeon louse
Wandering glider
Wandering violin mantid
Yellow fever mosquito

BARBADOS

Bed bug
German cockroach
Greenhouse camel cricket
Hair follicle mite
Honeybee
Human head/body louse
Indian mealmoth
Liposcelis bostrychophila
Long-bodied cellar spider
Lucerne flea
Silverfish
Wandering glider

BELARUS

American cockroach
Bed bug
Book scorpion
Brown mayfly
Common harvestman
Devil's coach-horse
European earwig
European stag beetle
German cockroach
Great water beetle
Greenhouse camel cricket
Gypsy moth
Hair follicle mite
Honeybee
Human head/body louse
Indian mealmoth
Large blue
Liposcelis bostrychophila
Long-bodied cellar spider
Long-winged conehead
Lucerne flea
Pea aphid
Schummel's inocelliid
  snakefly
Silverfish
Slender pigeon louse
Spoonwing lacewing
Triaenodes bicolor
Velvet ant
Western flower thrips
Zebra jumping spider

BELGIUM

American cockroach
Antlion
Bed bug
Book scorpion
Brown mayfly
Common harvestman
Devil's coach-horse
European earwig
European marsh crane fly
European stag beetle
Flat-backed millipede
German cockroach
Great water beetle
Greenhouse camel cricket
Gypsy moth
Hair follicle mite
Honeybee
Human head/body louse
Indian mealmoth
Large blue
Liposcelis bostrychophila
Long-bodied cellar spider
Long-winged conehead
Lucerne flea
Oriental cockroach
Petrobius brevistylis
Pill millipede
Silverfish
Slender pigeon louse
Spoonwing lacewing
Triaenodes bicolor
Velvet ant
Western flower thrips
Zebra jumping spider

BELIZE

American cockroach
Bed bug
Black-headed nasute termite
Brownbanded cockroach
Chigoe
Forest giant
German cockroach
Greenhouse camel cricket
Hair follicle mite

Hercules beetle
Honeybee
Horseshoe crab
Human head/body louse
Indian mealmoth
Liposcelis bostrychophila
Long-bodied cellar spider
Lucerne flea
Madeira cockroach
Mediterranean fruitfly
Pea aphid
Silverfish
Tailless whip scorpion
Wandering glider
Yellow fever mosquito

BENIN

American cockroach
Bed bug
Brownbanded cockroach
Chigoe
Death's head hawk moth
Emperor scorpion
European mantid
German cockroach
Greenhouse camel cricket
Greenhouse whitefly
Hair follicle mite
Honeybee
Human head/body louse
Indian mealmoth
Liposcelis bostrychophila
Long-bodied cellar spider
Long-winged conehead
Lucerne flea
Madeira cockroach
Silverfish
Slender pigeon louse
Tsetse fly
Variegated grasshopper
Wandering glider
Yellow fever mosquito

BHUTAN

American cockroach
Atlas moth

Bed bug
Brownbanded cockroach
Chinese mantid
Dead-leaf mantid
German cockroach
Greenhouse camel cricket
Greenhouse whitefly
Hair follicle mite
Honeybee
Human head/body louse
Indian mealmoth
Liposcelis bostrychophila
Long-bodied cellar spider
Lucerne flea
Oriental cockroach
Pea aphid
Silverfish
Wandering glider
Yellow fever mosquito

BOLIVIA
American cockroach
Backswimmer
Bed bug
Blue morpho
Brownbanded cockroach
Chigoe
Forest giant
German cockroach
Giant water bug
Greenhouse camel cricket
Greenhouse whitefly
Hair follicle mite
Hercules beetle
Honeybee
Human head/body louse
Indian mealmoth
Leaf-cutter ant
Liposcelis bostrychophila
Long-bodied cellar spider
Lucerne flea
Mediterranean fruitfly
Pea aphid
Silverfish
Wandering glider

BOSNIA AND HERZEGOVINA
American cockroach
Bed bug
Book scorpion
Brown mayfly
Brownbanded cockroach
Common harvestman
Devil's coach-horse
European mantid
European stag beetle
German cockroach
Great water beetle
Greenhouse camel cricket
Greenhouse whitefly
Gypsy moth
Hair follicle mite
Honeybee
House centipede
Human head/body louse
Indian mealmoth
Large blue
Liposcelis bostrychophila
Long-bodied cellar spider
Long-winged conehead
Lucerne flea
Mediterranean fruitfly
Pea aphid
Silverfish
Slender pigeon louse
Spoonwing lacewing
Triaenodes bicolor
Velvet ant
Western flower thrips
Yellow fever mosquito
Zebra jumping spider

BOTSWANA
American cockroach
Bed bug
Brownbanded cockroach
Death's head hawk moth
European mantid
German cockroach
Greenhouse camel cricket

Greenhouse whitefly
Hair follicle mite
Honeybee
Human head/body louse
Indian mealmoth
Liposcelis bostrychophila
Long-bodied cellar spider
Lucerne flea
Silverfish
Wandering glider
Western flower thrips
Yellow fever mosquito

BRAZIL
American cockroach
Backswimmer
Bed bug
Black-headed nasute termite
Blue morpho
Brownbanded cockroach
Chigoe
Cubacubana spelaea
German cockroach
Giant water bug
Greenhouse camel cricket
Greenhouse whitefly
Hair follicle mite
Hercules beetle
Honeybee
Human head/body louse
Indian mealmoth
Leaf-cutter ant
Linnaeus's snapping termite
Liposcelis bostrychophila
Long-bodied cellar spider
Lucerne flea
Magarhyssa nortoni
Mediterranean fruitfly
Pea aphid
Scolopender
Silverfish
Trissolcus basalis
Wandering glider
Yellow fever mosquito

BRUNEI

American cockroach
Atlas moth
Bed bug
Black macrotermes
Cyrtodiopsis dalmanni
Dead-leaf mantid
European earwig
German cockroach
Greenhouse camel cricket
Greenhouse whitefly
Hair follicle mite
Honeybee
Human head/body louse
Indian mealmoth
Javan leaf insect
Jungle nymph
Liposcelis bostrychophila
Long-bodied cellar spider
Lucerne flea
Orchid mantid
Pea aphid
Silverfish
Wandering glider
Yellow fever mosquito

BULGARIA

American cockroach
Bed bug
Book scorpion
Brown mayfly
Brownbanded cockroach
Common harvestman
Death's head hawk moth
Devil's coach-horse
European mantid
European stag beetle
German cockroach
Great water beetle
Greenhouse camel cricket
Greenhouse whitefly
Gypsy moth
Hair follicle mite
Honeybee
Human head/body louse

Indian mealmoth
Liposcelis bostrychophila
Long-bodied cellar spider
Long-winged conehead
Lucerne flea
Pea aphid
Sacred scarab
Silverfish
Slender pigeon louse
Spoonwing lacewing
Triaenodes bicolor
Velvet ant
Western flower thrips
Zebra jumping spider

BURKINA FASO

American cockroach
Bed bug
Brownbanded cockroach
Chigoe
Death's head hawk moth
Emperor scorpion
German cockroach
Greenhouse camel cricket
Greenhouse whitefly
Hair follicle mite
Honeybee
Human head/body louse
Indian mealmoth
Liposcelis bostrychophila
Long-bodied cellar spider
Lucerne flea
Silverfish
Slender pigeon louse
Tsetse fly
Variegated grasshopper
Wandering glider
Yellow fever mosquito

BURUNDI

American cockroach
Bed bug
Brownbanded cockroach
Chigoe
Death's head hawk moth
European earwig

European mantid
German cockroach
Greenhouse camel cricket
Greenhouse whitefly
Hair follicle mite
Honeybee
Human head/body louse
Indian mealmoth
Liposcelis bostrychophila
Long-bodied cellar spider
Lucerne flea
Silverfish
Slender pigeon louse
Wandering glider
Yellow fever mosquito

CAMBODIA

American cockroach
Atlas moth
Bed bug
Black macrotermes
Brownbanded cockroach
German cockroach
Greenhouse camel cricket
Greenhouse whitefly
Hair follicle mite
Honeybee
Human head/body louse
Indian mealmoth
Liposcelis bostrychophila
Long-bodied cellar spider
Lucerne flea
Oriental cockroach
Pea aphid
Silverfish
Wandering glider
Yellow fever mosquito

CAMEROON

American cockroach
Bed bug
Brownbanded cockroach
Chigoe
Death's head hawk moth
Emperor scorpion

European mantid
German cockroach
Greenhouse camel cricket
Greenhouse whitefly
Hair follicle mite
Honeybee
Human head/body louse
Indian mealmoth
Liposcelis bostrychophila
Long-bodied cellar spider
Long-winged conehead
Lucerne flea
Madeira cockroach
Scolopender
Silverfish
Tsetse fly
Variegated grasshopper
Wandering glider
Yellow fever mosquito

CANADA
American cockroach
American horseshoe crab
Bed bug
Big black horse fly
Brownbanded cockroach
Common American
  walkingstick
Common harvestman
Eastern dobsonfly
Eastern subterranean termite
European earwig
European mantid
European marsh crane fly
German cockroach
Giant salmonfly
Greenhouse camel cricket
Greenhouse whitefly
Gypsy moth
Hair follicle mite
Honeybee
House centipede
Human head/body louse
Indian mealmoth
Liposcelis bostrychophila
Long-bodied cellar spider

Lucerne flea
Oriental cockroach
Pea aphid
Petrobius brevistylis
Potter wasp
Rock-crawler
Rocky Mountain wood tick
Silverfish
Wandering glider
Western flower thrips
Zebra jumping spider

CAPE VERDE
Bed bug
Death's head hawk moth
German cockroach
Greenhouse camel cricket
Hair follicle mite
Honeybee
Human head/body louse
Indian mealmoth
Liposcelis bostrychophila
Long-bodied cellar spider
Lucerne flea
Silverfish
Wandering glider
Yellow fever mosquito

CENTRAL AFRICAN REPUBLIC
American cockroach
Bed bug
Brownbanded cockroach
Chigoe
Death's head hawk moth
Emperor scorpion
European mantid
German cockroach
Greenhouse camel cricket
Greenhouse whitefly
Hair follicle mite
Honeybee
Human head/body louse
Indian mealmoth
Liposcelis bostrychophila

Long-bodied cellar spider
Lucerne flea
Silverfish
Slender pigeon louse
Tsetse fly
Variegated grasshopper
Wandering glider
Yellow fever mosquito

CHAD
American cockroach
Bed bug
Brownbanded cockroach
Camel spider
Chigoe
Death's head hawk moth
Emperor scorpion
German cockroach
Greenhouse camel cricket
Greenhouse whitefly
Hair follicle mite
Honeybee
Human head/body louse
Indian mealmoth
Liposcelis bostrychophila
Long-bodied cellar spider
Lucerne flea
Silverfish
Slender pigeon louse
Tsetse fly
Variegated grasshopper
Wandering glider
Yellow fever mosquito

CHILE
American cockroach
Bed bug
Brownbanded cockroach
Chigoe
Chiloporter eatoni
European earwig
German cockroach
Greenhouse camel cricket
Greenhouse whitefly
Hair follicle mite

Honeybee
Human head/body louse
Indian mealmoth
Liposcelis bostrychophila
Long-bodied cellar spider
Lucerne flea
Oriental cockroach
Pea aphid
Silverfish
Wandering glider

CHINA

American cockroach
Atlas moth
Bed bug
Brownbanded cockroach
Chinese mantid
German cockroach
Greenhouse camel cricket
Greenhouse whitefly
Hair follicle mite
Honeybee
Human head/body louse
Indian mealmoth
Javan leaf insect
Large blue
Liposcelis bostrychophila
Long-bodied cellar spider
Lucerne flea
Oriental cockroach
Pea aphid
Scolopender
Sheep and goat flea
Silkworm
Silverfish
Wandering glider
Yellow fever mosquito
Zebra jumping spider

COLOMBIA

American cockroach
Bed bug
Black-headed nasute termite
Blue morpho
Brownbanded cockroach

Chigoe
Forest giant
German cockroach
Giant water bug
Greenhouse camel cricket
Greenhouse whitefly
Hair follicle mite
Hercules beetle
Honeybee
Human head/body louse
Indian mealmoth
Leaf-cutter ant
Liposcelis bostrychophila
Long-bodied cellar spider
Lucerne flea
Madeira cockroach
Mediterranean fruitfly
Pea aphid
Silverfish
Wandering glider
Western flower thrips
Yellow fever mosquito

COMOROS

Bed bug
Death's head hawk moth
German cockroach
Greenhouse camel cricket
Hair follicle mite
Honeybee
Human head/body louse
Indian mealmoth
Liposcelis bostrychophila
Long-bodied cellar spider
Lucerne flea
Scolopender
Silverfish
Wandering glider
Yellow fever mosquito

COSTA RICA

American cockroach
Bed bug
Black-headed nasute termite
Brownbanded cockroach
Chigoe

Dead leaf mimetica
Forest giant
German cockroach
Greenhouse camel cricket
Hair follicle mite
Hercules beetle
Honeybee
Human head/body louse
Indian mealmoth
Leaf-cutter ant
Liposcelis bostrychophila
Long-bodied cellar spider
Lucerne flea
Madeira cockroach
Mediterranean fruitfly
Pea aphid
Silverfish
Tailless whip scorpion
Tarantula hawk
Wandering glider
Yellow fever mosquito

CROATIA

American cockroach
Bed bug
Book scorpion
Brown mayfly
Brownbanded cockroach
Common harvestman
Death's head hawk moth
Devil's coach-horse
European earwig
European mantid
European stag beetle
German cockroach
Great water beetle
Greenhouse camel cricket
Greenhouse whitefly
Gypsy moth
Hair follicle mite
Honeybee
House centipede
Human head/body louse
Indian mealmoth
Large blue
Liposcelis bostrychophila

Long-bodied cellar spider
Long-winged conehead
Lucerne flea
Mediterranean fruitfly
Pea aphid
Silverfish
Slender pigeon louse
Spoonwing lacewing
Triaenodes bicolor
Velvet ant
Western flower thrips
Yellow fever mosquito
Zebra jumping spider

CUBA
Bed bug
Chigoe
German cockroach
Greenhouse camel cricket
Greenhouse whitefly
Hair follicle mite
Human head/body louse
Indian mealmoth
Liposcelis bostrychophila
Long-bodied cellar spider
Lucerne flea
Madeira cockroach
Mediterranean fruitfly
Pea aphid
Saunders embiid
Silverfish
Tarantula hawk
Trissolcus basalis
Wandering glider
Yellow fever mosquito

CYPRUS
Bed bug
Book scorpion
German cockroach
Greenhouse camel cricket
Hair follicle mite
Honeybee
Human head/body louse
Indian mealmoth
Liposcelis bostrychophila

Long-bodied cellar spider
Lucerne flea
Silverfish

CZECH REPUBLIC
American cockroach
Bed bug
Book scorpion
Brown mayfly
Common harvestman
Devil's coach-horse
European earwig
European marsh crane fly
European stag beetle
Flat-backed millipede
German cockroach
Great water beetle
Greenhouse camel cricket
Greenhouse whitefly
Gypsy moth
Hair follicle mite
Honeybee
Human head/body louse
Indian mealmoth
Large blue
Liposcelis bostrychophila
Long-bodied cellar spider
Long-winged conehead
Lucerne flea
Pea aphid
Pill millipede
Silverfish
Slender pigeon louse
Spoonwing lacewing
Triaenodes bicolor
Velvet ant
Western flower thrips
Zebra jumping spider

DEMOCRATIC REPUBLIC OF THE CONGO
American cockroach
Bed bug
Brownbanded cockroach
Chigoe

Death's head hawk moth
Emperor scorpion
European mantid
German cockroach
Greenhouse camel cricket
Greenhouse whitefly
Hair follicle mite
Honeybee
Human head/body louse
Indian mealmoth
Liposcelis bostrychophila
Long-bodied cellar spider
Lucerne flea
Madeira cockroach
Silverfish
Tsetse fly
Variegated grasshopper
Wandering glider
Yellow fever mosquito

DENMARK
American cockroach
Antlion
Bed bug
Book scorpion
Brown mayfly
Devil's coach-horse
European earwig
European marsh crane fly
European stag beetle
Flat-backed millipede
German cockroach
Great water beetle
Greenhouse camel cricket
Gypsy moth
Hair follicle mite
Honeybee
Human head/body louse
Indian mealmoth
Large blue
Liposcelis bostrychophila
Long-bodied cellar spider
Long-winged conehead
Lucerne flea
Oriental cockroach
Petrobius brevistylis

Pill millipede
Silverfish
Slender pigeon louse
Spoonwing lacewing
Triaenodes bicolor
Velvet ant
Western flower thrips

DJIBOUTI

Bed bug
Chigoe
Death's head hawk moth
European earwig
German cockroach
Greenhouse camel cricket
Hair follicle mite
Honeybee
Human head/body louse
Indian mealmoth
Liposcelis bostrychophila
Long-bodied cellar spider
Lucerne flea
Silverfish
Wandering glider
Yellow fever mosquito

DOMINICAN REPUBLIC

Bed bug
Chigoe
German cockroach
Greenhouse camel cricket
Greenhouse whitefly
Hair follicle mite
Hispaniola hooded catydid
Human head/body louse
Indian mealmoth
Liposcelis bostrychophila
Long-bodied cellar spider
Lucerne flea
Madeira cockroach
Mediterranean fruitfly
Pea aphid
Scolopender
Silverfish
Trissolcus basalis

Wandering glider
Yellow fever mosquito

ECUADOR

American cockroach
Bed bug
Black-headed nasute termite
Blue morpho
Brownbanded cockroach
Chigoe
Forest giant
German cockroach
Giant water bug
Greenhouse camel cricket
Greenhouse whitefly
Hair follicle mite
Honeybee
Human head/body louse
Indian mealmoth
Leaf-cutter ant
Liposcelis bostrychophila
Long-bodied cellar spider
Lucerne flea
Mediterranean fruitfly
Pea aphid
Silverfish
Tarantula hawk
Wandering glider
Western flower thrips
Yellow fever mosquito

EGYPT

American cockroach
Bed bug
Brownbanded cockroach
Camel spider
Death's head hawk moth
European earwig
German cockroach
Greenhouse camel cricket
Greenhouse whitefly
Hair follicle mite
Honeybee
House centipede
Human head/body louse

Indian mealmoth
Liposcelis bostrychophila
Long-bodied cellar spider
Long-winged conehead
Lucerne flea
Mediterranean fruitfly
Sacred scarab
Scolopender
Silverfish
Slender pigeon louse
Trissolcus basalis
Wandering glider
Yellow fever mosquito

EL SALVADOR

American cockroach
Bed bug
Black-headed nasute termite
Brownbanded cockroach
Chigoe
Forest giant
German cockroach
Greenhouse camel cricket
Greenhouse whitefly
Hair follicle mite
Hercules beetle
Honeybee
Human head/body louse
Indian mealmoth
Liposcelis bostrychophila
Long-bodied cellar spider
Lucerne flea
Madeira cockroach
Mediterranean fruitfly
Pea aphid
Silverfish
Wandering glider
Yellow fever mosquito

EQUATORIAL GUINEA

American cockroach
Bed bug
Brownbanded cockroach
Chigoe
Death's head hawk moth

Emperor scorpion
German cockroach
Greenhouse camel cricket
Greenhouse whitefly
Hair follicle mite
Honeybee
Human head/body louse
Indian mealmoth
Liposcelis bostrychophila
Long-bodied cellar spider
Lucerne flea
Madeira cockroach
Silverfish
Tsetse fly
Variegated grasshopper
Wandering glider
Yellow fever mosquito

ERITREA
Bed bug
Chigoe
Death's head hawk moth
European earwig
German cockroach
Greenhouse camel cricket
Hair follicle mite
Honeybee
Human head/body louse
Indian mealmoth
Liposcelis bostrychophila
Long-bodied cellar spider
Lucerne flea
Silverfish
Slender pigeon louse
Wandering glider
Yellow fever mosquito

ESTONIA
American cockroach
Bed bug
Brown mayfly
Common harvestman
European earwig
European marsh crane fly
German cockroach
Great water beetle

Greenhouse camel cricket
Gypsy moth
Hair follicle mite
Honeybee
Human head/body louse
Indian mealmoth
Large blue
Liposcelis bostrychophila
Long-bodied cellar spider
Long-winged conehead
Lucerne flea
Petrobius brevistylis
Schummel's inocelliid
  snakefly
Silverfish
Slender pigeon louse
Spoonwing lacewing
Triaenodes bicolor
Velvet ant
Western flower thrips
Zebra jumping spider

ETHIOPIA
Bed bug
Brownbanded cockroach
Chigoe
Death's head hawk moth
European earwig
German cockroach
Greenhouse camel cricket
Greenhouse whitefly
Hair follicle mite
Honeybee
Human head/body louse
Indian mealmoth
Liposcelis bostrychophila
Long-bodied cellar spider
Lucerne flea
Silverfish
Slender pigeon louse
Wandering glider
Yellow fever mosquito

FIJI
Bed bug
German cockroach

Greenhouse camel cricket
Hair follicle mite
Honeybee
Human head/body louse
Indian mealmoth
Liposcelis bostrychophila
Long-bodied cellar spider
Lucerne flea
Silverfish
Wandering glider

FINLAND
American cockroach
Bed bug
Brown mayfly
Common harvestman
European marsh crane fly
German cockroach
Great water beetle
Greenhouse camel cricket
Gypsy moth
Hair follicle mite
Honeybee
Human head/body louse
Indian mealmoth
Liposcelis bostrychophila
Long-bodied cellar spider
Lucerne flea
Petrobius brevistylis
Schummel's inocelliid
  snakefly
Silverfish
Slender pigeon louse
Triaenodes bicolor
Velvet ant
Zebra jumping spider

FRANCE
American cockroach
Antlion
Bed bug
Book scorpion
Brown mayfly
Brownbanded cockroach
Common harvestman

Death's head hawk moth
Devil's coach-horse
European earwig
European mantid
European marsh crane fly
European stag beetle
Flat-backed millipede
German cockroach
Great water beetle
Greenhouse camel cricket
Greenhouse whitefly
Gypsy moth
Hair follicle mite
Honeybee
House centipede
Human head/body louse
Indian mealmoth
Large blue
Liposcelis bostrychophila
Long-bodied cellar spider
Long-winged conehead
Lucerne flea
Mediterranean fruitfly
Oriental cockroach
Pea aphid
Petrobius brevistylis
Pill millipede
Sacred scarab
Silverfish
Slender pigeon louse
Spoonwing lacewing
Triaenodes bicolor
Trissolcus basalis
Velvet ant
Western flower thrips
Yellow fever mosquito
Zebra jumping spider

FRENCH GUIANA
American cockroach
Bed bug
Black-headed nasute termite
Blue morpho
Brownbanded cockroach
Chigoe
German cockroach

Giant water bug
Greenhouse camel cricket
Greenhouse whitefly
Hair follicle mite
Honeybee
Human head/body louse
Indian mealmoth
Linnaeus's snapping termite
Liposcelis bostrychophila
Long-bodied cellar spider
Lucerne flea
Madeira cockroach
Mediterranean fruitfly
Pea aphid
Silverfish
Tarantula hawk
Wandering glider
Western flower thrips

GABON
American cockroach
Bed bug
Brownbanded cockroach
Chigoe
Death's head hawk moth
Emperor scorpion
German cockroach
Greenhouse camel cricket
Greenhouse whitefly
Hair follicle mite
Honeybee
Human head/body louse
Indian mealmoth
Liposcelis bostrychophila
Long-bodied cellar spider
Lucerne flea
Madeira cockroach
Silverfish
Tsetse fly
Variegated grasshopper
Wandering glider
Yellow fever mosquito

GAMBIA
American cockroach
Bed bug

Brownbanded cockroach
Chigoe
Death's head hawk moth
Emperor scorpion
German cockroach
Greenhouse camel cricket
Hair follicle mite
Honeybee
Human head/body louse
Indian mealmoth
Liposcelis bostrychophila
Long-bodied cellar spider
Lucerne flea
Madeira cockroach
Oriental cockroach
Silverfish
Slender pigeon louse
Tsetse fly
Wandering glider
Yellow fever mosquito

GEORGIA
American cockroach
Bed bug
Brown mayfly
Death's head hawk moth
Devil's coach-horse
European mantid
German cockroach
Greenhouse camel cricket
Greenhouse whitefly
Hair follicle mite
Honeybee
Human head/body louse
Indian mealmoth
Liposcelis bostrychophila
Long-bodied cellar spider
Long-winged conehead
Lucerne flea
Pea aphid
Silverfish
Slender pigeon louse
Yellow fever mosquito
Zebra jumping spider

GERMANY
American cockroach
Antlion
Bed bug
Book scorpion
Brown mayfly
Common harvestman
Devil's coach-horse
European earwig
European mantid
European marsh crane fly
European stag beetle
Flat-backed millipede
German cockroach
Great water beetle
Greenhouse camel cricket
Greenhouse whitefly
Gypsy moth
Hair follicle mite
Honeybee
Human head/body louse
Indian mealmoth
Large blue
Liposcelis bostrychophila
Long-bodied cellar spider
Long-winged conehead
Lucerne flea
Oriental cockroach
Pea aphid
Petrobius brevistylis
Pill millipede
Schummel's inocelliid
  snakefly
Silverfish
Slender pigeon louse
Spoonwing lacewing
Triaenodes bicolor
Velvet ant
Western flower thrips
Zebra jumping spider

GHANA
American cockroach
Bed bug
Brownbanded cockroach
Chigoe

Death's head hawk moth
Emperor scorpion
European mantid
German cockroach
Greenhouse camel cricket
Greenhouse whitefly
Hair follicle mite
Honeybee
Human head/body louse
Indian mealmoth
Liposcelis bostrychophila
Long-bodied cellar spider
Long-winged conehead
Lucerne flea
Madeira cockroach
Oriental cockroach
Silverfish
Slender pigeon louse
Tsetse fly
Variegated grasshopper
Wandering glider
Yellow fever mosquito

GREECE
American cockroach
Bed bug
Book scorpion
Brown mayfly
Brownbanded cockroach
Common harvestman
Death's head hawk moth
European earwig
European mantid
European stag beetle
German cockroach
Great water beetle
Greenhouse camel cricket
Greenhouse whitefly
Gypsy moth
Hair follicle mite
Honeybee
House centipede
Human head/body louse
Indian mealmoth
Liposcelis bostrychophila
Long-bodied cellar spider

Long-winged conehead
Lucerne flea
Mediterranean fruitfly
Pea aphid
Sacred scarab
Silverfish
Slender pigeon louse
Spoonwing lacewing
Velvet ant
Western flower thrips
Yellow fever mosquito
Zebra jumping spider

GREENLAND
German cockroach
Greenhouse camel cricket
Hair follicle mite
Human head/body louse
Indian mealmoth
Liposcelis bostrychophila

GRENADA
Bed bug
German cockroach
Greenhouse camel cricket
Hair follicle mite
Honeybee
Human head/body louse
Indian mealmoth
Liposcelis bostrychophila
Long-bodied cellar spider
Lucerne flea
Silverfish
Wandering glider

GUAM
Bed bug
German cockroach
Greenhouse camel cricket
Hair follicle mite
Honeybee
Human head/body louse
Indian mealmoth
Liposcelis bostrychophila
Long-bodied cellar spider

Lucerne flea
Silverfish

GUATEMALA
American cockroach
Bed bug
Black-headed nasute termite
Brownbanded cockroach
Chigoe
Forest giant
German cockroach
Greenhouse camel cricket
Greenhouse whitefly
Hair follicle mite
Hercules beetle
Honeybee
Human head/body louse
Indian mealmoth
Liposcelis bostrychophila
Long-bodied cellar spider
Lucerne flea
Madeira cockroach
Mediterranean fruitfly
Pea aphid
Silverfish
Tailless whip scorpion
Wandering glider
Yellow fever mosquito

GUINEA
American cockroach
Bed bug
Beetle cricket
Brownbanded cockroach
Chigoe
Death's head hawk moth
Emperor scorpion
German cockroach
Greenhouse camel cricket
Greenhouse whitefly
Hair follicle mite
Honeybee
Human head/body louse
Indian mealmoth
Liposcelis bostrychophila

Long-bodied cellar spider
Lucerne flea
Madeira cockroach
Oriental cockroach
Silverfish
Slender pigeon louse
Tsetse fly
Variegated grasshopper
Wandering glider
Yellow fever mosquito

GUINEA-BISSAU
American cockroach
Bed bug
Brownbanded cockroach
Chigoe
Death's head hawk moth
Emperor scorpion
German cockroach
Greenhouse camel cricket
Greenhouse whitefly
Hair follicle mite
Honeybee
Human head/body louse
Indian mealmoth
Liposcelis bostrychophila
Long-bodied cellar spider
Lucerne flea
Madeira cockroach
Oriental cockroach
Silverfish
Slender pigeon louse
Tsetse fly
Variegated grasshopper
Wandering glider
Yellow fever mosquito

GUYANA
American cockroach
Bed bug
Black-headed nasute termite
Blue morpho
Brownbanded cockroach
Chigoe
German cockroach

Giant water bug
Greenhouse camel cricket
Greenhouse whitefly
Hair follicle mite
Honeybee
Human head/body louse
Indian mealmoth
Leaf-cutter ant
Linnaeus's snapping termite
Liposcelis bostrychophila
Long-bodied cellar spider
Lucerne flea
Madeira cockroach
Mediterranean fruitfly
Pea aphid
Silverfish
Tarantula hawk
Wandering glider
Western flower thrips

HAITI
Bed bug
Chigoe
German cockroach
Greenhouse camel cricket
Greenhouse whitefly
Hair follicle mite
Human head/body louse
Indian mealmoth
Liposcelis bostrychophila
Long-bodied cellar spider
Lucerne flea
Madeira cockroach
Mediterranean fruitfly
Pea aphid
Scolopender
Silverfish
Trissolcus basalis
Wandering glider
Yellow fever mosquito

HONDURAS
American cockroach
Bed bug
Black-headed nasute termite

Brownbanded cockroach
Chigoe
Forest giant
German cockroach
Greenhouse camel cricket
Greenhouse whitefly
Hair follicle mite
Hercules beetle
Honeybee
Human head/body louse
Indian mealmoth
Liposcelis bostrychophila
Long-bodied cellar spider
Lucerne flea
Madeira cockroach
Mediterranean fruitfly
Pea aphid
Silverfish
Wandering glider
Yellow fever mosquito

HUNGARY

American cockroach
Bed bug
Book scorpion
Brown mayfly
Common harvestman
Devil's coach-horse
European earwig
European mantid
European stag beetle
German cockroach
Great water beetle
Greenhouse camel cricket
Greenhouse whitefly
Gypsy moth
Hair follicle mite
Honeybee
Human head/body louse
Indian mealmoth
Large blue
Liposcelis bostrychophila
Long-bodied cellar spider
Long-winged conehead
Lucerne flea
Pea aphid

Silverfish
Slender pigeon louse
Spoonwing lacewing
Triaenodes bicolor
Velvet ant
Western flower thrips
Zebra jumping spider

ICELAND

German cockroach
Greenhouse camel cricket
Hair follicle mite
Human head/body louse
Indian mealmoth
Liposcelis bostrychophila
Long-bodied cellar spider
Lucerne flea
Petrobius brevistylis

INDIA

American cockroach
Atlas moth
Bed bug
Brownbanded cockroach
German cockroach
Greenhouse camel cricket
Greenhouse whitefly
Hair follicle mite
Honeybee
Human head/body louse
Indian mealmoth
Indian stick insect
Javan leaf insect
Liposcelis bostrychophila
Long-bodied cellar spider
Lucerne flea
Oriental cockroach
Pea aphid
Saunders embiid
Silkworm
Silverfish
Slender pigeon louse
Wandering glider
Wandering violin mantid
Western flower thrips
Yellow fever mosquito

INDIAN OCEAN

Colossendeis megalonyx
Sea skater

INDONESIA

Atlas moth
Bed bug
Cyrtodiopsis dalmanni
Dead-leaf mantid
European earwig
European mantid
German cockroach
Greenhouse camel cricket
Greenhouse whitefly
Hair follicle mite
Honeybee
Human head/body louse
Indian mealmoth
Javan leaf insect
Liposcelis bostrychophila
Long-bodied cellar spider
Lucerne flea
Orchid mantid
Pea aphid
Saunders embiid
Scolopender
Silverfish
Stalk-eyed fly
Wandering glider

IRAN

American cockroach
Bed bug
Brownbanded cockroach
Death's head hawk moth
German cockroach
Greenhouse camel cricket
Greenhouse whitefly
Hair follicle mite
Honeybee
Human head/body louse
Indian mealmoth
Liposcelis bostrychophila
Long-bodied cellar spider
Lucerne flea
Silverfish

Slender pigeon louse
Wandering glider
Yellow fever mosquito

IRAQ
Bed bug
Brownbanded cockroach
Camel spider
Death's head hawk moth
German cockroach
Greenhouse camel cricket
Greenhouse whitefly
Hair follicle mite
Honeybee
Human head/body louse
Indian mealmoth
Liposcelis bostrychophila
Long-bodied cellar spider
Lucerne flea
Mediterranean fruitfly
Pea aphid
Sacred scarab
Silverfish
Slender pigeon louse
Wandering glider
Yellow fever mosquito

IRELAND
American cockroach
Antlion
Bed bug
Book scorpion
Common harvestman
Devil's coach-horse
European earwig
European marsh crane fly
Flat-backed millipede
German cockroach
Great water beetle
Greenhouse camel cricket
Greenhouse whitefly
Gypsy moth
Hair follicle mite
Honeybee
Human head/body louse

Indian mealmoth
Large blue
Liposcelis bostrychophila
Long-bodied cellar spider
Lucerne flea
Oriental cockroach
Petrobius brevistylis
Silverfish
Slender pigeon louse
Spoonwing lacewing
Triaenodes bicolor
Zebra jumping spider

ISRAEL
American cockroach
Bed bug
Brownbanded cockroach
Camel spider
German cockroach
Greenhouse camel cricket
Greenhouse whitefly
Hair follicle mite
Honeybee
Human head/body louse
Indian mealmoth
Liposcelis bostrychophila
Long-bodied cellar spider
Long-winged conehead
Lucerne flea
Mediterranean fruitfly
Oriental cockroach
Sacred scarab
Silverfish
Slender pigeon louse
Wandering glider
Yellow fever mosquito

ITALY
American cockroach
Antlion
Bed bug
Book scorpion
Brown mayfly
Brownbanded cockroach
Common harvestman

Death's head hawk moth
Devil's coach-horse
European earwig
European mantid
European stag beetle
Flat-backed millipede
German cockroach
Great water beetle
Greenhouse camel cricket
Greenhouse whitefly
Gypsy moth
Hair follicle mite
Honeybee
House centipede
Human head/body louse
Indian mealmoth
Large blue
Liposcelis bostrychophila
Long-bodied cellar spider
Long-winged conehead
Lucerne flea
Mediterranean fruitfly
Pea aphid
Sacred scarab
Silverfish
Slender pigeon louse
Spoonwing lacewing
Triaenodes bicolor
Trissolcus basalis
Velvet ant
Western flower thrips
Yellow fever mosquito
Zebra jumping spider

IVORY COAST
American cockroach
Bed bug
Brownbanded cockroach
Chigoe
Death's head hawk moth
Emperor scorpion
German cockroach
Greenhouse camel cricket
Greenhouse whitefly
Hair follicle mite

Honeybee
Human head/body louse
Indian mealmoth
Liposcelis bostrychophila
Long-bodied cellar spider
Long-winged conehead
Lucerne flea
Madeira cockroach
Oriental cockroach
Silverfish
Slender pigeon louse
Trissolcus basalis
Tsetse fly
Variegated grasshopper
Wandering glider
Yellow fever mosquito

JAMAICA
Bed bug
Chigoe
German cockroach
Greenhouse camel cricket
Greenhouse whitefly
Hair follicle mite
Human head/body louse
Indian mealmoth
Liposcelis bostrychophila
Long-bodied cellar spider
Lucerne flea
Madeira cockroach
Mediterranean fruitfly
Pea aphid
Silverfish
Wandering glider
Yellow fever mosquito

JAPAN
American cockroach
Bed bug
Chinese mantid
European mantid
German cockroach
Greenhouse camel cricket
Greenhouse whitefly

Gypsy moth
Hair follicle mite
Human head/body louse
Indian mealmoth
Liposcelis bostrychophila
Long-bodied cellar spider
Lucerne flea
Pea aphid
Silkworm
Silverfish
Sinetomon yoroi
Wandering glider

JORDAN
American cockroach
Bed bug
Brownbanded cockroach
Camel spider
German cockroach
Greenhouse camel cricket
Greenhouse whitefly
Hair follicle mite
Honeybee
Human head/body louse
Indian mealmoth
Liposcelis bostrychophila
Long-bodied cellar spider
Lucerne flea
Mediterranean fruitfly
Sacred scarab
Scolopender
Silverfish
Slender pigeon louse
Wandering glider
Yellow fever mosquito

KAZAKHSTAN
Bed bug
Brown mayfly
Common harvestman
European mantid
German cockroach
Greenhouse camel cricket
Hair follicle mite
Honeybee

Human head/body louse
Indian mealmoth
Large blue
Liposcelis bostrychophila
Long-bodied cellar spider
Lucerne flea
Silverfish
Slender pigeon louse
Zebra jumping spider

KENYA
American cockroach
Bed bug
Brownbanded cockroach
Chigoe
Death's head hawk moth
European earwig
European mantid
German cockroach
Greenhouse camel cricket
Greenhouse whitefly
Hair follicle mite
Honeybee
Human head/body louse
Indian mealmoth
Liposcelis bostrychophila
Long-bodied cellar spider
Lucerne flea
Saunders embiid
Scolopender
Silverfish
Slender pigeon louse
Trissolcus basalis
Wandering glider
Yellow fever mosquito

KIRIBATI
Bed bug
German cockroach
Greenhouse camel cricket
Hair follicle mite
Honeybee
Human head/body louse
Indian mealmoth
Liposcelis bostrychophila
Long-bodied cellar spider

Lucerne flea
Silverfish
Wandering glider

KUWAIT
Bed bug
Camel spider
German cockroach
Greenhouse camel cricket
Hair follicle mite
Honeybee
Human head/body louse
Indian mealmoth
Liposcelis bostrychophila
Long-bodied cellar spider
Lucerne flea
Silverfish
Slender pigeon louse
Wandering glider
Yellow fever mosquito

KYRGYZSTAN
Atlas moth
Bed bug
Brownbanded cockroach
European mantid
German cockroach
Greenhouse camel cricket
Hair follicle mite
Honeybee
Human head/body louse
Indian mealmoth
Large blue
Liposcelis bostrychophila
Long-bodied cellar spider
Lucerne flea
Silverfish
Wandering glider
Western flower thrips
Zebra jumping spider

LAOS
American cockroach
Atlas moth

Bed bug
Brownbanded cockroach
German cockroach
Greenhouse camel cricket
Greenhouse whitefly
Hair follicle mite
Honeybee
Human head/body louse
Indian mealmoth
Liposcelis bostrychophila
Long-bodied cellar spider
Lucerne flea
Oriental cockroach
Pea aphid
Scolopender
Silverfish
Wandering glider
Yellow fever mosquito

LATVIA
American cockroach
Bed bug
Book scorpion
Brown mayfly
Common harvestman
European earwig
European marsh crane fly
German cockroach
Great water beetle
Greenhouse camel cricket
Gypsy moth
Hair follicle mite
Honeybee
Human head/body louse
Indian mealmoth
Large blue
Liposcelis bostrychophila
Long-bodied cellar spider
Long-winged conehead
Lucerne flea
Oriental cockroach
Petrobius brevistylis
Schummel's inocelliid
  snakefly
Silverfish
Slender pigeon louse

Spoonwing lacewing
Triaenodes bicolor
Velvet ant
Western flower thrips
Zebra jumping spider

LEBANON
American cockroach
Bed bug
Brownbanded cockroach
Camel spider
German cockroach
Greenhouse camel cricket
Greenhouse whitefly
Hair follicle mite
Honeybee
Human head/body louse
Indian mealmoth
Liposcelis bostrychophila
Long-bodied cellar spider
Long-winged conehead
Lucerne flea
Mediterranean fruitfly
Sacred scarab
Silverfish
Slender pigeon louse
Wandering glider
Yellow fever mosquito

LESOTHO
American cockroach
Bed bug
Brownbanded cockroach
Death's head hawk moth
European mantid
German cockroach
Greenhouse camel cricket
Greenhouse whitefly
Hair follicle mite
Honeybee
House centipede
Human head/body louse
Indian mealmoth
Liposcelis bostrychophila
Long-bodied cellar spider

Lucerne flea
Oriental cockroach
Silverfish
Wandering glider
Western flower thrips
Yellow fever mosquito

LESSER ANTILLES
Bed bug
German cockroach
Greenhouse camel cricket
Hair follicle mite
Honeybee
Human head/body louse
Indian mealmoth
Liposcelis bostrychophila
Long-bodied cellar spider
Lucerne flea
Silverfish

LIBERIA
American cockroach
Bed bug
Brownbanded cockroach
Chigoe
Death's head hawk moth
Emperor scorpion
European mantid
German cockroach
Greenhouse camel cricket
Greenhouse whitefly
Hair follicle mite
Honeybee
Human head/body louse
Indian mealmoth
Liposcelis bostrychophila
Long-bodied cellar spider
Long-winged conehead
Lucerne flea
Madeira cockroach
Scolopender
Silverfish
Slender pigeon louse
Tsetse fly
Variegated grasshopper

Wandering glider
Yellow fever mosquito

LIBYA
American cockroach
Bed bug
Brownbanded cockroach
Camel spider
Death's head hawk moth
European earwig
German cockroach
Greenhouse camel cricket
Greenhouse whitefly
Gypsy moth
Hair follicle mite
Honeybee
House centipede
Human head/body louse
Indian mealmoth
Liposcelis bostrychophila
Long-bodied cellar spider
Long-winged conehead
Lucerne flea
Mediterranean fruitfly
Sacred scarab
Silverfish
Slender pigeon louse
Wandering glider
Yellow fever mosquito

LIECHTENSTEIN
American cockroach
Antlion
Bed bug
Book scorpion
Brown mayfly
Common harvestman
Devil's coach-horse
European earwig
European marsh crane fly
European stag beetle
Flat-backed millipede
German cockroach
Great water beetle
Greenhouse camel cricket

Gypsy moth
Hair follicle mite
Honeybee
House centipede
Human head/body louse
Indian mealmoth
Large blue
Liposcelis bostrychophila
Long-bodied cellar spider
Long-winged conehead
Lucerne flea
Pill millipede
Silverfish
Slender pigeon louse
Spoonwing lacewing
Triaenodes bicolor
Velvet ant
Western flower thrips
Zebra jumping spider

LITHUANIA
American cockroach
Bed bug
Book scorpion
Brown mayfly
Common harvestman
European earwig
European marsh crane fly
German cockroach
Great water beetle
Greenhouse camel cricket
Gypsy moth
Hair follicle mite
Honeybee
Human head/body louse
Indian mealmoth
Large blue
Liposcelis bostrychophila
Long-bodied cellar spider
Long-winged conehead
Lucerne flea
Oriental cockroach
Petrobius brevistylis
Schummel's inocelliid
  snakefly
Silverfish

Slender pigeon louse
Spoonwing lacewing
Triaenodes bicolor
Velvet ant
Western flower thrips
Zebra jumping spider

LUXEMBOURG

American cockroach
Antlion
Bed bug
Book scorpion
Brown mayfly
Common harvestman
Devil's coach-horse
European earwig
European stag beetle
Flat-backed millipede
German cockroach
Great water beetle
Greenhouse camel cricket
Gypsy moth
Hair follicle mite
Honeybee
Human head/body louse
Indian mealmoth
Large blue
Liposcelis bostrychophila
Long-bodied cellar spider
Long-winged conehead
Lucerne flea
Pill millipede
Silverfish
Slender pigeon louse
Spoonwing lacewing
Triaenodes bicolor
Velvet ant
Western flower thrips
Zebra jumping spider

MACEDONIA

American cockroach
Bed bug
Book scorpion
Brown mayfly
Brownbanded cockroach

Common harvestman
Death's head hawk moth
Devil's coach-horse
European earwig
European mantid
European stag beetle
German cockroach
Great water beetle
Greenhouse camel cricket
Greenhouse whitefly
Gypsy moth
Hair follicle mite
Honeybee
House centipede
Human head/body louse
Indian mealmoth
Liposcelis bostrychophila
Long-bodied cellar spider
Long-winged conehead
Lucerne flea
Mediterranean fruitfly
Pea aphid
Sacred scarab
Silverfish
Slender pigeon louse
Spoonwing lacewing
Triaenodes bicolor
Velvet ant
Western flower thrips
Yellow fever mosquito
Zebra jumping spider

MADAGASCAR

Chigoe
Death's head hawk moth
German cockroach
Giraffe-necked weevil
Greenhouse camel cricket
Greenhouse whitefly
Hair follicle mite
Human head/body louse
Indian mealmoth
Indian stick insect
Javan leaf insect
Liposcelis bostrychophila
Lucerne flea

Saunders embiid
Scolopender
Silverfish
Wandering glider
Yellow fever mosquito

MALAWI

American cockroach
Bed bug
Brownbanded cockroach
Chigoe
Death's head hawk moth
European mantid
German cockroach
Greenhouse camel cricket
Greenhouse whitefly
Hair follicle mite
Honeybee
Human head/body louse
Indian mealmoth
Liposcelis bostrychophila
Long-bodied cellar spider
Lucerne flea
Silverfish
Wandering glider
Yellow fever mosquito

MALAYSIA

American cockroach
Atlas moth
Bed bug
Black macrotermes
Cyrtodiopsis dalmanni
Dead-leaf mantid
European earwig
German cockroach
Greenhouse camel cricket
Greenhouse whitefly
Hair follicle mite
Honeybee
Human head/body louse
Indian mealmoth
Javan leaf insect
Jungle nymph
Liposcelis bostrychophila
Long-bodied cellar spider

Lucerne flea
Orchid mantid
Pea aphid
Silverfish
Stalk-eyed fly
Wandering glider
Yellow fever mosquito

MALDIVES
Bed bug
German cockroach
Greenhouse camel cricket
Hair follicle mite
Honeybee
Human head/body louse
Indian mealmoth
Liposcelis bostrychophila
Long-bodied cellar spider
Lucerne flea
Silverfish
Wandering glider

MALI
American cockroach
Bed bug
Brownbanded cockroach
Chigoe
Death's head hawk moth
Emperor scorpion
German cockroach
Greenhouse camel cricket
Hair follicle mite
Honeybee
Human head/body louse
Indian mealmoth
Liposcelis bostrychophila
Long-bodied cellar spider
Lucerne flea
Mediterranean fruitfly
Silverfish
Slender pigeon louse
Tsetse fly
Variegated grasshopper
Wandering glider
Yellow fever mosquito

MALTA
Bed bug
German cockroach
Greenhouse camel cricket
Gypsy moth
Hair follicle mite
Honeybee
Human head/body louse
Indian mealmoth
Large blue
Liposcelis bostrychophila
Long-bodied cellar spider
Lucerne flea
Silverfish
Velvet ant
Western flower thrips

MARIANA ISLANDS
Bed bug
German cockroach
Greenhouse camel cricket
Hair follicle mite
Honeybee
Human head/body louse
Indian mealmoth
Liposcelis bostrychophila
Long-bodied cellar spider
Lucerne flea
Silverfish

MARSHALL ISLANDS
Bed bug
German cockroach
Greenhouse camel cricket
Hair follicle mite
Honeybee
Human head/body louse
Indian mealmoth
Liposcelis bostrychophila
Long-bodied cellar spider
Lucerne flea
Silverfish
Wandering glider

MAURITANIA
Bed bug
Chigoe
Death's head hawk moth
German cockroach
Greenhouse camel cricket
Hair follicle mite
Honeybee
Human head/body louse
Indian mealmoth
Liposcelis bostrychophila
Long-bodied cellar spider
Lucerne flea
Mediterranean fruitfly
Sacred scarab
Silverfish
Slender pigeon louse
Tsetse fly
Wandering glider
Western flower thrips
Yellow fever mosquito

MAURITIUS
Bed bug
Death's head hawk moth
German cockroach
Greenhouse camel cricket
Hair follicle mite
Honeybee
Human head/body louse
Indian mealmoth
Javan leaf insect
Liposcelis bostrychophila
Long-bodied cellar spider
Lucerne flea
Scolopender
Silverfish
Wandering glider
Yellow fever mosquito

MEXICO
American cockroach
Bed bug
Black-headed nasute termite
Brownbanded cockroach

Chigoe
Common harvestman
European earwig
Forest giant
German cockroach
Giant whip scorpion
Greenhouse camel cricket
Greenhouse whitefly
Hair follicle mite
Halictophagus naulti
Honeybee
Horseshoe crab
Human head/body louse
Indian mealmoth
Liposcelis bostrychophila
Long-bodied cellar spider
Lucerne flea
Madeira cockroach
Oriental cockroach
Panorpa nuptialis
Pea aphid
Rocky Mountain wood tick
Saunders embiid
Scolopender
Silverfish
Tarantula hawk
Wandering glider
Western flower thrips
Wide-headed rottenwood termite
Yellow fever mosquito
Zebra jumping spider

MICRONESIA
Bed bug
German cockroach
Greenhouse camel cricket
Hair follicle mite
Honeybee
Human head/body louse
Indian mealmoth
Liposcelis bostrychophila
Long-bodied cellar spider
Lucerne flea
Silverfish
Wandering glider

MOLDOVA
American cockroach
Bed bug
Book scorpion
Brown mayfly
Common harvestman
Death's head hawk moth
Devil's coach-horse
European earwig
European stag beetle
German cockroach
Great water beetle
Greenhouse camel cricket
Greenhouse whitefly
Gypsy moth
Hair follicle mite
Honeybee
Human head/body louse
Indian mealmoth
Large blue
Liposcelis bostrychophila
Long-bodied cellar spider
Long-winged conehead
Lucerne flea
Pea aphid
Silverfish
Slender pigeon louse
Spoonwing lacewing
Triaenodes bicolor
Velvet ant
Western flower thrips
Zebra jumping spider

MONACO
American cockroach
Antlion
Bed bug
Book scorpion
Brown mayfly
Brownbanded cockroach
Death's head hawk moth
Devil's coach-horse
European earwig
European mantid
European stag beetle
Flat-backed millipede

German cockroach
Great water beetle
Greenhouse camel cricket
Greenhouse whitefly
Gypsy moth
Hair follicle mite
Honeybee
House centipede
Human head/body louse
Indian mealmoth
Large blue
Liposcelis bostrychophila
Long-bodied cellar spider
Long-winged conehead
Lucerne flea
Mediterranean fruitfly
Pea aphid
Silverfish
Slender pigeon louse
Spoonwing lacewing
Triaenodes bicolor
Velvet ant
Western flower thrips
Yellow fever mosquito

MONGOLIA
Bed bug
Chinese mantid
Common harvestman
European mantid
German cockroach
Greenhouse camel cricket
Hair follicle mite
Honeybee
Human head/body louse
Indian mealmoth
Large blue
Liposcelis bostrychophila
Long-bodied cellar spider
Lucerne flea
Sheep and goat flea
Silverfish
Wandering glider
Western flower thrips
Zebra jumping spider

MOROCCO

American cockroach
Bed bug
Brownbanded cockroach
Chigoe
Death's head hawk moth
Devil's coach-horse
European earwig
European mantid
German cockroach
Greenhouse camel cricket
Greenhouse whitefly
Gypsy moth
Hair follicle mite
Honeybee
House centipede
Human head/body louse
Indian mealmoth
Liposcelis bostrychophila
Long-bodied cellar spider
Long-winged conehead
Lucerne flea
Mediterranean fruitfly
Sacred scarab
Scolopender
Silverfish
Slender pigeon louse
Spoonwing lacewing
Trissolcus basalis
Velvet ant
Wandering glider
Western flower thrips
Yellow fever mosquito

MOZAMBIQUE

American cockroach
Bed bug
Brownbanded cockroach
Chigoe
Death's head hawk moth
European mantid
German cockroach
Greenhouse camel cricket
Greenhouse whitefly
Hair follicle mite
Honeybee

Human head/body louse
Indian mealmoth
Liposcelis bostrychophila
Long-bodied cellar spider
Lucerne flea
Oriental cockroach
Saunders embiid
Scolopender
Silverfish *Trissolcus basalis*
Wandering glider
Western flower thrips
Yellow fever mosquito

MYANMAR

American cockroach
Atlas moth
Bed bug
Brownbanded cockroach
Dead-leaf mantid
European mantid
German cockroach
Greenhouse camel cricket
Greenhouse whitefly
Hair follicle mite
Honeybee
Human head/body louse
Indian mealmoth
Liposcelis bostrychophila
Long-bodied cellar spider
Lucerne flea
Orchid mantid
Oriental cockroach
Pea aphid
Silverfish
Wandering glider
Wandering violin mantid
Yellow fever mosquito

NAMIBIA

American cockroach
Bed bug
Brownbanded cockroach
Death's head hawk moth
European mantid
German cockroach
Gladiator

Greenhouse camel cricket
Greenhouse whitefly
Hair follicle mite
Honeybee
Human head/body louse
Indian mealmoth
Liposcelis bostrychophila
Long-bodied cellar spider
Lucerne flea
Scolopender
Silverfish
Wandering glider
Western flower thrips
Yellow fever mosquito

NAURU

Bed bug
German cockroach
Greenhouse camel cricket
Hair follicle mite
Honeybee
Human head/body louse
Indian mealmoth
Liposcelis bostrychophila
Long-bodied cellar spider
Lucerne flea
Silverfish
Wandering glider

NEPAL

American cockroach
Atlas moth
Bed bug
Brownbanded cockroach
German cockroach
Greenhouse camel cricket
Greenhouse whitefly
Hair follicle mite
Honeybee
Human head/body louse
Indian mealmoth
Liposcelis bostrychophila
Long-bodied cellar spider
Lucerne flea
Pea aphid
Scolopender

Silkworm
Silverfish
Slender pigeon louse
Wandering glider
Western flower thrips
Yellow fever mosquito

NETHERLANDS
American cockroach
Antlion
Bed bug
Book scorpion
Brown mayfly
Common harvestman
Devil's coach-horse
European earwig
European marsh crane fly
European stag beetle
Flat-backed millipede
German cockroach
Great water beetle
Greenhouse camel cricket
Gypsy moth
Hair follicle mite
Honeybee
Human head/body louse
Indian mealmoth
Large blue
Liposcelis bostrychophila
Long-bodied cellar spider
Long-winged conehead
Lucerne flea
Oriental cockroach
Petrobius brevistylis
Pill millipede
Schummel's inocelliid
  snakefly
Scolopender
Silverfish
Slender pigeon louse
Spoonwing lacewing
Triaenodes bicolor
Velvet ant
Western flower thrips
Zebra jumping spider

NEW ZEALAND
Colossendeis megalonyx
European earwig
German cockroach
Greenhouse camel cricket
Greenhouse whitefly
Hair follicle mite
Human head/body louse
Indian mealmoth
Liposcelis bostrychophila
Long-bodied cellar spider
Lucerne flea
Megarhyssa nortoni
Pea aphid
Silverfish
Wandering glider
Western flower thrips

NICARAGUA
American cockroach
Bed bug
Black-headed nasute termite
Brownbanded cockroach
Chigoe
Forest giant
German cockroach
Greenhouse camel cricket
Greenhouse whitefly
Hair follicle mite
Hercules beetle
Honeybee
Human head/body louse
Indian mealmoth
Liposcelis bostrychophila
Long-bodied cellar spider
Lucerne flea
Madeira cockroach
Mediterranean fruitfly
Pea aphid
Scolopender
Silverfish
Yellow fever mosquito

NIGER
American cockroach
Bed bug

Brownbanded cockroach
Camel spider
Chigoe
Death's head hawk moth
Emperor scorpion
German cockroach
Greenhouse camel cricket
Hair follicle mite
Honeybee
Human head/body louse
Indian mealmoth
Liposcelis bostrychophila
Long-bodied cellar spider
Lucerne flea
Silverfish
Slender pigeon louse
Tsetse fly
Variegated grasshopper
Wandering glider
Yellow fever mosquito

NIGERIA
American cockroach
Bed bug
Brownbanded cockroach
Chigoe
Death's head hawk moth
Emperor scorpion
European mantid
German cockroach
Greenhouse camel cricket
Greenhouse whitefly
Hair follicle mite
Honeybee
Human head/body louse
Indian mealmoth
Liposcelis bostrychophila
Long-bodied cellar spider
Long-winged conehead
Lucerne flea
Madeira cockroach
Silverfish
Slender pigeon louse
Tsetse fly
Variegated grasshopper

Wandering glider
Yellow fever mosquito

NORTH KOREA
American cockroach
Bed bug
Chinese mantid
Common harvestman
European mantid
German cockroach
Greenhouse camel cricket
Hair follicle mite
Honeybee
Human head/body louse
Indian mealmoth
Large blue
Liposcelis bostrychophila
Long-bodied cellar spider
Lucerne flea
Pea aphid
Silkworm
Silverfish
Wandering glider
Western flower thrips
Zebra jumping spider

NORWAY
American cockroach
Bed bug
Brown mayfly
Common harvestman
European marsh crane fly
Flat-backed millipede
German cockroach
Great water beetle
Greenhouse camel cricket
Gypsy moth
Hair follicle mite
Honeybee
Human head/body louse
Indian mealmoth
Liposcelis bostrychophila
Long-bodied cellar spider
Lucerne flea
Oriental cockroach

Petrobius brevistylis
Pill millipede
Silverfish
Slender pigeon louse
Spoonwing lacewing
Triaenodes bicolor
Velvet ant
Zebra jumping spider

OMAN
Bed bug
Camel spider
German cockroach
Greenhouse camel cricket
Hair follicle mite
Honeybee
Human head/body louse
Indian mealmoth
Liposcelis bostrychophila
Long-bodied cellar spider
Lucerne flea
Scolopender
Silverfish
Slender pigeon louse
Wandering glider
Yellow fever mosquito

PACIFIC OCEAN
Colossendeis megalonyx
Sea skater

PAKISTAN
American cockroach
Atlas moth
Bed bug
Brownbanded cockroach
German cockroach
Greenhouse camel cricket
Greenhouse whitefly
Hair follicle mite
Honeybee
Human head/body louse
Indian mealmoth
Liposcelis bostrychophila

Long-bodied cellar spider
Lucerne flea
Pea aphid
Silkworm
Silverfish
Slender pigeon louse
Wandering glider
Western flower thrips
Yellow fever mosquito

PALAU
Bed bug
German cockroach
Greenhouse camel cricket
Hair follicle mite
Honeybee
Human head/body louse
Indian mealmoth
Liposcelis bostrychophila
Long-bodied cellar spider
Lucerne flea
Silverfish
Wandering glider

PANAMA
American cockroach
Bed bug
Black-headed nasute termite
Brownbanded cockroach
Chigoe
Dead leaf mimetica
Forest giant
German cockroach
Greenhouse camel cricket
Greenhouse whitefly
Hair follicle mite
Hercules beetle
Honeybee
Human head/body louse
Indian mealmoth
Leaf-cutter ant
Liposcelis bostrychophila
Long-bodied cellar spider
Lucerne flea
Madeira cockroach

Mediterranean fruitfly
Pea aphid
Silverfish
Tarantula hawk
Wandering glider
Yellow fever mosquito

PAPUA NEW GUINEA
Bed bug
Cyrtodiopsis dalmanni
German cockroach
Greenhouse camel cricket
Greenhouse whitefly
Hair follicle mite
Honeybee
Human head/body louse
Indian mealmoth
Liposcelis bostrychophila
Long-bodied cellar spider
Lucerne flea
Mantid lacewing
Pea aphid
Silverfish
Stalk-eyed fly
Wandering glider
Yellow fever mosquito

PARAGUAY
American cockroach
Backswimmer
Bed bug
Blue morpho
Brownbanded cockroach
Chigoe
German cockroach
Greenhouse camel cricket
Greenhouse whitefly
Hair follicle mite
Honeybee
Human head/body louse
Indian mealmoth
Leaf-cutter ant
Liposcelis bostrychophila
Long-bodied cellar spider
Lucerne flea

Mediterranean fruitfly
Pea aphid
Silverfish
Wandering glider

PERU
American cockroach
Bed bug
Black-headed nasute termite
Blue morpho
Brownbanded cockroach
Chigoe
Forest giant
German cockroach
Greenhouse camel cricket
Greenhouse whitefly
Hair follicle mite
Honeybee
Human head/body louse
Indian mealmoth
Leaf-cutter ant
Liposcelis bostrychophila
Long-bodied cellar spider
Lucerne flea
Mediterranean fruitfly
Pea aphid
Scolopender
Silverfish
Tarantula hawk
Wandering glider
Yellow fever mosquito

PHILIPPINES
American cockroach
Atlas moth
Bed bug
European earwig
German cockroach
Greenhouse camel cricket
Greenhouse whitefly
Hair follicle mite
Honeybee
Human head/body louse
Indian mealmoth
Liposcelis bostrychophila

Long-bodied cellar spider
Lucerne flea
Oriental cockroach
Pea aphid
Scolopender
Silverfish
Wandering glider

POLAND
American cockroach
Bed bug
Book scorpion
Brown mayfly
Common harvestman
Devil's coach-horse
European earwig
European marsh crane fly
European stag beetle
German cockroach
Great water beetle
Greenhouse camel cricket
Greenhouse whitefly
Gypsy moth
Hair follicle mite
Honeybee
Human head/body louse
Indian mealmoth
Large blue
Liposcelis bostrychophila
Long-bodied cellar spider
Long-winged conehead
Lucerne flea
Oriental cockroach
Pea aphid
Petrobius brevistylis
Pill millipede
Schummel's inocelliid
  snakefly
Silverfish
Slender pigeon louse
Spoonwing lacewing
Triaenodes bicolor
Velvet ant
Western flower thrips
Zebra jumping spider

PORTUGAL

American cockroach
Antlion
Bed bug
Book scorpion
Brown mayfly
Brownbanded cockroach
Common harvestman
Death's head hawk moth
Devil's coach-horse
European earwig
European mantid
German cockroach
Greenhouse camel cricket
Greenhouse whitefly
Gypsy moth
Hair follicle mite
Honeybee
House centipede
Human head/body louse
Indian mealmoth
Large blue
Liposcelis bostrychophila
Long-bodied cellar spider
Long-winged conehead
Lucerne flea
Mediterranean fruitfly
Oriental cockroach
Pea aphid
Sacred scarab
Silverfish
Slender pigeon louse
Spoonwing lacewing
Trissolcus basalis
Velvet ant
Western flower thrips
Yellow fever mosquito
Zebra jumping spider

PUERTO RICO

Bed bug
German cockroach
Greenhouse camel cricket
Hair follicle mite
Honeybee
Human head/body louse
Indian mealmoth
Liposcelis bostrychophila
Long-bodied cellar spider
Lucerne flea
Silverfish
Wandering glider

QATAR

Bed bug
Camel spider
German cockroach
Greenhouse camel cricket
Hair follicle mite
Honeybee
Human head/body louse
Indian mealmoth
Liposcelis bostrychophila
Long-bodied cellar spider
Lucerne flea
Silverfish
Slender pigeon louse
Wandering glider
Yellow fever mosquito

REPUBLIC OF THE CONGO

American cockroach
Bed bug
Brownbanded cockroach
Chigoe
Death's head hawk moth
Emperor scorpion
German cockroach
Greenhouse camel cricket
Greenhouse whitefly
Hair follicle mite
Honeybee
Human head/body louse
Indian mealmoth
Liposcelis bostrychophila
Long-bodied cellar spider
Lucerne flea
Madeira cockroach
Silverfish
Tsetse fly

Variegated grasshopper
Wandering glider
Yellow fever mosquito

ROMANIA

American cockroach
Bed bug
Book scorpion
Brown mayfly
Common harvestman
Death's head hawk moth
Devil's coach-horse
European earwig
European mantid
European stag beetle
German cockroach
Great water beetle
Greenhouse camel cricket
Greenhouse whitefly
Gypsy moth
Hair follicle mite
Honeybee
Human head/body louse
Indian mealmoth
Large blue
Liposcelis bostrychophila
Long-bodied cellar spider
Long-winged conehead
Lucerne flea
Pea aphid
Silverfish
Slender pigeon louse
Spoonwing lacewing
Triaenodes bicolor
Velvet ant
Western flower thrips
Zebra jumping spider

RUSSIA

American cockroach
Bed bug
Brown mayfly
Common harvestman
Death's head hawk moth
Devil's coach-horse

European earwig
European mantid
European marsh crane fly
European stag beetle
German cockroach
Great water beetle
Greenhouse camel cricket
Greenhouse whitefly
Gypsy moth
Hair follicle mite
Honeybee
Human head/body louse
Indian mealmoth
Large blue
Liposcelis bostrychophila
Long-bodied cellar spider
Long-winged conehead
Lucerne flea
Pea aphid
Sacred scarab
Schummel's inocelliid
  snakefly
Sheep and goat flea
Silverfish
Slender pigeon louse
Triaenodes bicolor
Velvet ant
Western flower thrips
Zebra jumping spider

RWANDA
American cockroach
Bed bug
Brownbanded cockroach
Chigoe
Death's head hawk moth
European earwig
European mantid
German cockroach
Greenhouse camel cricket
Greenhouse whitefly
Hair follicle mite
Honeybee
Human head/body louse
Indian mealmoth

Liposcelis bostrychophila
Long-bodied cellar spider
Lucerne flea
Silverfish
Slender pigeon louse
Wandering glider
Yellow fever mosquito

ST. KITTS-NEVIS
Bed bug
German cockroach
Greenhouse camel cricket
Hair follicle mite
Honeybee
Human head/body louse
Indian mealmoth
Liposcelis bostrychophila
Long-bodied cellar spider
Lucerne flea
Silverfish
Wandering glider

ST. LUCIA
Bed bug
German cockroach
Greenhouse camel cricket
Hair follicle mite
Honeybee
Human head/body louse
Indian mealmoth
Liposcelis bostrychophila
Long-bodied cellar spider
Lucerne flea
Silverfish
Wandering glider

ST. VINCENT
Bed bug
German cockroach
Greenhouse camel cricket
Hair follicle mite
Honeybee
Human head/body louse
Indian mealmoth
Liposcelis bostrychophila

Long-bodied cellar spider
Lucerne flea
Silverfish
Wandering glider

SAMOA
Bed bug
German cockroach
Greenhouse camel cricket
Hair follicle mite
Honeybee
Human head/body louse
Indian mealmoth
Liposcelis bostrychophila
Long-bodied cellar spider
Lucerne flea
Silverfish
Wandering glider

SAN MARINO
American cockroach
Antlion
Bed bug
Book scorpion
Brown mayfly
Brownbanded cockroach
Common harvestman
Death's head hawk moth
Devil's coach-horse
European earwig
European mantid
European stag beetle
Flat-backed millipede
German cockroach
Great water beetle
Greenhouse camel cricket
Greenhouse whitefly
Gypsy moth
Hair follicle mite
Honeybee
House centipede
Human head/body louse
Indian mealmoth
Large blue
Liposcelis bostrychophila

Long-bodied cellar spider
Long-winged conehead
Lucerne flea
Mediterranean fruitfly
Pea aphid
Sacred scarab
Silverfish
Slender pigeon louse
Spoonwing lacewing
Triaenodes bicolor
Velvet ant
Western flower thrips
Yellow fever mosquito
Zebra jumping spider

SÃO TOMÉ AND PRÍNCIPE
Bed bug
Death's head hawk moth
Emperor scorpion
German cockroach
Greenhouse camel cricket
Hair follicle mite
Honeybee
Human head/body louse
Indian mealmoth
Liposcelis bostrychophila
Long-bodied cellar spider
Lucerne flea
Silverfish
Wandering glider
Yellow fever mosquito

SAUDI ARABIA
Bed bug
Brownbanded cockroach
Camel spider
German cockroach
Greenhouse camel cricket
Hair follicle mite
Honeybee
Human head/body louse
Indian mealmoth
Liposcelis bostrychophila
Long-bodied cellar spider

Lucerne flea
Mediterranean fruitfly
Sacred scarab
Silverfish
Slender pigeon louse
Wandering glider
Yellow fever mosquito

SENEGAL
American cockroach
Bed bug
Brownbanded cockroach
Chigoe
Death's head hawk moth
Devil's coach-horse
Emperor scorpion
German cockroach
Greenhouse camel cricket
Greenhouse whitefly
Hair follicle mite
Honeybee
Human head/body louse
Indian mealmoth
Liposcelis bostrychophila
Long-bodied cellar spider
Lucerne flea
Madeira cockroach
Oriental cockroach
Silverfish
Slender pigeon louse
Tsetse fly
Variegated grasshopper
Wandering glider
Yellow fever mosquito

SERBIA AND MONTENEGRO
American cockroach
Bed bug
Book scorpion
Brown mayfly
Brownbanded cockroach
Common harvestman
Death's head hawk moth
Devil's coach-horse

European earwig
European mantid
European stag beetle
German cockroach
Great water beetle
Greenhouse camel cricket
Greenhouse whitefly
Gypsy moth
Hair follicle mite
Honeybee
House centipede
Human head/body louse
Indian mealmoth
Large blue
Liposcelis bostrychophila
Long-bodied cellar spider
Long-winged conehead
Lucerne flea
Mediterranean fruitfly
Pea aphid
Sacred scarab
Silverfish
Slender pigeon louse
Spoonwing lacewing
Triaenodes bicolor
Velvet ant
Western flower thrips
Yellow fever mosquito
Zebra jumping spider

SEYCHELLES
Bed bug
Death's head hawk moth
German cockroach
Greenhouse camel cricket
Hair follicle mite
Honeybee
Human head/body louse
Indian mealmoth
Javan leaf insect
Liposcelis bostrychophila
Long-bodied cellar spider
Lucerne flea
Scolopender
Silverfish
Wandering glider
Yellow fever mosquito

SIERRA LEONE

American cockroach
Bed bug
Brownbanded cockroach
Chigoe
Death's head hawk moth
Emperor scorpion
European mantid
German cockroach
Greenhouse camel cricket
Greenhouse whitefly
Hair follicle mite
Honeybee
Human head/body louse
Indian mealmoth
Liposcelis bostrychophila
Long-bodied cellar spider
Lucerne flea
Madeira cockroach
Oriental cockroach
Silverfish
Slender pigeon louse
Tsetse fly
Variegated grasshopper
Wandering glider
Yellow fever mosquito

SINGAPORE

American cockroach
Atlas moth
Bed bug
Black macrotermes
Brownbanded cockroach
Cyrtodiopsis dalmanni
Dead-leaf mantid
European earwig
European mantid
German cockroach
Greenhouse camel cricket
Greenhouse whitefly
Hair follicle mite
Honeybee
Human head/body louse
Indian mealmoth
Javan leaf insect

Jungle nymph
Liposcelis bostrychophila
Lucerne flea
Orchid mantid
Silverfish
Stalk-eyed fly
Wandering glider
Yellow fever mosquito

SLOVAKIA

American cockroach
Bed bug
Book scorpion
Brown mayfly
Common harvestman
Devil's coach-horse
European earwig
European mantid
European stag beetle
German cockroach
Great water beetle
Greenhouse camel cricket
Greenhouse whitefly
Gypsy moth
Hair follicle mite
Honeybee
Human head/body louse
Indian mealmoth
Large blue
Liposcelis bostrychophila
Long-bodied cellar spider
Long-winged conehead
Lucerne flea
Pea aphid
Silverfish
Slender pigeon louse
Spoonwing lacewing
Triaenodes bicolor
Velvet ant
Western flower thrips
Zebra jumping spider

SLOVENIA

American cockroach
Bed bug

Book scorpion
Brown mayfly
Brownbanded cockroach
Common harvestman
Death's head hawk moth
Devil's coach-horse
European earwig
European mantid
European stag beetle
Flat-backed millipede
German cockroach
Great water beetle
Greenhouse camel cricket
Greenhouse whitefly
Gypsy moth
Hair follicle mite
Honeybee
House centipede
Human head/body louse
Indian mealmoth
Large blue
Liposcelis bostrychophila
Long-bodied cellar spider
Long-winged conehead
Lucerne flea
Mediterranean fruitfly
Pea aphid
Pill millipede
Silverfish
Slender pigeon louse
Spoonwing lacewing
Triaenodes bicolor
Velvet ant
Western flower thrips
Yellow fever mosquito
Zebra jumping spider

SOLOMON ISLANDS

Bed bug
German cockroach
Greenhouse camel cricket
Hair follicle mite
Honeybee
Human head/body louse
Indian mealmoth
Liposcelis bostrychophila

Long-bodied cellar spider
Lucerne flea
Silverfish
Wandering glider

SOMALIA
Bed bug
Brownbanded cockroach
Chigoe
Death's head hawk moth
European earwig
European mantid
German cockroach
Greenhouse camel cricket
Greenhouse whitefly
Hair follicle mite
Honeybee
Human head/body louse
Indian mealmoth
Liposcelis bostrychophila
Long-bodied cellar spider
Lucerne flea
Saunders embiid
Scolopender
Silverfish
Slender pigeon louse
Wandering glider
Yellow fever mosquito

SOUTH AFRICA
American cockroach
Bed bug
Brownbanded cockroach
Death's head hawk moth
European mantid
German cockroach
Gladiator
Greenhouse camel cricket
Greenhouse whitefly
Hair follicle mite
Honeybee
House centipede
Human head/body louse
Indian mealmoth
Liposcelis bostrychophila

Long-bodied cellar spider
Lucerne flea
Oriental cockroach
Scolopender
Silverfish
Wandering glider
Western flower thrips
Yellow fever mosquito

SOUTH KOREA
American cockroach
Bed bug
Chinese mantid
Common harvestman
German cockroach
Greenhouse camel cricket
Hair follicle mite
Honeybee
Human head/body louse
Indian mealmoth
Liposcelis bostrychophila
Long-bodied cellar spider
Lucerne flea
Pea aphid
Silkworm
Silverfish
Wandering glider
Western flower thrips
Zebra jumping spider

SPAIN
American cockroach
Antlion
Bed bug
Book scorpion
Brown mayfly
Brownbanded cockroach
Common harvestman
Death's head hawk moth
Devil's coach-horse
European earwig
European mantid
European marsh crane fly
European stag beetle
German cockroach

Great water beetle
Greenhouse camel cricket
Greenhouse whitefly
Gypsy moth
Hair follicle mite
Honeybee
House centipede
Human head/body louse
Indian mealmoth
Large blue
Liposcelis bostrychophila
Long-bodied cellar spider
Long-winged conehead
Lucerne flea
Mediterranean fruitfly
Oriental cockroach
Pea aphid
Sacred scarab
Silverfish
Slender pigeon louse
Spoonwing lacewing
Velvet ant
Western flower thrips
Yellow fever mosquito
Zebra jumping spider

SRI LANKA
Atlas moth
Bed bug
Brownbanded cockroach
German cockroach
Greenhouse camel cricket
Greenhouse whitefly
Hair follicle mite
Honeybee
Human head/body louse
Indian mealmoth
Javan leaf insect
Liposcelis bostrychophila
Long-bodied cellar spider
Lucerne flea
Scolopender
Silverfish
Wandering glider
Wandering violin mantid

SUDAN

Bed bug
Brownbanded cockroach
Camel spider
Chigoe
Death's head hawk moth
European mantid
German cockroach
Greenhouse camel cricket
Hair follicle mite
Honeybee
Human head/body louse
Indian mealmoth
Liposcelis bostrychophila
Long-bodied cellar spider
Lucerne flea
Scolopender
Silverfish
Slender pigeon louse
Tsetse fly
Wandering glider
Yellow fever mosquito

SURINAME

American cockroach
Bed bug
Black-headed nasute termite
Blue morpho
Brownbanded cockroach
Chigoe
German cockroach
Giant water bug
Greenhouse camel cricket
Greenhouse whitefly
Hair follicle mite
Honeybee
Human head/body louse
Indian mealmoth
Linnaeus's snapping termite
Liposcelis bostrychophila
Long-bodied cellar spider
Lucerne flea
Madeira cockroach
Mediterranean fruitfly
Pea aphid
Silverfish

Tarantula hawk
Wandering glider
Western flower thrips

SWAZILAND

American cockroach
Bed bug
Brownbanded cockroach
Death's head hawk moth
European mantid
German cockroach
Greenhouse camel cricket
Greenhouse whitefly
Hair follicle mite
Honeybee
House centipede
Human head/body louse
Indian mealmoth
Liposcelis bostrychophila
Long-bodied cellar spider
Lucerne flea
Oriental cockroach
Silverfish
Wandering glider
Western flower thrips
Yellow fever mosquito

SWEDEN

American cockroach
Bed bug
Brown mayfly
Common harvestman
Devil's coach-horse
European marsh crane fly
Flat-backed millipede
German cockroach
Great water beetle
Greenhouse camel cricket
Gypsy moth
Hair follicle mite
Honeybee
Human head/body louse
Indian mealmoth
Liposcelis bostrychophila
Long-bodied cellar spider
Long-winged conehead
Lucerne flea

Oriental cockroach
Petrobius brevistylis
Pill millipede
Schummel's inocelliid
  snakefly
Silverfish
Slender pigeon louse
Spoonwing lacewing
Triaenodes bicolor
Velvet ant
Zebra jumping spider

SWITZERLAND

American cockroach
Antlion
Bed bug
Book scorpion
Brown mayfly
Brownbanded cockroach
Common harvestman
Devil's coach-horse
European earwig
European mantid
European marsh crane fly
European stag beetle
Flat-backed millipede
German cockroach
Great water beetle
Greenhouse camel cricket
Greenhouse whitefly
Gypsy moth
Hair follicle mite
Honeybee
House centipede
Human head/body louse
Indian mealmoth
Large blue
Liposcelis bostrychophila
Long-bodied cellar spider
Long-winged conehead
Lucerne flea
Pea aphid
Pill millipede
Silverfish
Slender pigeon louse
Spoonwing lacewing
Triaenodes bicolor

Velvet ant
Western flower thrips
Zebra jumping spider

SYRIA
American cockroach
Bed bug
Brownbanded cockroach
Camel spider
Death's head hawk moth
German cockroach
Greenhouse camel cricket
Greenhouse whitefly
Hair follicle mite
Honeybee
Human head/body louse
Indian mealmoth
Liposcelis bostrychophila
Long-bodied cellar spider
Long-winged conehead
Lucerne flea
Mediterranean fruitfly
Pea aphid
Sacred scarab
Silverfish
Slender pigeon louse
Wandering glider
Yellow fever mosquito

TAIWAN
Bed bug
German cockroach
Greenhouse camel cricket
Hair follicle mite
Honeybee
Human head/body louse
Indian mealmoth
Liposcelis bostrychophila
Long-bodied cellar spider
Lucerne flea
Silverfish

TAJIKISTAN
American cockroach
Atlas moth

Bed bug
Brownbanded cockroach
German cockroach
Greenhouse camel cricket
Greenhouse whitefly
Hair follicle mite
Honeybee
Human head/body louse
Indian mealmoth
Liposcelis bostrychophila
Long-bodied cellar spider
Lucerne flea
Silverfish
Slender pigeon louse
Wandering glider
Western flower thrips

TANZANIA
American cockroach
Bed bug
Brownbanded cockroach
Chigoe
Death's head hawk moth
European earwig
European mantid
German cockroach
Gladiator
Greenhouse camel cricket
Greenhouse whitefly
Hair follicle mite
Honeybee
Human head/body louse
Indian mealmoth
Liposcelis bostrychophila
Long-bodied cellar spider
Lucerne flea
Saunders embiid
Scolopender
Silverfish
Slender pigeon louse
Wandering glider
Yellow fever mosquito

THAILAND
American cockroach
Atlas moth

Bed bug
Black macrotermes
Brownbanded cockroach
German cockroach
Greenhouse camel cricket
Greenhouse whitefly
Hair follicle mite
Honeybee
Human head/body louse
Indian mealmoth
Jungle nymph
Liposcelis bostrychophila
Long-bodied cellar spider
Lucerne flea
Oriental cockroach
Pea aphid
Silverfish
Wandering glider
Yellow fever mosquito

TIMOR-LESTE
Bed bug
Dead-leaf mantid
German cockroach
Greenhouse camel cricket
Honeybee
Human head/body louse
Indian mealmoth
Liposcelis bostrychophila
Long-bodied cellar spider
Lucerne flea
Silverfish

TOGO
American cockroach
Bed bug
Brownbanded cockroach
Chigoe
Death's head hawk moth
Emperor scorpion
European mantid
German cockroach
Greenhouse camel cricket
Greenhouse whitefly
Hair follicle mite
Honeybee

Human head/body louse
Indian mealmoth
Liposcelis bostrychophila
Long-bodied cellar spider
Long-winged conehead
Lucerne flea
Madeira cockroach
Silverfish
Slender pigeon louse
Tsetse fly
Variegated grasshopper
Wandering glider
Yellow fever mosquito

TONGA
Bed bug
German cockroach
Greenhouse camel cricket
Hair follicle mite
Honeybee
Human head/body louse
Indian mealmoth
Liposcelis bostrychophila
Long-bodied cellar spider
Lucerne flea
Silverfish
Wandering glider

TRINIDAD AND TOBAGO
Bed bug
German cockroach
Greenhouse camel cricket
Hair follicle mite
Honeybee
Human head/body louse
Indian mealmoth
Linnaeus's snapping termite
Liposcelis bostrychophila
Long-bodied cellar spider
Lucerne flea
Silverfish
Wandering glider

TUNISIA
American cockroach
Bed bug

Brownbanded cockroach
Death's head hawk moth
Devil's coach-horse
European earwig
European mantid
German cockroach
Greenhouse camel cricket
Greenhouse whitefly
Gypsy moth
Hair follicle mite
Honeybee
House centipede
Human head/body louse
Indian mealmoth
Liposcelis bostrychophila
Long-bodied cellar spider
Long-winged conehead
Lucerne flea
Mediterranean fruitfly
Sacred scarab
Scolopender
Silverfish
Slender pigeon louse
Spoonwing lacewing
Wandering glider
Western flower thrips
Yellow fever mosquito

TURKEY
American cockroach
Bed bug
Book scorpion
Brown mayfly
Devil's coach-horse
European earwig
European mantid
European stag beetle
German cockroach
Great water beetle
Greenhouse camel cricket
Greenhouse whitefly
Gypsy moth
Hair follicle mite
Honeybee
House centipede
Human head/body louse

Indian mealmoth
Liposcelis bostrychophila
Long-bodied cellar spider
Long-winged conehead
Lucerne flea
Mediterranean fruitfly
Pea aphid
Sacred scarab
Silverfish
Slender pigeon louse
Velvet ant
Western flower thrips
Yellow fever mosquito
Zebra jumping spider

TURKMENISTAN
Bed bug
Brownbanded cockroach
German cockroach
Greenhouse camel cricket
Greenhouse whitefly
Hair follicle mite
Honeybee
Human head/body louse
Indian mealmoth
Liposcelis bostrychophila
Long-bodied cellar spider
Lucerne flea
Pea aphid
Silverfish
Wandering glider
Zebra jumping spider

TUVALU
Bed bug
German cockroach
Greenhouse camel cricket
Hair follicle mite
Honeybee
Human head/body louse
Indian mealmoth
Liposcelis bostrychophila
Long-bodied cellar spider
Lucerne flea
Silverfish
Wandering glider

UGANDA

American cockroach
Bed bug
Brownbanded cockroach
Chigoe
Death's head hawk moth
European earwig
European mantid
German cockroach
Greenhouse camel cricket
Greenhouse whitefly
Hair follicle mite
Honeybee
Human head/body louse
Indian mealmoth
Liposcelis bostrychophila
Long-bodied cellar spider
Lucerne flea
Silverfish
Slender pigeon louse
Wandering glider
Yellow fever mosquito

UKRAINE

American cockroach
Bed bug
Book scorpion
Brown mayfly
Common harvestman
Death's head hawk moth
Devil's coach-horse
European earwig
European mantid
European stag beetle
German cockroach
Great water beetle
Greenhouse camel cricket
Greenhouse whitefly
Gypsy moth
Hair follicle mite
Honeybee
Human head/body louse
Indian mealmoth
Large blue
Liposcelis bostrychophila
Long-bodied cellar spider

Long-winged conehead
Lucerne flea
Pea aphid
Sacred scarab
Schummel's inocelliid
 snakefly
Silverfish
Slender pigeon louse
Spoonwing lacewing
Velvet ant
Western flower thrips
Zebra jumping spider

UNITED ARAB EMIRATES

Bed bug
Camel spider
German cockroach
Great water beetle
Greenhouse camel cricket
Hair follicle mite
Honeybee
Human head/body louse
Indian mealmoth
Large blue
Liposcelis bostrychophila
Long-bodied cellar spider
Lucerne flea
Silverfish
Slender pigeon louse
Wandering glider
Yellow fever mosquito

UNITED KINGDOM

American cockroach
Antlion
Bed bug
Book scorpion
Common harvestman
Devil's coach-horse
European earwig
European marsh crane fly
Flat-backed millipede
German cockroach
Greenhouse camel cricket

Greenhouse whitefly
Gypsy moth
Hair follicle mite
Honeybee
Human head/body louse
Indian mealmoth
Liposcelis bostrychophila
Long-bodied cellar spider
Long-winged conehead
Lucerne flea
Oriental cockroach
Petrobius brevistylis
Pill millipede
Silverfish
Slender pigeon louse
Spoonwing lacewing
St. Helena earwig
Triaenodes bicolor
Velvet ant
Western flower thrips
Zebra jumping spider

UNITED STATES

Allopauropus carolinensis
American burying beetle
American cockroach
Bed bug
Big black horse fly
Brownbanded cockroach
Chinese mantid
Common American
 walkingstick
Common harvestman
Devil's coach-horse
Eastern dobsonfly
Eastern subterranean termite
European earwig
European mantid
European marsh crane fly
Flat-backed millipede
German cockroach
Giant salmonfly
Giant whip scorpion
Greenhouse camel cricket
Greenhouse whitefly
Gypsy moth

Hair follicle mite
Holijapyx diversiuguis
Honeybee
Horseshoe crab
House centipede
Hubbard's angel insect
Human head/body louse
Indian mealmoth
Liposcelis bostrychophila
Long-bodied cellar spider
Lucerne flea
Megarhyssa nortoni
Northern rock-crawler
Oriental cockroach
Panorpa nuptialis
Pea aphid
Potter wasp
Rocky Mountain wood tick
Saunders embiid
Seventeen-year cicada
Silverfish
Tarantula hawk
Trissolcus basalis
Wandering glider
Western flower thrips
Wide-headed rottenwood
 termite
Yellow fever mosquito
Zebra jumping spider

UNKNOWN
Garden symphylan

URUGUAY
American cockroach
Backswimmer
Bed bug
Brownbanded cockroach
German cockroach
Greenhouse camel cricket
Greenhouse whitefly
Hair follicle mite
Honeybee
Human head/body louse
Indian mealmoth
Liposcelis bostrychophila

Long-bodied cellar spider
Lucerne flea
Oriental cockroach
Pea aphid
Silverfish
Wandering glider
Yellow fever mosquito

UZBEKISTAN
Bed bug
Brownbanded cockroach
European mantid
German cockroach
Greenhouse camel cricket
Hair follicle mite
Honeybee
Human head/body louse
Indian mealmoth
Liposcelis bostrychophila
Long-bodied cellar spider
Lucerne flea
Silverfish
Wandering glider
Zebra jumping spider

VANUATU
Bed bug
German cockroach
Greenhouse camel cricket
Hair follicle mite
Honeybee
Human head/body louse
Indian mealmoth
Liposcelis bostrychophila
Long-bodied cellar spider
Lucerne flea
Silverfish
Wandering glider

VATICAN CITY
Bed bug
German cockroach
Greenhouse camel cricket
Hair follicle mite
Honeybee

Human head/body louse
Indian mealmoth
Liposcelis bostrychophila
Long-bodied cellar spider
Lucerne flea
Silverfish

VENEZUELA
American cockroach
Bed bug
Black-headed nasute termite
Blue morpho
Brownbanded cockroach
Chigoe
German cockroach
Giant water bug
Greenhouse camel cricket
Greenhouse whitefly
Hair follicle mite
Hercules beetle
Honeybee
Human head/body louse
Indian mealmoth
Leaf-cutter ant
Liposcelis bostrychophila
Long-bodied cellar spider
Lucerne flea
Madeira cockroach
Mediterranean fruitfly
Pea aphid
Saunders embiid
Silverfish
Tarantula hawk
Wandering glider
Western flower thrips
Yellow fever mosquito

VIETNAM
American cockroach
Atlas moth
Bed bug
Black macrotermes
Brownbanded cockroach
German cockroach
Greenhouse camel cricket

Greenhouse whitefly
Hair follicle mite
Honeybee
Human head/body louse
Indian mealmoth
Liposcelis bostrychophila
Long-bodied cellar spider
Lucerne flea
Oriental cockroach
Pea aphid
Silverfish
Wandering glider
Yellow fever mosquito

YEMEN
Bed bug
Camel spider
German cockroach
Greenhouse camel cricket
Hair follicle mite
Honeybee
Human head/body louse
Indian mealmoth
Liposcelis bostrychophila

Long-bodied cellar spider
Lucerne flea
Scolopender
Silverfish
Slender pigeon louse
Wandering glider
Yellow fever mosquito

ZAMBIA
American cockroach
Bed bug
Brownbanded cockroach
Chigoe
Death's head hawk moth
European mantid
German cockroach
Greenhouse camel cricket
Greenhouse whitefly
Hair follicle mite
Honeybee
Human head/body louse
Indian mealmoth
Liposcelis bostrychophila
Long-bodied cellar spider

Lucerne flea
Silverfish
Wandering glider
Yellow fever mosquito

ZIMBABWE
American cockroach
Bed bug
Brownbanded cockroach
Death's head hawk moth
European mantid
German cockroach
Greenhouse camel cricket
Greenhouse whitefly
Hair follicle mite
Honeybee
Human head/body louse
Indian mealmoth
Liposcelis bostrychophila
Long-bodied cellar spider
Lucerne flea
Silverfish
Wandering glider
Yellow fever mosquito

Index

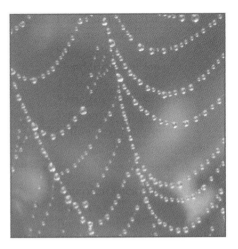

Italic type indicates volume number; **boldface** type indicates entries and their pages; (ill.) indicates illustrations.

Red List of Threatened Species. *See* World Conservation Union (IUCN) Red List of Threatened Species

Resilin, *2:* 329

Reticulitermes flavipes. See Eastern subterranean termites

Rhabdotogryllus caraboides. See Beetle crickets

Rhino cockroaches, *1:* 101

Rhinoceros katydids, *1:* 168

Rhyparobia maderae. See Madeira cockroaches

RimskiKorsakov, Nikolai, *2:* 395

Robber flies, *2:* 336, 339

Rockcrawlers, *1:* 152–57

Rocky Mountain wood ticks, *1:* 21–23, 21 (ill.), 22 (ill.)

Root miner flies, *2:* 341

Ross, Edward S., *2:* 213

Rove beetles, *2:* 290, 294, 295, 296

Russian steppe cockroaches, *1:* 103

S

Sacred scarabs, *2:* 297, 308–9, 308 (ill.), 309 (ill.)

Saintpaulia species, *2:* 439–40

Salmonflies, giant, *1:* 96–97, 96 (ill.), 97 (ill.)

Salticus scenicus. See Zebra jumping spiders

Sand flies, *2:* 340

Saunders embids, *2:* 214–15, 214 (ill.), 215 (ill.)

Sawflies, *2:* 390–414

Scale insects, *2:* 236, 237, 239, 240

Scarabaeus sacer. See Sacred scarabs

Scarabs, *2:* 294
dung, *2:* 297, 298
sacred, *2:* 297, 308–9, 308 (ill.), 309 (ill.)

Schummel's inocelliid snakeflies, *2:* 271–72, 271 (ill.), 272 (ill.)

Scoliid wasps, *2:* 393

Scolopenders, *2:* 417, 419–20, 419 (ill.), 420 (ill.)

Scolopendra abnormis. See Serpent Island centipedes

Scolopendra morsitans. See Scolopenders

Scorpionflies, *2:* 320–26

Scorpions, *1:* 9, 15–44, *2:* 238

Scutigera coleoptrata. See House centipedes

Scutigerella immaculata. See Garden symphylans

Scutigerella species, *2:* 435

Sea scorpions, *1:* 9

Sea skaters, *2:* 237, 252–53, 252 (ill.), 253 (ill.)

Sea spiders, *1:* 1–7

Serpent Island centipedes, *2:* 418

Seventeenyear cicadas, *2:* 245–47, 245 (ill.), 246 (ill.)

Sheep and goat fleas, *2:* 333–34, 333 (ill.), 334 (ill.)

Shellac, *2:* 240

Shieldbacks, Antioch dunes, *1:* 171

Shortfaced scorpionflies, *2:* 322

Silk, spider, *1:* 17

Silkworms, *2:* 372, 374–75, 374 (ill.), 375 (ill.)

Silky lacewings, *2:* 275

Silverfish, *1:* 61, 65–70, 67 (ill.), 68 (ill.)

Sinentomon yoroi, 1: 48–49, 48 (ill.), 49 (ill.)

Siphonaptera. *See* Fleas

Skin beetles, *2:* 293

Skippers, *2:* 366–89

Slender pigeon lice, *2:* 234–35, 234 (ill.), 235 (ill.)

Sminthurus viridis. See Lucerne fleas

Snakeflies, *2:* 268–72

Snapping termites, Linnaeus's, *1:* 130–31, 130 (ill.), 131 (ill.)

Snow fleas, *1:* 52

Snow scorpionflies, *2:* 320, 322

Social insects, *2:* 393–94

Soldier beetles, *2:* 289, 294

Sowbugs, *2:* 239

Spectres, Macleay's, *1:* 205–7, 205 (ill.), 206 (ill.)

Spider bat flies, *2:* 348–49, 348 (ill.), 349 (ill.)

Spider webs, *1:* 17

Spiders, *1:* 15–44
See also Sea spiders

Spirobolus species, *2:* 428

Splitfooted lacewings, *2:* 276

Spongilla flies, *2:* 274, 275

Spoonwing lacewings, *2:* 273, 274, 275, 286–88, 286 (ill.), 287 (ill.)

Spreadwings, *1:* 82

Springtails, *1:* 45, 50–54, 55

St. Helena earwigs, *1:* 160, 163–64, 163 (ill.), 164 (ill.)

Stable flies, *2:* 336

Stag beetles, *2:* 294, 303–5, 303 (ill.), 304 (ill.)

Stalkeyed flies, *2:* 344–45, 344 (ill.), 345 (ill.)

Stick insects, *1:* 158, 193–210

Stink bugs, *2:* 240

Stone centipedes, *2:* 417

Stoneflies, *1:* 92–98

Strepsiptera. *See* Twistedwing parasites

Sucking lice, *2:* 227–35

Sugarfoot moth flies, *2:* 341

Sun spiders, *1:* 15, 17

Supella longipalpa. See Brownbanded cockroaches

Swallowtail butterflies, *2:* 368

Sylvestri, Antonio, *1:* 46

Symphyla. *See* Symphylans

Symphylans, *2:* 434–37

T

Tabanus punctifer. See Big black horse flies

Tachycines asynamorus. See Greenhouse camel crickets

Tailless whip scorpions, 1: 24–26, 24 (ill.), 25 (ill.)

Tarantula hawks, 2: 407–8, 407 (ill.), 408 (ill.)

Tasmanian devils, 2: 328

Tasmanian torrent midges, 2: 341

Telson tails. See Proturans

Tenodera aridifolia sinensis. See Chinese mantids

Tent caterpillars, 2: 372

Termes fatalis. See Linnaeus's snapping termites

Termites, 1: 99, **117–34**, 136, 2: 395

Thousandleggers. See Millipedes

Thrips, 2: **257–61**

Thysanoptera. See Thrips

Thysanura. See Fire brats; Silverfish

Ticks, 1: **15–44**

Tiger beetles, 2: 293, 295

Tiger moths, 2: 370

Timemas, 1: **193–210**

Tipula paludosa. See European marsh crane flies

Toktokkies, 2: 295

Tortoise beetles, 2: 296

Trachelophorus giraffa. See Giraffenecked weevils

Tree crickets, 1: 168

Triaenodes bicolor, 2: 363–64, 363 (ill.), 364 (ill.)

Trichogramma species, 2: 372

Trichoptera. See Caddisflies

Trissolcus basalis, 2: 409–11, 409 (ill.), 410 (ill.)

Troides species. See Birdwing butterflies

True bugs, 2: **236–56**

Tsetse flies, 2: 340, 346–47, 346 (ill.), 347 (ill.)

Tunga penetrans. See Chigoes

Twistedwing parasites, 2: **315–19**, 318 (ill.), 319 (ill.)

U

United States Fish and Wildlife Service. See Fish and Wildlife Service (U.S.)

Uropsylla tasmanica, 2: 328

V

Varied springtails. See Lucerne fleas

Variegated grasshoppers, 1: 175–76, 175 (ill.), 176 (ill.)

Velvet ants, 2: 405–6, 405 (ill.), 406 (ill.)

Vine borers, 2: 372

Vinegaroons. See Giant whip scorpions

W

Walkingsticks, common American, 1: 202–4, 202 (ill.), 203 (ill.)

Wandering gliders, 1: 86–87, 86 (ill.), 87 (ill.)

Wandering violin mantids, 1: 139–41, 139 (ill.), 140 (ill.)

Waspmimicking katydids, 1: 169

Wasps, 2: 339, **390–414**

Water beetles, 2: 298, 301–2, 301 (ill.), 302 (ill.)

Water boatmen, 2: 240

Water bugs, giant, 2: 239, 240, 248–49, 248 (ill.), 249 (ill.)

Water loss, centipedes and, 2: 417

Water quality, stoneflies for, 1: 94

Water scavengers, 2: 294

Water scorpions, 2: 238

Water striders, 2: 238

Webs, spider, 1: 17

Webspinners, 2: **211–15**

Webworms, 2: 372

Weevils, 2: **289–314**

Western flower thrips, 2: 260–61, 260 (ill.), 261 (ill.)

Western pygmy blues, 2: 366

Wetas, giant, 1: 166, 170

Whip scorpions, 1: 16
  giant, 1: 39–41, 39 (ill.), 40 (ill.)
  tailless, 1: 24–26, 24 (ill.), 25 (ill.)

Whip spiders. See Tailless whip scorpions

Whirligig beetles, 2: 290, 291, 294

White ants. See Termites

Whiteflies, 2: 236, 237, 241–42, 241 (ill.), 242 (ill.)

Wideheaded rottenwood termites, 1: 132–33, 132 (ill.), 133 (ill.)

Wingless wood cockroaches, 1: 117

Woodboring beetles, 2: 293, 298

Wood ticks, Rocky Mountain, 1: 21–23, 21 (ill.), 22 (ill.)

Woodworms. See Thrips

World Conservation Union (IUCN) Red List of Threatened Species
  on arachnids, 1: 18
  on beetles, 2: 298, 311
  on caddisflies, 2: 361–62
  on centipedes, 2: 418
  on Chiloporter eatoni, 1: 77
  on cicadas, 2: 247
  on damselflies, 1: 85
  on dragonflies, 1: 85
  on earwigs, 1: 160, 164
  on emperor scorpions, 1: 44
  on flies, 2: 341
  on hemiptera, 2: 240

on horseshoe crabs, *1:* 11

on hymenoptera, *2:* 396

on large blues, *2:* 377

on lepidoptera, *2:* 372, 377

on lice, *2:* 229, 230

on Lord Howe stick insects, *1:* 196

on mantids, *1:* 138

on mayflies, *1:* 74

on midges, *2:* 341

on orthopterans, *1:* 171–72

on rockcrawlers, *1:* 154

on stoneflies, *1:* 94–95

Worms, blood, *2:* 340

Wound infection, maggots for, *2:* 340

Wrinkled beetles, *2:* 289

Y

Yellow fever mosquitoes, *2:* 342–43, 342 (ill.), 343 (ill.)

Yellow jackets, *2:* 393, 395

Z

Zebra jumping spiders, *1:* 29–31, 29 (ill.), 30 (ill.)

Zonocerus variegatus. See Variegated grasshoppers

Zootermopsis laticeps. See Wideheaded rottenwood termites

Zoraptera. *See* Angel insects

Zorapterans, *2:* **216–21**

Zorotypus hubbardi. See Hubbard's angel insects